**Australian Edition**

# Kokoda

## FOR

# DUMMIES®

**Australian Edition**

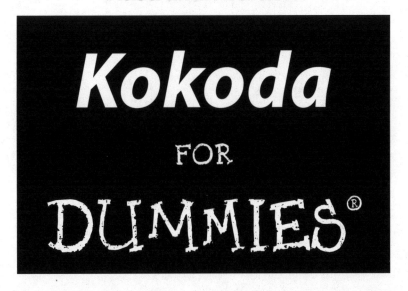

Kokoda
FOR
DUMMIES®

**by Dr Peter Williams**

WILEY

Wiley Publishing Australia Pty Ltd

**Kokoda For Dummies®, Australian Edition**

Published by
**Wiley Publishing Australia Pty Ltd**
42 McDougall Street
Milton, Qld 4064
www.dummies.com

Copyright © 2012 Wiley Publishing Australia Pty Ltd

The moral rights of the author have been asserted.

National Library of Australia
Cataloguing-in-Publication data:

| | |
|---|---|
| Author: | Williams, Peter |
| Title: | Kokoda For Dummies / Peter Williams. |
| Edition: | Australian ed. |
| ISBN: | 9780730376996 (pbk.) |
| Notes: | Includes index. |
| Subjects: | World War, 1939–1945 — Campaigns — Papua New Guinea. |
| | World War, 1939–1945 — Campaigns — Papua New Guinea — Kokoda. |
| | World War, 1939–1945 — Participation, Australian. |
| | World War, 1939–1945 — Participation, Japanese. |
| | World War, 1939–1945 — Australia. |
| | Kokoda Trail (Papua New Guinea) — History. |
| | Kokoda Trail (Papua New Guinea) — Description and travel. |
| Dewey Number: | 940.5426561 |

Cover image: © Australian War Memorial Archive, AWM 027081

Typeset by diacriTech, Chennai, India

Printed in China by
Printplus Limited

10 9 8 7 6 5 4 3 2 1

# About the Author

**Dr Peter Williams** is the author of six books and websites on Australian military history including *The Battle of Anzac Ridge 1915* (2006), *Australia's Involvement in the Korean War* (2010) and *The Kokoda Campaign 1942: Myth and Reality* (2012). Before he became a military historian, Peter was a teacher of history and English in Australia and Japan. He lives in Canberra where he is a researcher for the Defence Honours and Awards Appeals Tribunal.

# Dedication

I dedicate this book to my wife, Sammy, who, over the years, has become a reluctant expert on things Kokoda.

# Author's Acknowledgements

Without Gary Traynor, this book couldn't have been completed. Gary guides tours to Australian battlefields at Gallipoli and in Papua New Guinea and has walked Kokoda ten times. Drawing on his experiences, he contributed Chapters 14, 15, 16 and 18.

Thank you also to my editor, Catherine Spedding, and the team at Wiley.

## Publisher's Acknowledgements

We're proud of this book; please send us your comments through our online registration form located at http://dummies.custhelp.com.

Some of the people who helped bring this book to market include the following:

**Acquisitions, Editorial and Media Development**

**Project Editor:** Catherine Spedding

**Acquisitions Editor:** Rebecca Crisp

**Editorial Manager:** Hannah Bennett

**Special Contributor:** Gary Traynor

**Production**

**Graphics:** diacriTech

**Cartoons:** Glenn Lumsden

**Proofreader:** Charlotte Duff

**Indexer:** Don Jordan, Antipodes Indexing

The author and publisher would like to thank the following copyright holders, organisations and individuals for their permission to reproduce copyright material in this book:

- Pages 36 and 173: *Australia in the War of 1939–1945*. Series 1 — Army — Vol 5. South-West Pacific Area — First Year: Kokoda to Wau (1st edition, 1959) Author: Dudley McCarthy. Reproduced with permission of the Australian War Memorial.

- Pages 44, 47, 231, 251 and 274: Photos courtesy of the author. © Peter Williams.

- Page 181: By Arrangement with the Licensor, The David Campbell Estate c/-Curtis Brown (Aust) Pty Ltd.

Every effort has been made to trace the ownership of copyright material. Information that enables the publisher to rectify any error or omission in subsequent editions is welcome. In such cases, please contact the Permissions Section of John Wiley & Sons Australia, Ltd.

# Contents at a Glance

# Table of Contents

# Introduction

. . . . . . . . . . . . . . . . . . . . . . . . . . . . . . . . . . .

*A*ustralians are fond of their military history, but this fondness wasn't always so. When I was growing up in the 1960s, our wars — Vietnam was going on then — were rarely the subjects of television documentaries, movies and books as they are today. Now, websites are also devoted to warfare and new books appear every week. This is all very good news for authors and fans of military history.

The two campaigns Australians want to know most about are Gallipoli in 1915 and Kokoda in 1942. When I began writing military history, those were the two topics I decided to tackle first. I wanted to understand the nuts and bolts of strategy and tactics, battles and armies, how they're supplied and what makes some soldiers stand and die while others run away. Early on I learned that to best understand a battle you have to visit the place where it was fought. What I share in this book is based on my experiences travelling to the battlefields in Papua New Guinea.

## About This Book

Seven years ago I began studying the fighting on the Kokoda Trail. *Kokoda For Dummies* is a summary of what I've learnt so far, as well as a practical guide for those who are considering walking the track. Do walk the track. I've never met anyone who regretted it.

I talk about more than just the fighting on the track because understanding the other events in Papua in the six months Australians fought there is important. The final report of the Battles Nomenclature Committee in 1958 divided the war in Papua from July 1942 to January 1943 into three battles. The battle I focus on in *Kokoda For Dummies* is the Battle of Kokoda. The other battles I examine are the Battle of Milne Bay and the Battle of Buna–Gona, which was fought after Kokoda and saw the destruction of the Japanese force that had advanced along the track. In official jargon the fights along the track were not battles, they were called 'actions' or 'engagements'. I call them battles though because everybody else does.

Some of the questions this book answers are:

- Why did fighting occur along the track at all?
- What were the Australians and Japanese trying to achieve?
- How did the training and preparation of the armies affect the outcome of the battles?
- What kinds of weapons did the armies have?
- What was fighting in the mountainous jungle on the track really like?
- How do I prepare to walk the track and what will I see there?

# Conventions Used in This Book

In this book, I've used a number of conventions:

- Armies use a lot of technical words, like battalion and battery or company and casualty clearing station, to describe their structure. They have another list of tricky words to describe what they do: Flanking the enemy, making a pinning attack, bombarding. You don't need to know them all and I've used them only where necessary. Some of these technical words are explained in the Appendix.
- Names are written in their correct order. Australian and American people put their family name (surname) last, Japanese names have the family name first.
- I use the term *Buna* to describe the Japanese base in Papua. Buna is not strictly accurate because the Japanese base was spread over a large area and the centre was at Giruwa, near Buna. Buna itself was one of the less important parts of the base; however, Buna is a name a lot of Australians know so I've used it.
- When I use the word *Kokoda* I'm talking about the track or the fighting in general. When I mean the village of Kokoda after which the fighting was named, I make that clear. I also use Kokoda Trail — the official term — or track, not Kokoda Track.
- I use the terms used in 1942, when the north part of Papua New Guinea was called the Territory of New Guinea and the south part the Territory of Papua. If I use the term 'New Guinea', I am referring generally to the whole modern country.

# What You're Not to Read

The fighting in Papua was full of fascinating facts, stories and personalities that aren't vital to following the main story of Kokoda. I've placed some of these stories in sidebars — the shaded boxes — where I also include excerpts from interviews with war veterans, both Australian and Japanese. You can skip the sidebars and not lose the thread, but I think they're too good to miss out on.

# Foolish Assumptions

Many books about Kokoda or some aspect of it have been published and more appear each day. Some are technical and hard to understand and some are simple. Working out which is which can be difficult. I assume you've picked up this book because

- You plan to walk the track and you want to know if you should, what you will see and how to get ready.
- You want an overview of Kokoda that answers the where, what, when, who and how kinds of questions.
- You want a ready reference so you can look up a battle quickly.
- You wish you knew more about Kokoda, so you can join in on conversations.

# How This Book is Organised

This book is divided into six parts. I start by explaining the significance of the track and convincing you to walk the track if you haven't already. Then I talk about the battles and the practical steps you have to take before the trip if you want to see the battle sites.

## Part I: The Essentials of Kokoda

In this part, I tell you the basic information you need to make sense of the rest of the book. I explain why the track is significant, why you should go, what you will find and who has done it before you.

# Part II: Australians in Retreat

Australia and its Allies did a lot of retreating in the first ten months after Japan invaded Asia and the Pacific in December 1942. Here I explain the plans and objectives of both sides, and what went right with the Japanese plan and what went wrong with the Allied plan. I talk about what the Allies did in the war in the Pacific before the Japanese arrived in Papua and how we came to be fighting there. Part II ends at the end of the Australian retreat, at Imita Ridge 40 kilometres from Port Moresby.

# Part III: Fighting in the Jungle

Here I take a break from describing what happened and explain how war in the jungle is different from any other kind of warfare. I write about tactics and disease, supply and patrolling, and describe what the nitty gritty of jungle fighting was like.

# Part IV: Chasing the Japanese Out of Papua

After Imita Ridge in September 1942, the Australians went on the attack. I examine the four months of the Australian advance, from when we began driving the Japanese back along the track to January 1943 when the Japanese force in Papua was finally destroyed at the Battle of Buna–Gona.

# Part V: Walking the Kokoda Trail

This is the part that helps you decide if you're going to walk the track. Walking the track isn't easy and requires preparation. Here you learn about the practical stuff, how much training to do, what you should take with you and how to avoid illness.

# Part VI: The Part of Tens

In this part, I explain the common myths about the fighting in Papua. If you've read a bit about the fighting, you may be surprised by some of these myths. I also list ten things to look out for along the track and include ten interesting stories from Australian and Japanese veterans. The part of tens is a great place to start reading if you want to see if you'll like this book.

# Icons Used in This Book

Icons are those little pictures in the left margin. The picture on each gives you a clue to the content. Here's what they mean:

This icon shows where to go to find, or avoid, discussion about military strategy, tactics formation and doctrine.

This icon points you to interesting details that illuminate the story.

You may not want to read the technical details of organisation of equipment, especially if you're pressed for time. You can skip over the technical stuff, but it's difficult for me to imagine that many readers don't want to know how many rounds a .303 Lee-Enfield rifle held in its magazine.

When I want to summarise the key points I've just made at length I use this icon to point out an easy-to-remember sentence or two that captures the essence of the key points.

This icon serves as a warning, telling you to avoid something that's potentially harmful. Take heed!

This bulls-eye alerts you to on-target advice, insights or recommendations.

These highlight excerpts from interviews with Kokoda veterans that explain in their own words what being on the track was really like.

# *Where To Go From Here*

You can go anywhere you like from here because I've written the book so each part or chapter makes sense without having to read the other parts. Consult the table of contents to see where you want to go next. If you just want to read about the fighting, go to Parts II to IV. If you want to begin training for the track right now, go to Part V.

# Part I
# The Essentials of Kokoda

*Glenn Lumsden*

*'I can't believe my great-granddad did all this AND had people shooting at him as well.'*

# In this part ...

**W**hen I first went to Papua New Guinea in 1980, I wanted to see the Australian battlefields of World War II. I recall considering going to Kokoda but it didn't stand out in my mind. Instead I went to Buna, Lae, Shaggy Ridge, Finschhafen, Rabaul and Bougainville. Something has changed in 30 years because I can't now imagine a tourist, who wants to see where famous battles were fought in Papua New Guinea, who wouldn't have the Kokoda Trail at the top of the list.

In this part, I explore what has changed, what now gives that word 'Kokoda' a little magic, and why Kokoda is one of the best-known words in Australian military history. I explain why you should go to the track and what you're likely to see when you do.

# Chapter 1

# Understanding the Significance of the Kokoda Trail

*In This Chapter*

▶ Crossing the Owen Stanley Range over 2,000 years

▶ Examining the military history of the track

▶ Exploring the start and finish of the track

*I*n 1942 Australia lay in the shadow of war, a shadow starting on its very doorstep. The victorious Japanese forces were in Papua, and Australia was threatened. In the air, on land, at sea and on the home front, Australia was hard-pressed. Survival was the order of the day; victory was far from certain. On the Kokoda Trail, Australians fought to halt the advance towards Australia.

Kokoda is historically significant. The Kokoda Trail (or track, as some call it) stands as an icon for Australian participation in World War II, just as Gallipoli serves the same purpose for World War I. However, the track also stands as a potent symbol of Australia's shift in national identity, for Australians are conscious that the defeat of the Japanese on the track was a job Australians did themselves, without significant outside assistance.

Then there is proximity. Port Moresby is only 90 minutes by air from Cairns. The war in Papua was not a far-flung war, but one close to home. Australians see the significance of this. While people can argue about whether or not the fighting in Papua prevented an invasion of Australia, what is certain is that never before had the army of an enemy come close to our shores. Australians care about this, and the sacrifice of our troops in 1942. Why else do thousands of Australians make the Kokoda pilgrimage every year? It is because Kokoda holds a special place in national sentiment.

In this chapter, I explain the significance of the Kokoda Trail by looking at the track's history before World War II and during the key year of 1942. I also locate the track geographically and in the context of the other fighting in Papua.

# Looking at the Track Before the War

The Owen Stanley Range is the eastern extension of the central mountain range running east–west across New Guinea. In Papua, the 'tail' of the island of New Guinea, the range contains mountains almost 4,000 metres high.

For thousands of years, if Papuans wanted to cross the range from north to south, they threaded their way along rugged tracks through the lower parts of the range at altitudes of 2,000 metres. One of the several paths they might have chosen is the Kokoda Trail, which connects the Mambare River valley in the north to the south coast. Prior to the establishment of the British protectorate in New Guinea in 1884, the track was not the best known of the several ways to cross the Owen Stanley Range, but it most certainly is now and the track is still used as a thoroughfare. On it, you may well meet someone from Popondetta walking to visit a relative in Port Moresby.

In 1889, the Owen Stanley Range was first crossed by a non-Papuan, the British explorer George Bedford, though he didn't use the Kokoda Trail. Although other explorers set out with the intention of crossing the Owen Stanley mountains, the problems with hostile villagers and treacherous jungle conditions continued to be a deterrent.

## Mining at Yodda

The Kokoda Trail first came to prominence with the 1900 opening of the Yodda goldfield, north-west of Kokoda in the Mambare River valley. The success of the Yodda alluvial goldfield led to the establishment of the Kokoda Government Station on the flat-topped plateau that was the scene of battle in 1942.

By 1904, 1,000 miners and labourers were in the region, extracting almost one tonne of gold each year. The track was surveyed in an effort to improve communication with the new government station and with the miners. The then Lieutenant-Governor of Papua, Francis Barton, thought that the track might supplement the Sanananda–Kokoda track in servicing the new goldfield, but this didn't happen because gold finds at Yodda declined and many prospectors went elsewhere in search of richer deposits. The path out of Port Moresby towards the southern end of the track was upgraded to a vehicular road with the discovery of copper in the area.

Percy McDonald, who gave his name to McDonald's Corner, was the first to drive a vehicle along the new road in 1928. Until 1942, the track began at McDonald's Corner. See Chapter 3 to read more about this part of the track.

## Posting the mail to Kokoda

In 1904, a group led by Acting Administrator Francis Barton made its way through Bomana, Sogeri, Uberi, Nauro, Menari and Kagi and were the first whites to successfully traverse the Kokoda Trail, as the track is known today. Fittingly, a bottle of champagne was poured into tin mugs to commemorate the great success of the expedition.

Barton's expedition led, among other things, to the establishment of a fortnightly mail service between Port Moresby and Kokoda, which began the same year. Delivering civilian mail or official documents from Port Moresby by sea to Buna, then by land from Buna to Kokoda and Yodda along the Sanananda track had sometimes taken six weeks.

The new system was faster. Two policemen, each leaving from one end of the track with a mailbag, met halfway four days later and swapped bags, then returned. Though an airfield was built at Kokoda in 1932, the on-foot mail service continued until World War II.

# Coming to Terms with the Military History of the Kokoda Trail

From July 1942 to January 1943, the Japanese Army occupied Papua, the southern half of the country now known as Papua New Guinea. They invaded what was then an Australian territory with the purpose of capturing Port Moresby. The route they chose to come by was the Kokoda Trail over the Owen Stanley Mountain Range.

Most Australians think now that Australia was never invaded but this isn't strictly true. In 1942 the Australian territories of Papua and New Guinea were in law, if not in national sentiment, very nearly as much a part of Australia as the Northern Territory. Australian soil was, therefore, invaded by the Japanese in 1942 when the Japanese arrived in Rabaul and then invaded Papua. The Japanese soldiers had read that Papua was an Australian territory and some believed they were invading part of Australia. More than one Japanese veteran has said to me that the reason the Australians fought so hard in Papua was a natural one: That their country had been invaded.

In this section I consider whether the Allies saved Australia from Japanese invasion. I also discuss how history is told by the victors and how this relates to the stories told about the track.

## Saving Australia from invasion

The Australians prevented the Japanese from taking Port Moresby. If the Japanese had held Port Moresby, then they had the option to invade the east coast of Australia. Without Port Moresby they couldn't invade Australia. I discuss the importance of Port Moresby in Chapter 5.

So did the Australians on the Kokoda Trail save Australia from invasion? At the time, Australians believed that it was so. They didn't know that the Japanese didn't intend to invade, but military historians know that now, so the answer to the question must be no, they didn't save Australia from invasion.

But that's not the whole answer. In March 1942, Imperial headquarters in Tokyo discussed the possibility of an invasion of Australia and rejected it, deciding to examine the question again later. In June, their run of success ended when they lost the naval battle of Midway. After that their difficulties mounted and the question of invading Australia never came up again. We can't assume that, had the Japanese won at Midway, they wouldn't have come back to the question of Australia and decided to invade.

## Telling the story: History is made by the victors

The very popularity of Kokoda makes it likely that a lot of what you may read or see on television may contain a fraction too much legend and be slightly short on the facts. Stories of the bravery of our forefathers are stirring and, over time, the story can become just too good to be corrected by a few inconvenient truths that emerge later. Sometimes wartime propaganda doesn't disappear after the war, and instead becomes a part of the legend.

For example, it was widely said at the time that the Australian defeats in the first few months of fighting on the track (see Chapters 7 and 8) occurred because the Australians were massively outnumbered. This was untrue, but it allowed Australian authorities to claim, as General Sir Thomas Blamey did, that man for man the Australian was better trained, better led and a much better soldier than the Japanese. In 1942 that, perhaps, was not true but it was necessary to say it was as an aid to both military and civilian morale. After a war, wartime propaganda, such as Blamey's comment, tends to escape scrutiny and become part of the victors' accepted version of history.

# Defining 'casualty'

A casualty is a soldier removed from the front line owing to death, injury or illness. A battle casualty is a soldier killed or wounded by enemy action. A long list of sometimes odd categories were used in World War II to describe casualties. Some of these terms were

- *Killed in action.* Known to be killed by enemy fire.

- *Died of wounds.* Wounded in action but died soon after.

- *Died on active service.* Mostly those who died of illness.

- *Accidentally killed or wounded.* Covers a range of possibilities, from drowned while crossing a river to being run over by a truck.

- *Died of misadventure.* Covers those who died in some strange way. One Australian died in Port Moresby while trying to climb a flagpole while drunk.

- *Died while prisoner of war.* Used for those who died while in enemy captivity, from any of a number of causes, such as execution or starvation.

- *Missing in action.* Not with the unit after the battle and no witnesses to confirm that the person died.

- *Missing believed killed.* Not with the unit after the battle, but another soldier may have reported that the person was killed. If confirmed later, the record was changed to killed in action.

- *Evacuated sick.* A casualty removed to a hospital.

- *Died of exhaustion or privation.* Some Australians on the track, cut off from their own unit and lost in the jungle without food, died this way.

Another thing victors' history sometimes does is ignore our allies. While the Australians did their bit on the track, another larger battle was going on, where the Japanese and the Americans faced off on the island of Guadalcanal, east across the Solomon Sea from Papua. The Battle of Guadalcanal had a great influence on the fighting in Papua and without the American land, sea and air victories there the outcome in Papua would probably have been less happy for Australia. I look at this battle in Chapter 5.

And sometimes we hear only one side of the Kokoda story. We can read all about what each platoon of the 39th was doing during the fighting at Deniki (see Chapter 7), but the Japanese appear only as a big threatening red arrow on the battle map. Understanding an historical event when you don't hear half of the story, that of the enemy, is difficult.

This book aims to avoid the legendary and to tell both sides of the story, those of the Australians and the Japanese. If you're looking for the legend, you may be surprised at some of what you read here, and you may not agree with it.

# Deciding Where the Track Tour Starts and Finishes

The Kokoda Trail seems a lot longer when you're walking it, but the track is 96 kilometres long. It begins at Owers' Corner, 61 kilometres by road from Port Moresby, and ends on a plateau at Kokoda on which the Kokoda Government Station once stood.

Of course, if you start at Kokoda, the track ends at Owers' Corner, though most people walk from south to north rather than north to south.

Some say that starting at Kokoda makes following the sequence of events easier, but if you intend to go beyond Kokoda to see the battlefield of Buna–Gona, starting at the Port Moresby end is better. Whichever way you go, you can fly into three airports: Port Moresby, Kokoda or Popondetta near Buna.

In Chapter 3, I take an in-depth look at the geography of the track and some key battle sites on the track.

# Starting from Owers' Corner

The road from Port Moresby ends at Owers' Corner. If you ever go there, you quickly understand why. The track falls steeply to the Goldie River and you gaze on mountains so rugged you can see why no-one has yet tried to extend the road. Over the next few days, you'll walk up and down ridges, climbing up sometimes and sliding down on other occasions.

Chapter 3 and all of Part V are dedicated to the geography of the track and the trek along the track that you can make. But for now, Table 1-1 shows what a typical tour itinerary (perhaps slightly faster than most!) might look like.

| Table 1-1 | A Typical Itinerary for a Trek along the Kokoda Trail |
|---|---|
| *Day Number* | *Description of the Day's Walk* |
| Day 1 | Having camped overnight at Owers' Corner, climb down to and cross the Goldie River, the first of 11 river crossings, some with bridges, some without. Cross Imita Ridge and camp at Ioribaiwa. |
| Day 2 | Passing Japanese trenches, cross the Maguli Range and camp near Nauro. |
| Day 3 | Enjoy an hour of walking on flat ground — a rare terrain feature on the track — by the Brown River, cross the river and camp at Menari. |
| Day 4 | Climb to Brigade Hill and Mission Ridge, scene of an Australian defeat on 8 September 1942, then camp at Efogi. |
| Day 5 | Walk towards Templeton's Crossing and make a side trip to Myola to see where the Allies airdropped supplies. |
| Day 6 | Walk through Templeton's Crossing, scene of a battle both during the Australian retreat in September and another during the Australian advance in October. Camp at Isurava. |
| Day 7 | Visit the Isurava memorial then descend from the mountains into Kokoda. |

# Ending at Kokoda

Looking north from Isurava down Eora Gorge is a view of the lowlands near Kokoda. A few hours' walk takes you through the battle site of Deniki and from there the Kokoda airstrip comes into view, seven kilometres away.

Only a few hours' easy downhill walking remains. The last hour is flat, easy walking, allowing time to savour your achievement as the district office, which marks the end of the walk, comes into view. At the Kokoda plateau, most trekkers have a photograph taken at the district office to prove they got there. Nearby on the plateau is a museum and the site of the trench where Colonel Owen was mortally wounded on the night of 29 July 1942 (see Chapter 7).

## Moving beyond the track to Buna, Gona and Sanananda

After Kokoda you can see more, for the Kokoda Trail is only part of the story of what happened in Papua in 1942. Even better, you don't have to walk over any more mountains because there is a good road all the way.

Less than half an hour drive to the east along the Popondetta Road is the battlefield of Oivi–Gorari. The site of the largest battle of the Kokoda period of the fighting, Oivi–Gorari is not actually in the Owen Stanley Range but in gentler country that continues all the way to the north coast.

Further along are other scenes of fighting at Gorari, the Kumusi River and Awala. At Popondetta, where you can board a flight to Port Moresby, you're well placed to see the battlefields of Buna, Sanananda and Gona (see Chapter 12), each a 20 kilometre drive from Popondetta.

## Including Milne Bay

Not normally a part of a Kokoda tour is the site of the Battle of Milne Bay. Milne Bay is 400 kilometres, or less than an hour's flight, south-east of Port Moresby. While the Australians were fighting at Isurava on the track, the Japanese landed at Milne Bay. They were defeated and forced to evacuate after a ten-day battle. I cover the Battle of Milne Bay in Chapter 11.

While isolated, Milne Bay was of great strategic importance. Within the bay at the western end was flat and well-drained land suitable for airfields. Milne Bay is an isolated spot but valuable because of its location at the extreme eastern end of Papua facing the Coral Sea.

No road goes to Milne Bay, although roads around the bay take you to memorials and the sights of the fighting. The most popular of these sites is at No. 3 strip where the final Japanese attack was bloodily halted.

# Tracking or trailing?

Some people call it the Kokoda Track and some the Kokoda Trail. The terms Kokoda Track and Kokoda Trail were both in use during World War II and both are still used today, though the former term is more common. I use track because that's what all the diggers who fought there call it. But I'm wrong in a technical sense because the official name of that muddy up and down path is the Kokoda Trail and the official name of the battle fought along the track is the Battle of the Kokoda Trail.

When was the last time you heard the track called a trail unless you were arguing this very point? Considerable debate has occurred over which should be the preferred term. The Australian official historian of the Kokoda campaign, Dudley McCarthy, corresponded with and spoke to many Kokoda veterans. The fact that he chose 'track' carries authority. He was influenced by veterans, including senior officers such as Brigadier John Lloyd, 16th Brigade commander, who said 'we on the track referred to it as the track not the trail'.

No other jungle paths Australians fought over in Papua and New Guinea are called trails: The Sanananda Track, the Bulldog Track and Black Cat Track. The official memorial located at Isurava, constructed by the Australian Government during 2002 as part of the commemorations for the 60th anniversary of the 1942 battles on the track, uses the term track, but other memorials located along the track, erected by various individuals and organisations, use Kokoda Trail.

Other arguments in favour of 'trail' are that the Australian Army battle honour bears the name Kokoda Trail: The battle honour was established in 1959, well after the war, and careful thought was given to the name it bore. The Australian War Memorial also uses trail in its displays and the Papua New Guinea Government's place names committee also decided on Kokoda Trail in 1972.

Dr Karl James of the Australian War Memorial has tackled the issue and his points are worth repeating:

- No-one was too fussed at the time, but as the prominence of Kokoda rises, so too does the track or trail question.

- Supporters on both sides can become belligerent, so impassioned is the question in some quarters.

- The mail route over the Owen Stanley Range didn't have a formal name before the war; in fact, it was sometimes even called a road.

- Australian army survey maps of 1942 use track.

I use track but I am not wedded to it. In the end, I agree with James's conclusion:

*Too much time and energy has been spent on the 'track' versus 'trail' debate. It is clear that both words were used interchangeably during the war, and in a sense both are correct, so it is not possible to give a definitive ruling for one over the other. Rather than quibble over the name, it is far more important to remember the service and sacrifice of those Australians, Papuans, and Japanese who fought and died along it.*

# Chapter 2

# Reasons for Walking the Kokoda Trail

*W*alking the Kokoda Trail (referred to throughout this chapter as 'the track') puts you at the scene of one of the most famous events in Australian military history. Completing the track is a great way to honour the memory of the Australian soldiers, sailors and aircrew who were in combat on the track and to pay homage at the places where they fought. Walking the track, echoing the gruelling achievements of all of those who fought there, also commemorates and celebrates those who've walked the track before, in wartime and in peace.

Our rediscovery of and fascination with the track is relatively new and, some believe, dates from the then prime minister Paul Keating's ANZAC Day speech in Papua New Guinea in 1992. He said, 'They died in defence of Australia, and the civilisation and values which had grown up there. That's why it might be said that, for Australians, the battles of Papua New Guinea were the most important ever fought'. They were fighting for 'the democracy they had built ... the life they had made and the future they believed their country held'. Since 1992, the Australian Government has done much to imprint the meaning of the track on Australia's collective consciousness.

People who aren't Australian have other reasons to walk the track. Honouring the sites of battle of Japanese, Americans and Papuans who played their part in Kokoda is a portion of the story that doesn't belong to Australia alone. The track also serves as an opportunity to undertake a physical and spiritual challenge. Walking in the footsteps of the men of 1942 serves as an inspiration to overcome personal and professional adversities in people's everyday lives.

In this chapter, I tell you why you should walk the track, whose footsteps you'll tread in, what the experience is like, and about the organisations that take care of the track.

# Honouring Heritage and Paying Homage

The Kokoda campaign as part of Australia's heritage is now a focus of national commemoration and reflection. The arduous physical act of negotiating the track demonstrates respect, admiration or dedication to those who have gone before.

The Battle of Kokoda was a four-month struggle that began with the Japanese landing in Papua in July 1942. The Japanese strategy was to take Port Moresby via a track over the Owen Stanley Range. From Port Moresby, they could threaten an invasion of Queensland. The Japanese failed; the Australians drove them back and ejected the Japanese Army from Papua.

The track resonates today as a significantly Australian military achievement because it represents a moment in our history when Australia's forces were no longer fighting as a junior partner in the British Empire, as happened at Gallipoli and Singapore. Kokoda was a battle fought and won by Australians, on the Australian territory of Papua, and fought in the belief that if Australian forces were defeated, the Australian mainland might be invaded.

The Australian memorials to all participants honour the attributes of the *diggers* (Australian soldiers). Loyalty and, above all else, mateship, have come to be closely associated with Australian values. The Japanese also have their memorials on the track. The Japanese Bone Man of Kokoda, who has collected Japanese bones from their final resting places and built memorials to the Japanese dead, honours the Japanese Nankai Shitai (South Sea Forces) warrior spirit of Bushido, a code encompassing frugality, loyalty and honour unto death.

The commercial success of the books by Peter Brune (*A Bastard of a Place*, 2003), Peter Fitzsimons (*Kokoda*, 2004) and Paul Ham (*Kokoda*, 2004), as well as Alister Grierson's film *Kokoda* (2006), demonstrate the wide interest in the Kokoda campaign, as does the increasing number of trekkers each year. Even for those people who aren't so interested in the military history of the track, the intense physical challenge of the Kokoda Trail as a test of endurance holds a great attraction. Those who have completed the track are proud of their achievement, but be warned — walking the track is hard work; the unprepared should stay at home.

When you walk the track, you have the opportunity to soak up the feeling of being at the battlefields, to remember the deeds of the soldiers who fought there and admire their courage, and to join the list of the famous and not-yet-famous who have made the trek.

## Remembering their deeds

Standing on a battlefield on the track is a great aid to remembrance. Sitting at home, we can read accounts and imagine the fear, noise and confusion of battle, but nothing compares to being on the spot where the action happened.

The unfamiliar smells and sounds of the jungle-covered mountains, the rusty remains of rifle cartridges and water bottles, and the shallow outline in the ground of a trench transport you closer to the events of 1942 than any book or battle map.

Those who have a relative who served on the track can, with a little research, often find the place where he fought. Nowhere is better to stand to reflect on his contribution and sacrifice.

## Naming those to be honoured

For those who fought in Papua in 1942, the largest group were Australians, 56,000 of whom were in our land, sea and air forces in Papua during that year. Perhaps 12,000 of these soldiers actually walked the track in World War II and more Australians have walked the track since. The Americans, allied to the Australians, contributed 24,000 men but none were on the track, though many of their aircrew fought in the air over the track. Their enemy, the Japanese, had 27,000 men, some not from Japan but from Japan's empire, involved in Papuan operations. About 18,000 people from what is now Papua New Guinea, but was then the Australian Territories of Papua and New Guinea, fought, scouted and carried supplies for both sides. In total, about 125,000 people participated in the campaign on either side, in one capacity or another.

The dead are especially remembered. We can't name all of them here but we honour them. Among the 625 Australians who died along the track are famous diggers like Butch Bisset (see the sidebar 'Brothers on the track') and Bruce Kingsbury (see the section 'Admiring Victoria Cross winners'), whose graves can be visited at Bomana Cemetery near Port Moresby. Others, such as Private Harold Bould of 39th Battalion who was killed at Kokoda on 29 July 1942 and whose body was never found, aren't famous, but they're also remembered.

IN THEIR OWN WORDS

# Brothers on the track

Stan Bisset tells the story of his brother Hal 'Butch' Bisset:

Back home, I joined the 2/14th Battalion. My older brother, Hal, had already joined. He was known throughout the battalion as Butch. We were both pretty good marksmen. We grew up mostly in Melbourne, but we spent a couple of years at Warrandyte in the Victorian countryside. We had some wonderful times there. We used to build rafts and raft down the Yarra River for miles and miles. We had .22 rifles and we learned to shoot a flame out at 25 metres. We could also shoot rabbits on the run.

We went with the battalion to the Middle East and fought in Syria, but after Pearl Harbor was bombed we were all pretty keen to get back home to defend Australia against the Japanese. We were sent up the Kokoda Track to relieve the 39th Battalion, who had been fighting the Japanese for weeks and were holding out against the enemy at Isurava.

Butch and his platoon were sent up to the higher ground, to a position the Japanese were aiming to capture so they could overlook the battlefield. In two days Butch's platoon of about 35 men was confronted by 11 Japanese attacks. In each attack there were over 100 Japanese. We lost a lot of casualties and Butch got a burst from a Japanese machine gun through his tummy when he was going around distributing grenades. He was badly wounded, but I didn't learn about it for several hours as I was busy doing my rounds as intelligence officer. I got within 30 metres of Butch's platoon and I came across one of his Bren gunners who had lost his hand when a grenade he was throwing went off prematurely, so I whizzed him back through to the medical aid post.

Later, I heard Butch had been hit and stretcher bearers were bringing him back. So I went up the track and caught up with them. We laid Butch down off the side of the track. Our medical officer, Don Duffy, had a look at Butch and could see there was no hope for him. By then it was about 10 o'clock at night. The doc gave him some morphine and I said. 'I'll stay with him, doc.' I sat with him for six hours. He was quite conscious at times. We talked about Mum and Dad, our good times and bad times, what we did as kids. I sat with him until about 4 am, when he finally left us. We buried him beside the track.

Butch is now buried at Bomana Cemetery.

Some of the Australians who fought on the Kokoda Trail who received military honours and awards during WWII include the following:

- Stan Bisset — Military Cross for bravery during the Ramu valley campaign 1943
- Ben Buckler — Order of the British Empire for service rendered during World War II

- John French — Victoria Cross for valour at the Battle of Milne Bay
- Bruce Kingsbury — Victoria Cross for valour at the Battle of Isurava
- William Owen — Distinguished Service Cross (United States) for bravery during the fighting at Kokoda, where he was killed
- Arnold Potts — Distinguished Service Order awarded for Syrian Campaign 1941
- Phillip Rhoden — Order of the British Empire for services rendered during World War II

# Admiring Victoria Cross winners

The Victoria Cross (VC) is the highest award for acts of valour in the face of the enemy. The Victoria Cross was instituted in 1856 by Queen Victoria and is designed in the form of the Maltese Cross. In the centre of the medal is a lion guardant standing upon the Royal Crown. The words 'For valour' are inscribed below.

Two Australians earned the Victoria Cross during the fighting in Papua:

- **John French**, of 2/9th Battalion, was born near Toowoomba, Queensland in 1914. Before the war he worked as a barber in his father's business.

  At Milne Bay on 4 September 1942, French's battalion attacked a Japanese position, encountering heavy rifle and machine gun fire. The section's advance was held up by fire from three Japanese machine gun posts. French ordered his section to take cover, advanced and silenced one of the posts with grenades, then gathered more grenades, advanced again and silenced the second post.

  Armed with a Thompson submachine gun, French then attacked the third post. He was badly wounded, but continued to advance. The Japanese ceased fire and his section pushed on to find that all of the three Japanese gun crews had been killed, as had French, who died in front of the third gun pit. French's courage saved his section from heavy casualties and was responsible for the successful conclusion of the attack.

✔ **Bruce Kingsbury**, of 2/14th Battalion, was born in Melbourne. He enlisted in the AIF in May 1940 and was posted to the 2/14th Battalion in June. After serving in Egypt and Syria, he returned to Australia with the 7th Division in March 1942. His unit was sent to Port Moresby and in late August he was fighting the Japanese on the track.

Kingsbury was awarded the first Victoria Cross ever gained on territory administered by Australia and the first awarded in the south-west Pacific for his actions at the Battle of Isurava on 29 August 1942. Kingsbury Rock on the track near Isurava is said to mark the location of his act of gallantry. At Kingsbury Rock, when the Japanese broke through the Australian positions, Kingsbury rushed forward firing his Bren gun, causing a number of casualties and clearing a path through the enemy that enabled his mates to push the Japanese back. After the war, Japanese records confirmed that Kingsbury, and the soldiers attacking with him, killed almost an entire Japanese headquarters, including the company commander Lieutenant Watanabe, of the first company of the first battalion of 144 Regiment. Kingsbury was shot dead by another member of the company at the moment of success. He is buried at the Bomana War Cemetery at Port Moresby, Papua New Guinea. Figure 2-1 shows his grave.

**Figure 2-1:** An Australian soldier tends the grave of Private Bruce Kingsbury VC.

*Source: Australian War Memorial Archive, AWM 072431*

# Trekking in good company

People from all walks of life, sporting and corporate groups and other organisations report a spiritual bonding among their group, with the harsh and difficult terrain and climate of the track. Trekkers, usually exhausted and overcome, often describe an epiphany occurring through the ordeal.

Most trekkers are everyday people and include those retracing the steps of their ancestors, school and non-government groups, the young and the old.

However, the list of famous people who've walked the track is long; examples include:

- ✔ **Authors:** Paul Ham, Peter FitzSimons
- ✔ **Celebrities and business figures:** John Singleton, Lachlan Murdoch, Holly Brisley, Angry Anderson
- ✔ **Media personalities:** Mike Munro, David Koch
- ✔ **Ex-military personnel:** General Peter Cosgrove
- ✔ **Politicians:** Kevin Rudd, Mal Brough, Joe Hockey
- ✔ **Sporting legends:** Mal Meninga, Vicki Wilson, Allan Border, Jane Flemming

Completing the track is difficult enough for most able bodied people, but Paralympic champion Kurt Fearnley (see Chapter 14) and former commando Damien Thomlinson, who lost his legs when he was wounded by a bomb in Afghanistan, set a very high bar for physical and mental endurance. Fearnley's journey was to raise awareness of men's health issues and was inspired by the story of Corporal John Metson, who, wounded in 1942, crawled back along the track for three weeks, refusing the assistance of a stretcher so he wouldn't burden his comrades. Thomlinson's journey was no less poignant; he completed the track for a fallen mate and all fallen soldiers, walking on legs made of carbon fibre.

# Protecting Pilgrimage and Commemoration

A pilgrimage refers to a journey to a place of great significance to the traveller. On a pilgrimage, pilgrims usually pass by memorial sites where they may stop and reflect.

Australians (and New Zealanders) pause to remember their war dead at shrines and memorials across the country on 25 April and 11 November each year. Another way to honour the memory of our soldiers, sailors and aircrew is to visit the battle sites where diggers fought and fell. For this reason, thousands of Australians each year walk the Kokoda Trail, even though walking it is a difficult ten-day endeavour.

So many Australians now walk the track that considerable organisation is needed to keep them safe, ensure the track is maintained for future generations and to care for the interests of the locals whose land the track passes through. Both the Papua New Guinean and the Australian governments co-operate in this endeavour. The Commonwealth War Graves Commission cares for the graves of members of the Commonwealth, while the Department of Veterans' Affairs administers the Office of Australian War Graves.

# Commonwealth War Graves Commission

The Commonwealth War Graves Commission (CWGC) was established in 1917 to care for the graves of members of the Commonwealth who died in war. Australian war graves units have been exhuming the bodies buried in field graves and re-interring the remains since 1943.

No official graves or war cemeteries now exist along the track or in the beachhead areas of Buna, Gona and Sanananda. Remains have been identified and re-interred by the Army graves registration units and now by the CWGC in the Bomana Cemetery, although doubtless some remains are yet to be found in the Owen Stanley Range.

The war cemetery at Bomana, northeast of Port Moresby, which holds Australian, British, New Zealand, Dutch and other allied nationals, was established in 1942 and officially opened on 5 August 1944. The Bomana War Cemetery contains 3,779 burial sites, of which 701 are unidentified but some are believed to be British Royal Artillery personnel.

Some graves in this cemetery that may be of interest are

- Harold 'Butch' Bisset, brother of Stan Bisset (see the sidebar 'Brothers on the track'), Section C6, Grave F13
- Bruce Kingsbury, Victoria Cross, Section C6, Grave E1
- Charlie McCallum, Distinguished Conduct Medal, Section B3, Grave C7

✔ John Metson, British Empire Medal, Section B7, Grave C26
  (see Chapter 10)

✔ William Owen, Distinguished Service Cross (US), Section C6, Grave E4
  (see Chapter 7)

If you want to find out more about the CWGC, go to the website at
www.cwgc.org.

## Department of Veterans' Affairs

The role of the Commemorations Group of the Department of Veterans'
Affairs Australia is to acknowledge and commemorate the service and
sacrifice of all those who served Australia and Australia's allies in wars,
conflicts and peace operations.

The Department of Veterans' Affairs also administers the Office of Australian
War Graves. The Office of Australian War Graves maintains war cemeteries
and individual war graves in Australia and the region, builds and maintains
national memorials overseas and commemorates eligible veterans who died
postwar and whose deaths were caused by their war service.

The department constructed the Isurava memorial in 2002 and in 2010
refurbished the Milne Bay waterfront memorial and the Turnbull Field
memorial.

If you want to know more about the Department of Veterans' Affairs and the
Office of Australian War Graves, the websites are

✔ Department of Veteran Affairs: www.dva.gov.au/Pages/home.aspx

✔ Office of Australian War Graves: www.dva.gov.au/commems_oawg/
  OAWG/Pages/index.aspx

## Kokoda Initiative: The joint venture between the Papua New Guinean and Australian governments

In 2008, the Australian and Papua New Guinean governments signed a Joint
Understanding to work together to protect the track and Owen Stanley
Range, ultimately to improve the livelihoods of communities living along
the track. This joint work is being delivered through the *Kokoda Initiative*,
which runs a development program aimed at improving the lives of the

people living along the track by providing access to basic services such as water, sanitation, health, education and transport. The Kokoda Initiative also supports the Sustainable Livelihoods Project, which looks for ways to increase the economic benefits of tourism while at the same time protecting the integrity of village life.

The Australian interest in the track is also important for those who live in the region. The track passes through Oro Province and Central Province. The two main communities in these provinces are the Orokaiva in the north and the Koiari people to the south. An important part of their income is now generated by tourism. Fees are paid to the Papuans for camping and some are employed as tour guides.

The Kokoda Track Authority has responsibility for administering trekking permits, coordinating activities on the track and distributing funds to communities. By preserving the track's historic areas and natural environment, and maintaining and improving the track's special qualities for trekkers, the aim of the Authority is to provide a sustainable future for the track, the trekking industry and local communities. Improvements to some sections of the track that are becoming unsafe are planned.

In 2009, the Kokoda trekking industry code of conduct was endorsed to minimise adverse effects and maximise benefits for local people. You can read the code of conduct at kokodatrackauthority.org.

The Authority's commission is to

- ✔ Assist communities on the track to secure a sustainable future
- ✔ Collect and manage fees and permits
- ✔ Consult landowners along the track
- ✔ Deliver community development programs
- ✔ Regulate the conduct of tour operators
- ✔ Work with tourism providers to develop and maintain the tourism industry on the track

# Walking the Kokoda Trail Today

Walking the track isn't for the faint of heart. The track is 96 kilometres long and you can walk in either direction.

The northern end of the track starts 40 kilometres outside Port Moresby and leads you over the Owen Stanley Range to Kokoda station near Kokoda Village. The southern end of the track begins at Owers' Corner, 61 kilometres by road north-east of Port Moresby.

## Walking the Kokoda Trail (by someone who has)

From my own experience, walking may not be quite the right word to use to describe progress across the Owen Stanley Range: I spent almost all of the 50-hour trip (an average of five hours of walking per day, over ten days) descending or ascending; carefully negotiating my way down a narrow track, crossing a slippery log bridge over a fast-flowing stream at the bottom, then climbing steeply and slowly. Sometimes the ascent is almost vertical and both hands and feet are required to progress at all. In the worst places, the rate of advance is as slow as one kilometre an hour.

Those who complete the trip from south to north, as I did, will remember, about one-third of the way through the journey, that hour when the track follows along the bank of the Brown River. Apart from the last hour into Kokoda, this section is the only decent length of flat walking

on the track. This luxurious hour beside the Brown River is paid for, in full, by 'the wall', an incredibly steep climb that follows hard upon the river flats.

A typical day's effort may be crossing from one to three ridges, which usually run at right angles to the track. The southern half of the walk, though not the highest above sea level, is nevertheless the more difficult half. The ups and downs are more frequent and precipitous.

The rain can find you at any height and cloud sometimes descends to 1,000 metres, giving the feeling of walking through thick mist. In the Mt Bellamy–Templeton's Crossing region, the track rises to more than 2,000 metres above sea level. Here temperatures can drop at night to as low as 5° Celsius.

Starting at Kokoda may seem easier but in fact you climb an extra 500 metres from that direction!

Whichever direction you walk you must consider the physical and mental challenge. The following sections help you decide if you're capable of completing the track (see also Chapter 14).

## The physical challenge

The track serves as an opportunity to undertake a physical and spiritual challenge. The efforts of the Australians and Papuans before, during and after the events of 1942 serve as an inspiration to overcome everyday personal and professional adversities.

Various walkers describe being overwhelmed by the spiritual significance of what they're doing, putting into perspective the annoyances and inconvenience of problems at work or at home.

Other trekkers report euphoria, an epiphany in their weariness. Just when you think you're seeing the peak as you put hand over hand to climb a ridge face, the peak disappears and you realise you're still some distance from the crest. Scaling ravines to wash in small gully streams and constantly drying out clothes becomes commonplace. Freezing at night in the wet jungle segues into the steamy wetness of the day, occasionally broken by treacherous river crossings.

If you're trekking with carriers, imagine the extra burden of carrying wartime necessities of food, ammunition, and personal and medical supplies.

## Don't walk alone: Touring with others

You can cross the track alone, but some very good reasons exist not to. During wartime, the track was treacherous, with poor visibility, and death was only a sniper attack away. In peace time, the only thing that has changed is the awaiting sniper. You may experience some or all of these factors:

- Hot, humid days
- Intensely cold nights
- Risk of endemic tropical diseases, such as malaria
- Torrential rainfall

These days, death on the track is not unknown and the Kokoda Track Authority provides no liability. Each year, between 80 and 100 hikers have to be evacuated.

However, don't let all of this put you off! Trekking and health authorities are demanding more rigorous health and fitness training and testing requirements prior to walking the track, so you're allowed to go only if you're in good physical shape.

Walking in a group has many benefits. Groups experience different things and individuals are also subject to different experiences. Sharing recollections and adversity can inspire a track pilgrim and the fellowship caused by bonding in hardship can provide the strength to complete the walk. A group also provides safety in numbers and, if you're walking with a good guide, you're likely to see more than you might if you were on your own. Trek organisers can show you features of the terrain and sites of military interest. Go with a reputable tour operator to minimise the risk of injury and illness (see Chapter 14 for more about selecting a tour company).

# Some trekker trivia

Some call walking the Kokoda Trail trekking. The dictionary defines trekking as 'a slow and arduous journey on foot'. Not a bad description.

I've collated interesting track stats for you. Let's start with the big one: How many people have walked the Kokoda Trail since 1990?

A whopping 28,000 people. And the number of people who have died walking the track since 1990? Just six people.

In fact, the number of people walking the track each year has increased as time passes, as the following table shows.

### Number of Walkers along the Kokoda Trail, 2001–2010

| Year | Walkers |
| --- | --- |
| 2001 | 76 |
| 2002 | 365 |
| 2003 | 1,074 |
| 2004 | 1,584 |
| 2005 | 2,374 |
| 2006 | 3,747 |
| 2007 | 5,146 |
| 2008 | 5,600 |
| 2009 | 4,364 |
| 2010 | 5,800 |

Okay, let's get into some special categories of statistics:

- First trekker: John Landy, the long distance runner, walked the track in four days, 1955

- Youngest Australian male trekker: Nicholas Lawson (7), 2005

- Youngest Australian female trekker: Ellie Hargrave (12), 2004

- Oldest male trekker: Don Vale (83), 2009

- Oldest female trekker: Sybil Dwyer (74), 2010

- Youngest Papua New Guinean trekker: Malik Suma (6), 2007

- Guides with the most number of treks: John Derick Eroro (400+ treks) and Russell Eroro (287+ treks)

# Is the original Kokoda Trail the same as today's track?

The short answer is not exactly. The Kokoda Trail has been there for a long time and was once simply a track that mountain villagers used to get from one village to the next. The track links the villages along the way and the villagers sometimes change the location of the village, so the track alters a bit too.

## Describing the Kokoda Trail in detail

In 1942, Sir Frank Kingsley Norris, the senior medical officer of the Australian 7th Division, wrote a description of the track which is yet to be bettered (fortunately, the track is in much better condition these days, although you can still get a sense of the terrible conditions that the soldiers had to deal with):

> Imagine an area of approximately one hundred miles long. Crumple and fold this into a series of ridges, each rising higher and higher until seven thousand feet is reached, then declining in ridges to three thousand feet. Cover this thickly with jungle, short trees and tall trees, tangled with great, entwining savage vines. Through an oppression of this density, cut a little native track, two or three feet wide, up the ridges, over the spurs, round gorges and down across swiftly-flowing, happy mountain streams. Where the track clambers up the mountain sides, cut steps—big steps, little steps, steep steps—or clear the soil from the tree roots.

> Every few miles, bring the track through a small patch of sunlit kunai grass, or an old deserted native garden, and every seven or ten miles, build a group of dilapidated grass huts — as staging shelters — generally set in a foul, offensive clearing. Every now and then, leave beside the track dumps of discarded, putrifying food, occasional dead bodies and human foulings. In the morning, flicker the sunlight through the tall trees, flutter green and blue and purple and white butterflies lazily through the air, and hide birds of deep-throated song, or harsh cockatoos, in the foliage.

> About midday, and through the night, pour water over the forest, so that the steps become broken, and a continual yellow stream flows downwards, and the few level areas become pools and puddles of putrid black mud. In the high ridges above Myola, drip this water day and night over the track through a foetid forest grotesque with moss and glowing phosphorescent fungi. Such is the ... route for ten days to be covered from [Owers' Corner] to Deniki.

The location of the track has changed since 1942 and the location is likely to change again. Menari and Efogi villages, for example, have changed their locations by a few kilometres twice since 1942. At Ioribaiwa, the current track is two kilometres east of the 1942 track. In some cases, the change moves away from the original track but then moves back near the original location so you'll be back on the original track.

The track is also shorter than in 1942. At the Port Moresby end, the track once began at McDonald's Corner. In mid 1942, two Australian units, 7th Field Company and 2/14th Field Company, constructed a road from McDonald's Corner to Owers' Corner, shaving seven kilometres off the length of the track.

Despite these changes to the track over the years, overall you're walking on about three-quarters of the original track. You can still get a good feel for what the original track was like, and the hardships that the soldiers would've faced as they trekked along the path.

## Doing Kokoda the restful way

If you're interested in the battle sites of Kokoda and the arena of war in 1942, but baulk at the mountainous terrain (and that's quite understandable!) consider easier ways to visit the battlefields than walking the Kokoda Trail. From Port Moresby to Kokoda, the track is a tough walk over the Owen Stanley Range. However, the route onwards from Kokoda to the north coast at Sanananda is much easier. This route is reasonably flat and can be driven in a few hours.

## Doing Kokoda the energetic way

While most of us walk for 50 hours over eight or ten days to get from one end of the track to the other, you can run if you like.

The Kokoda Challenge Race is held in August each year, starting at Owers' Corner and finishing at Kokoda Station, covering a distance of 96 kilometres, the full length of the track.

The current records for the Kokoda Challenge Race are:

✔ Fastest man on the Kokoda Trail (porter): Brendan Buka, August 2008, 16 hours, 34 minutes, 5 seconds

✔ Fastest female: Nesta Gipine, August 2008, 22 hours, 8 minutes, 38 seconds

✔ Fastest man (non-porter): Damon Goerke, August 2006, 19 hours, 28 minutes

To find out more about the Kokoda Challenge Race, go the website www.kokodatrail.com.au/kokodachallenge.html.

The easy way to see some of the Papuan battlefields is to take a short flight from Port Moresby to Popondetta on the north coast (see Chapter 12). From Popondetta, the battlefields of Buna, Gona and Sanananda are less than 20 kilometres away by road. Popondetta has a hotel and basic accommodation is available right on the beach in the village of Sanananda.

Several hours drive to the west along the Popondetta–Kokoda road is the battlefield of Oivi–Gorari, the largest battle of the Kokoda period of the fighting. Oivi–Gorari is 16 kilometres east of Kokoda and not actually in the Owen Stanley Range. Proceeding along this road also takes the visitor past two other scenes of fighting in the early stages of the campaign at Awala and at the Kumusi River crossing. A half-hour drive further west from Oivi is the village of Kokoda. The airstrip here was the objective of two small but furious engagements in 1942 between the Australians and the Japanese. The airstrip is still in use and you can fly direct from Port Moresby to Kokoda.

None of the places described in this section require any hill climbing and all are accessible by vehicle, with the exception of times in the wet season when the rivers flood. For the slightly more adventurous, a steep climb up from Kokoda into the Owen Stanley Range, a six-hour walk, takes you to Deniki and to the iconic battlefield of Isurava. An overnight stay in tents or huts can be arranged at nearby Alola.

# Chapter 3

# Finding Places of Military Importance

*Y*ou can walk the Kokoda Trail beginning from either end. Some argue that, because Australians are often more interested in the period of Australian retreat from Kokoda than the subsequent advance, starting from Kokoda and following the Japanese advance from there makes more sense. However, most who make the Kokoda pilgrimage begin at Port Moresby and walk north to Kokoda, then either fly back to Port Moresby or go by road through Oivi and Gorari to the northern beach battle sites at Buna, Gona and Sanananda.

This chapter follows the order most people walk: From Port Moresby to Kokoda. I focus on visiting sites of interest and finding plaques and memorials along the track.

The trip falls naturally into three parts:

✔ Sites to see by vehicle on the 60 kilometres of road from Port Moresby to where the track begins at Owers' Corner

✔ The Kokoda battlefields along the track, each usually located by plaques or memorials

✔ The trip beyond Kokoda by vehicle to the north coast

Figure 3-1 shows a map of the Kokoda Trail in its entirety; this map is useful for locating the places I discuss in this chapter.

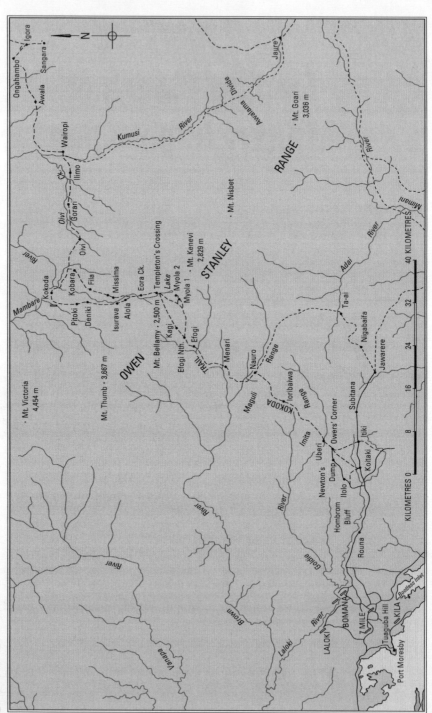

**Figure 3-1:**
The Kokoda
Trail.

# Completing the First Part: Port Moresby to Owers' Corner

Port Moresby was named after Captain John Moresby, who was the first European to visit in 1873. Until World War II, Port Moresby wasn't the foremost town in New Guinea. Lae took prominence as the supply base for the gold rushes in Wau, Bulolo and Rabaul, but during the Kokoda campaign Port Moresby grew to be a military base containing 60,000 personnel.

Port Moresby was bombed more than 100 times from January 1942 to September 1943. The rusty remains of ships sunk by Japanese bombing, aircraft wrecks and Australian anti-aircraft gun positions on hill crests can still be seen.

Outside Port Moresby, on the road to the start of the track, are the sites of airfields and other places of interest (including a famous cricket pitch!) connected to the story of 1942.

## Seven Mile Strip

Jackson International Airport, where flights from Australia arrive, was originally called Seven Mile Strip (named because it was seven miles — 12 kilometres — by road from the port), and later became known as Jackson's Field after Johnny Jackson, a Queenslander who commanded 75 Squadron RAAF.

From March 1942, the squadron defended Port Moresby from air attack and in one of these dogfights, on 28 April, Jackson was killed. On the far side of the runway from the airport terminal, U-shaped earthworks that protected aircraft from shrapnel can still be seen.

From a single runway, the area around Seven Mile Strip eventually became the largest air base in New Guinea, with six airfields. The other wartime airfields in Port Moresby and nearby were

- Kila Drome (3 miles or 5 kilometres from the port to the airstrip by road) airfield for fighters and bombers
- Ward Drome (5 miles or 8 kilometres) airfield for heavy bombers and transport planes
- Berry Drome (12 miles or 20 kilometres) fighter and medium bomber base near Bomana

- Schwimmer (14 miles or 24 kilometres) fighter and medium bomber base

- Durand (17 miles or 29 kilometres) fighter and medium bomber base

- Rogers (Rarona, 30 miles or 50 kilometres) fighter and medium bomber

- Fishermen's (Daugo) emergency landing strip on an offshore island

## Bomana Cemetery

Outside Port Moresby on the way to Owers' Corner is Bomana Cemetery. Bomana was established in 1942. Over the next several years those who had been temporarily buried elsewhere in New Guinea, or in other cemeteries around Port Moresby, were re-interred at Bomana.

Bomana Cemetery is the largest Commonwealth war cemetery in the Pacific. Interred in the 3,779 graves are:

- 3,069 known Australians

- 267 unknown Australians

- 443 Allied soldiers, sailors and airmen

## Wreck of the Macdhui

In Port Moresby harbour, the wreck of the liner MV *Macdhui*, sunk by Japanese air attack, can still be seen from one of the hilltop anti-aircraft defences.

The *Macdhui*, of 4,630 tonnes, was built in Glasgow, Scotland, in 1930. It was owned and operated on the Australia–Papua New Guinea service by Burns Philp and Company Limited. When the war began, the ship was commandeered by the Royal Australian Navy and used to evacuate civilians from New Guinea and to carry Australian troops to Port Moresby.

On 17 June 1942, the *Macdhui* was attacked by Japanese bombers in Port Moresby harbour. It sustained damage but managed to dock alongside the main wharf to unload dead and wounded. Attacked again the next day, the *Macdhui* took four direct hits and keeled over onto a reef. Sixty-seven crew survived but ten were killed, along with five Australians from 39th Battalion. The *Macdhui*'s mast now stands outside the Royal Papua Yacht Club as a memorial to those who died.

Port Moresby (Bomana) War Cemetery lies approximately 19 kilometres north of Port Moresby on the road to Nine Mile, and is approached from the main road by a short side road called Pilgrims Way.

The Stone of Remembrance is located near the forecourt, with the altar and Cross of Sacrifice. On the hill behind stands pillars that record the names of Australian military personnel and others who lost their lives in battle but have no known grave.

One particular monument at Bomana deserves mention. It honours the Papuan and New Guinean servicemen, police and carriers who served their country during the campaigns in Papua New Guinea during 1942 to 1945. The monument is adjacent to the cemetery car park. The plaque is flanked by two bronze relief impressions of a Papuan Infantry Battalion soldier and a Papuan Constabulary officer, each armed with a Lee Enfield .303 rifle.

# Koitaki

Koitaki is a side trip from the main road to Owers' Corner. This site is famous because on 9 November 1942, General Sir Thomas Blamey gave an address to the troops of the 21st Brigade at the Koitaki Cricket Pitch.

The text of the speech was not kept but reactions to the speech are found in personal records and other historical accounts. This speech is referred to as the 'rabbit speech' and was perceived very differently by different people present.

In essence, the men of the brigade being addressed were expecting praise from Blamey, but instead found themselves insulted by what General Blamey had to say. The troops believed Blamey hinted that they had run like rabbits from the Japanese in the battles along the Kokoda Trail.

Others present have said that Blamey was misunderstood and had no intention of giving offence. However, many veterans' dislike of Blamey stems from this event.

You can read more about the speech in the sidebar 'The rabbit speech'.

# The rabbit speech

On 9 November 1942, Blamey addressed the men of the 21st Infantry Brigade (see Chapter 8 for what the brigade did on the track) on a cricket oval. The members of Maroubra Force (which was what the Australian force on the Kokoda Trail was called) expected congratulations for their efforts in holding back the Japanese. However, instead of praising them, Blamey told the brigade that they had been 'beaten' by inferior forces, and that 'no soldier should be afraid to die'.

'Remember', Blamey was reported as saying, 'it's the rabbit who runs who gets shot, not the man holding the gun'. In a later letter to his wife, an enraged Brigadier Potts swore to 'fry his [Blamey's] soul in the afterlife' over this incident. According to witnesses, when Blamey subsequently visited Australian wounded in the camp hospital, inmates nibbled lettuce, while wrinkling their noses and whispering 'run, rabbit, run' (the chorus of a popular song during the war). Thereafter some troops referred to him as 'that bastard Blamey'.

Even Blamey's closest colleague, Lieutenant Colonel Norman Carlyon OBE, wrote that he was amazed that Blamey could deal so insensitively with the men of such a well proven brigade. The medical officer of the 2/16th Battalion, Major General Henry Steward, who was also present at the parade, wrote that he was shocked that Blamey could talk to the men the way he did: 'The entire parade, men and officers, were almost molten with rage'.

Another witness, Brigadier Dougherty, the brigade's new commander, thought differently:

> It never entered my head as I stood there on parade that the general had any idea he was being offensive, or that he intended to be so. But the Brigade gave to what he said the interpretation that 'they ran like rabbits'. This interpretation of what he said spread through New Guinea and indeed back home and resulted in bitter feelings.

Following his address to the whole brigade, General Blamey addressed the officers separately. He was direct with them and said that a few officers had failed. This caused bitterness. But after both addresses, Blamey told me that he thought highly of the brigade and repeated to me what he would have told the whole brigade, 'that I, as their new brigade commander, would be very proud of them'.

When the brigade was reorganised at Ravenshoe in 1943, Blamey's assistant one day asked me if Blamey could speak to my officers. He had been genuinely upset at having hurt my brigade when he addressed them at Koitaki, as he had not intended to do so. When speaking to the officers on this occasion he referred to the Koitaki incident. He said that he had said certain things to the officers, and he had meant all that he had said. He endeavoured to explain the meaning of what he had said then, and to put his remarks into their correct perspective. His comments on this occasion, frank and sincere, were well received.

# On the road to Owers' Corner

At a crossroads on the way to Owers' Corner is a cairn with three plaques:

- One plaque is in memory of the officers, NCOs (non-commissioned officers) and men of the Australian military forces who gave their lives on the track July to November 1942. It bears the motto 'To strive, to seek, to find and not to yield'.

- The next plaque recognises the support of the Ianari clan of Sogeri. It was erected by the Australian Government on the 48th anniversary of the battle in November 1990.

- The third plaque on this cairn recognises the 7th Australian Infantry Brigade and 2nd Australian Watercraft Workshop who designed and built the memorial in 1943.

At McDonald's Corner (at the base of the metal soldier figurine) lies a plaque laid on 14 August 1967 to commemorate a pilgrimage by members of the 39th Battalion on the 25th anniversary of the campaign. (For more about the 39th Battalion, see Chapter 7.) At the base of the pole is a plate laid by R J McDonald, commemorating the exploits of the 39th Infantry Battalion. The plate recognises that this was the first unit to engage the Japanese along the Kokoda Trail and records that 138 members of that unit lost their lives in New Guinea. It also remembers P J McDonald, himself a veteran of World War I and after whom this corner is named.

A sign at Owers' Corner sheds light on how this southern end of the track received its name. Captain Noel 'Jerry' Owers was the officer in charge of the 2nd Survey Corps, 8th Division AIF. He was ordered to survey a road from Port Moresby to Kokoda. No road was constructed; however, Owers and his team did survey a track. In honour of his work, this point was named after Owers. Between two flag poles is a concrete memorial with a bronze relief map of the Kokoda Trail. This monument was laid in 1999 and was sculpted by Ross J Bastiaan (see the sidebar 'The plaque maker'). An almost identical bronze relief map has been mounted at Kokoda Plateau.

The beginning of the track is marked by the 1999 Kokoda Memorial Arch. The six uprights, representing the six states of the Australian Commonwealth, support the arch. The arch, in its turn, represents the connection between the people of Papua New Guinea and Australia. Nearby is an Australian 25 pounder field gun.

## The plaque maker

Ross Bastiaan is a Victorian periodontist and self-taught bronze sculptor who's passionate about history and ensuring that Australians are commemorated on the battlefields where they have fought worldwide.

Bastiaan's interest in history began when he was a young boy. He was raised in a family where many members fought in World War I or World War II. He was also very close to Lawrence McCarthy, a World War I veteran who was awarded the Victoria Cross.

Bastiaan travelled to Gallipoli but was very disappointed by the lack of information for visitors to this battlefield which has such an iconic place in Australian history. Bastiaan set about placing information plaques, written in plain English, around Gallipoli. Since then he has placed more than 120 commemorative plaques at battlefields around the world where Australians have fought, as a way of commemorating the role Australians have played in history.

# Walking the Second Part: Owers' Corner to Kokoda

If you've made it from Port Moresby (refer to the preceding section), the walking really begins now. Over the next eight or ten days, starting from the Memorial Arch and ending at Kokoda plateau, the trekker passes through the battlefields of the Kokoda Trail where more than 50 memorials of all shapes and sizes record the campaign.

## Imita Ridge — end of retreat and beginning of the Australian advance

Imita Ridge was the furthest point of the Australian withdrawal. Under orders not to retreat, the Australians waited here in late September 1942 for a Japanese attack that never came.

On Imita Ridge, where the track crosses the saddle, is a bronze plaque that differs from the standard Ross Bastiaan style plaque, in that it displays a figure of an Australian digger armed with an Owen Gun. It also shows the *disposition* (the way the military formations were placed) of the Australian troops deployed along Imita Ridge.

## Ioribaiwa Ridge

The next ridge along the track to the north is Ioribaiwa where the Japanese advance halted. The Australians were defeated and driven off this ridge on 16 September 1942 (see Chapter 8).

At the top of Ioribaiwa Ridge lies a small, privately laid plaque to Ian Andrew Bergman who, as a trekker, sadly lost his life while walking the track on 14 June 2006, aged 35.

In new Ioribaiwa Village, on the 1942 Ponoon Track, is another Ross Bastiaan plaque, commemorating the battle for Ioribaiwa.

## Menari

Passing over the Maguli range, where the Australians fought a rearguard action in early September 1942, the track enters Menari, where war photographer and correspondent Damien Parer is remembered.

Parer participated in the Australian retreat and took the now famous film and photographs of Kokoda fighting. Renowned for his Academy Award winning film *Kokoda Front Line*, Damien Parer was killed in action on 16 September 1944 while filming a US Marine attack on the island of Peleliu. A plaque was laid near Menari by relatives and friends of Parer in July 2004.

The plaque is easily missed. Follow the track down to the Menari airstrip, then descend a series of steps to the creek. Here the track turns left but the plaque is to the right on a large boulder.

Figure 3-2 shows a signpost at Menari; as you can see, Menari is nearly halfway along the track (if you're coming from Owers' Corner, that is; it's more than halfway if you've come from Kokoda!).

## Menari to Efogi

Leaving Menari, the track climbs to Brigade Hill (see Chapter 8) where Maroubra Force (which was what the Australian force on the Kokoda Trail was called) was defeated by the Japanese on 8 September 1942. On the grassy knoll of Brigade Hill stands a Ross Bastiaan memorial commemorating the battle. The plaque also recognises the preservation of this site through the generosity of the Koiari people.

**Figure 3-2:**
Signpost at
Menari.

A small plaque commemorates NX135511 Private Reginald Joseph Holles. The plaque was laid by his family.

See Chapter 8 for lots more information on this part of the Kokoda campaign.

## Efogi to Myola

A side trip from the track leads to Myola 1 and 2, impressive dry lakes used for the airdropping of supplies. At the guesthouse/campsite of Myola 2 are two plaques set onto low rocks near aircraft wreckage (which is believed to be that of a Ford tri-motor that crashed while attempting to evacuate wounded troops):

✔ One plaque commemorates the service of No. 36 Squadron RAAF, who dropped supplies and transported troops in New Guinea during World War II. This plaque was laid during Anzac week (25 April) 2010 by members of No. 36 Squadron (RAAF) Association. An identical copy of this memorial was also laid within the Bert Kienzle Museum on Kokoda plateau.

> ✔ The second plaque at Myola 2 was laid by Soc Kienzle and his family, to recognise the discovery of Myola. The plaque also acknowledges the part played by the Koiari people in helping to locate Myola 1. The plaque reveals that these two drop zones were named by Captain Herbert 'Bert' Kienzle after Myola, the wife of Australian New Guinea Administrative Unit (ANGAU) officer Major Elliot-Smith. From March 1942, the civil administration of Papua and New Guinea was handed to the Australian Army, which ran ANGAU.

# Templeton's Crossing

Fighting occurred at Templeton's Crossing during both the Australian retreat in September and the Australian advance the following month (see Chapter 8). The two separate battles are known as Eora–Templeton's 1 and Eora–Templeton's 2. They're remembered at the upper end of the campsite on the Myola side of the track on the bank of the creek. There, a small plaque is embedded into a large rock. The plaque explains that this area was the staging camp, also called Dump 2, and is the junction of the old Kokoda mail track and the new track that was blazed by Captain 'Bert' Kienzle (father of Soc Kienzle) on 4 August 1942. Kienzle named the crossing in honour of 'Uncle Sam' Templeton who was captured and killed by the Japanese near Oivi on 26 July 1942.

# Eora

On the flat area of ground that's commonly, yet incorrectly, regarded as the 1942 location of a village at Eora Creek, stands a Ross Bastiaan plaque commemorating the battle for Eora Creek that took place during the Australian advance from 22 to 29 October 1942. According to Kokoda authority Soc Kienzle, this area was merely a conglomeration of huts and shelters and was never a village site. However, this location was filmed by Damien Parer during the Australian withdrawal and is often the subject of photographs in books depicting the Kokoda Trail, where the site is described as Eora Village. As you approach from the direction of Owers' Corner, this location is at the bottom of a long descent.

The 3rd Australian Infantry Battalion (AMF) plaque at Eora Creek is commonly referred to by trek leaders as the Bede Tongs plaque. Bede Tongs was awarded his military medal during fighting between Templeton's Crossing and Eora Creek on the opposite side of the creek from the plaque. Bede laid the plaque on 26 June 1980 while participating in Peter Luck's documentary about Kokoda.

The plaque at Eora Creek commemorates the involvement of the 3rd Militia Battalion in the campaign. Not many people know that the 3rd Battalion, recruited from the Canberra-Queanbeyan region, was the longest continuously serving Australian unit in the Kokoda campaign. This plaque is located at Eora Creek crossing, below the Japanese mountain gun position on the high ground to the north west.

Trekkers heading to Kokoda from the direction of Owers' Corner need to cross Eora Creek to view this plaque; however, you may to need to search the bank to locate this memorial.

## Isurava

During the Battle of Isurava (see Chapter 8 for more about this battle), the Australians held two positions. The second of these, the one found first when walking from the south, was at Isurava Rest House. Here lies a privately laid plaque in honour of Lieutenant Thomas Harold ('Butch') Bisset, 10 Platoon, B Company 2/14th Battalion. This plaque depicts a photograph of Butch Bisset and his brother, Captain Stan Bisset in Australia, prior to deployment to Papua. It was laid by members of their family on 30 August 2005, the 63rd anniversary of Butch's death. This plaque is located approximately 300 metres on the Owers' Corner side of the area known as the Isurava Rest House position. The plaque is adjacent to a flat 'diamond' shaped rock that's called Con's Rock. The rock is also known as Surgeon's Rock, where Medical Orderly Con Vapp of the 2/14th Battalion is said to have conducted an amputation. Approximately 50 metres further south is where Stan Bissett held his dying brother's hand and comforted Butch during his last hours.

The most northern of the two Australian positions at Isurava was between two creeks called 'front' and 'back' creeks. The newest memorial here is a privately laid plaque in memory of Sergeant W J 'Bill' Guest, VX103114, 39th Infantry Battalion. This plaque was laid by his family on the occasion of the scattering of his ashes near the Isurava Memorial on 29 August 2007, the 65th anniversary of the battle for Isurava. Guest's memorial is on the lower slope of the area occupied by the four pillars of the official memorial and can be seen as you look uphill from the Eora Creek side of Kingsbury's Rock.

Further north, the 'new' Isurava Village is situated between the Isurava battlefield site, where the official memorial is placed, and Deniki. A Ross Bastiaan memorial is in the centre of the village. It was laid at new Isurava prior to 2002 when the official main memorial was constructed by the Department of Veterans' Affairs. The four Australian black granite pillars making up the memorial are each inscribed with a single word — courage, endurance, mateship and sacrifice (the memorial is shown in Figure 3-3). Information panels near the memorial provide background about the battles and the history of the Isurava battle site. This is also where to look for Kingsbury's Rock and the commemorative plaque to Private Bruce Kingsbury, who was awarded the Victoria Cross for his valour at Isurava. This memorial probably marks the site where he was killed.

**Figure 3-3:** The Isurava Memorial to fallen Australian and Papuan soldiers.

# Kokoda

The battlefield of Deniki is along the track from Isurava to Kokoda. Look for shallow two-man fighting pits close by on either side of the track as you get your first glimpse of Kokoda airstrip.

The official end to the Kokoda Trail is on the plateau at Kokoda, which once contained the government station. On 28 July Australians were attacked and driven off the plateau but retook it briefly on 9 August (see Chapter 7 for all the exciting action). These two encounters are known as first and second Kokoda.

In early 1945, General Sir Thomas Blamey (who was knighted in 1942) initiated a scheme for a series of historical monuments to be erected throughout Papua and New Guinea to commemorate the Australian Military Force's achievements during the war. When the first large pilgrimage of veterans returned to Kokoda in November 1967, to mark the 25th anniversary of the re-taking of the village, the commemorative program centred on the Kokoda memorial and parade ground. The oldest is the Kokoda memorial cairn located at the edge of the parade ground in front of what was the government station.

Alongside the Kokoda memorial is the memorial to the native carriers. This memorial was initiated and funded by Bert Kienzle and was dedicated in November 1959. The memorial forms a stone base surmounted by two stone pillars, linked at the top by a bronze bar, with a bronze plaque on either side of the memorial. The bronze symbolises the alliance of the Australians and the Papuans.

A third memorial is nearby. It was built by the Japan–Papua New Guinea Goodwill Society in cooperation with the Kienzles. In February 1980, the memorial was dedicated to all of the campaign's war dead (Japanese, Australian and Papuan). Other commemorative plaques are also in the station's grounds. In 1995, prime ministers Paul Keating (Australia) and Julius Chan (Papua New Guinea) opened the Kokoda War Museum.

On the Kokoda airstrip (near the entrance to the Oro Haven Guest House), is a wall that displays a number of private plaques, dedicated to the Kokoda trekkers who lost their lives as a result of an aircraft crash on 11 August 2009. One plaque is dedicated to Hannah Louise Kinross and Kelly Louise Weire. Another remembers Kingsley Eroro, who was a trek leader for a trekking company.

On the Kokoda plateau is a series of large white monuments, each dedicated to various combatants who fought on the Kokoda Trail. One cairn bears a bronze relief map by Ross Bastiaan of the track. Of particular note is the memorial to the 'Fuzzy Wuzzy Angels' and other Papuans who gave invaluable service during the Kokoda campaign.

# Covering the Third Part: The North Coast

After Kokoda, you don't need to walk over any more mountains. A (good) road leads east on flat ground to the north coast where Papua New Guinea meets the Solomon Sea.

While the Kokoda Trail is the centrepiece of the story of the fighting in Papua, much is to be seen on this road. From Kokoda, 100 kilometres of road leads east to the site of the last battle in Papua, that of Buna–Gona.

Along this route in July 1942 the Papuans and Australians fell back before the Japanese advance, but in November it was the scene of the defeat of the Nankai Shitai (South Sea Force) at the Battle of Oivi–Gorari.

## Oivi–Gorari

Oivi and Gorari (see Chapter 11) were the scene of fighting both during the Australian retreat and subsequent advance.

At the village of Gorari is a bronze plaque, laid on 29 September 2010 by an Australian trekking company. The plaque was dedicated to the 39th Australian Infantry Battalion for their actions during the Australian retreat. In particular, it honours Captain Samuel Templeton, and privates Sydney Moffatt, Thomas Herbert, Harry Lubansky and Leslie Speechley who lost their lives near Oivi. The plaque was unveiled by Kokoda veteran, Alan 'Kanga' Moore.

## Crossing the Kumusi River

The Kumusi River is halfway between Kokoda and the north coast. The Kumusi River is the largest river to be crossed from Port Moresby to the sea on the north coast of Papua.

Called Papaki by the Japanese and Wairopi by the Papuans ('wire rope', after the way the original bridge was constructed), where the bridge crosses the river now was where the Japanese built several bridges on their supply line from the coast to Kokoda.

These bridges were subject to continual Australian and American air attack. All of the Australians who marched from Kokoda to the beachhead battles passed through this area.

## Awala

On a cairn at the village of Awala is a plaque that identifies the area where the first action in Papua took place on 25 July 1942, between elements of the Papuan Infantry Battalion and the Imperial Japanese Army. The cairn is situated on the left side of the road as you drive towards Popondetta from Kokoda.

Be aware that a tariff may be demanded by the local landholders should you stop and take a photograph of the cairn at Awala. This 'demand for tariff' is often the case for many plaques that are located on privately owned land on areas that aren't often visited by Kokoda pilgrims.

# Popondetta

Popondetta makes an ideal base for excursions to the scenes of the fighting at Buna, Gona and Sanananda. Nearby Dobodura, a large Allied airfield complex built for the Battle of Buna–Gona, has wrecks of aircraft, including a B24 Liberator bomber. At the Popondetta airport is a B25 Mitchell bomber. The plane's nose art reveals its name was Bat Outta Hell.

A memorial park with several plaques and Japanese anti-aircraft guns on display is in the middle of Popondetta. Some of the other buildings in town have propellers or bomb casings in front of them. The house where the Bone Man of Kokoda lived may also be visited (read the sidebar 'The Bone Man of Kokoda' to understand more about this veteran).

# Gona

One thousand Japanese held Gona in December 1942 (see Chapter 12 for more about the fighting in Gona). By the time the Australians took Gona on 9 December, almost all the Japanese had been killed.

Prior to entering Gona village from Popondetta, on your right side is another Ross Bastiaan plaque that commemorates the battle. A short distance away and hidden from the roadway is a privately laid plaque placed in memory of Lieutenant E R L Allnutt of the 2/16th Infantry Battalion, AIF. The plaque was put in place by his son, R L Allnutt, on 4 August 1994.

The local landowner may ask for a small gratuity to view the plaque for Lieutenant Allnutt, situated on private land.

A memorial cairn, commemorating the battle for Gona, is situated adjacent to the May Hayman Memorial Hospital at Gona Village. This area is on the left side of the road as you enter the village proper. The memorial lists all of the units, both army and RAAF, that served during the action at Gona. A short distance from the May Hayman Memorial Hospital is the 1942 Gona Cross.

# Sanananda

Sanananda was in the centre of the Japanese defences from Gona in the north to Buna in the south. American troops from 32 Division joined the Australians in capturing Sanananda.

Four kilometres from the current Sanananda coastline is a sign erected by The American Legion, commemorating Captain Meredith M Huggins of the 3rd Battalion, 126th Regiment of the US 32nd Division. It marks the location of Huggins Roadblock, an American defensive position during the fighting in December 1942. As you drive from Popondetta, the sign can be seen on the right side of the road. However, the sign was erected on privately owned land and is vigilantly guarded by the local landowner who has the uncanny knack of appearing from nowhere and firmly requesting a gratuity if you stop and take a photograph.

The Huggins Roadblock commemorative sign, erected during April 1992 on behalf of The American Legion by then National Commander, Dominic D Difrancesco, was erected before the exact location of Huggins Roadblock was re-opened for Kokoda trekkers in 2005. The sign should have been erected several hundred metres to the north of its current location and on the opposite side of the road. The wartime road actually parallels the current road and is about 100 metres to the west.

To the west of Sanananda Point, where the road ends, lies another Ross Bastiaan plaque, commemorating the battle for Sanananda that commenced on 15 November 1942. Sanananda fell on 21 January 1943 and was the last Japanese stronghold in Papua to fall. A small concrete monument and plaque commemorating the 161 men of the 55/53rd Infantry Battalion, AMF who lost their lives in this battle are on the mainland side of the village. The memorial is lovingly cared for by local landowner, Annanius Mongagi, and a small memorial service is held there just before Anzac Day each year.

# Buna

Near the eastern shoreline of the area that once housed the Buna Government Station is a Ross Bastiaan plaque commemorating the battle that took place here between 19 November 1942 and 2 January 1943.

The plaque is adjacent to the Buna Medical Centre and nearby is a cairn that lists the units that participated in the Sanananda and Buna actions (see Chapter 12 for more on the fighting in Sanananda and Buna). For those arriving at Buna by vehicle, the memorial is beyond the western end of the

Old Strip, where on New Year's Day 1943, 2/12th Battalion made a battalion attack across the strip to eliminate the last Japanese position at Buna.

In the same vicinity is a sign erected by The American Legion, commemorating the actions of Staff Sergeant Herman J Bottcher, Platoon Commander of 'G' Company, 126th Regiment of the US 32nd Division. This plaque is of the same construction as the sign situated near Huggins Roadblock at Sanananda (refer to preceding section). The commemorative sign was erected during April 1992 on behalf of The American Legion by then National Commander, Dominic D Difrancesco. Just like the Huggins Roadblock sign, this commemorative sign is incorrectly located because it describes an action that took place on the western shoreline of the Buna Government Station site, a short distance from the 1942 Buna village locality. This area earned the name Maggot Beach as a result of the large number of Japanese dead who fell victim to the guns of Bottcher's party.

# Noting Japanese Memorials

As the Japanese retreated along the Kokoda Trail towards the sea, they left simple memorials to their dead. Most of these memorials haven't survived but after the war, mainly from 1955 to 1995, Japanese veterans and the Japanese government returned to find their many dead. These men built memorials, which can still be seen paying silent tribute to their fallen comrades: The Shinto altar on the Sanananda road, the modest memorial on Brigade Hill, and the impressive white monument with a Japanese mountain gun barrel on Kokoda plateau.

Many trips have been made to the Kokoda area over the past 60 years by Japanese groups:

- **1950s:** The first Japanese War Dead Mission, sponsored by the Japanese Government, was sent to the 'South Seas Islands' in February 1955. The mission spent just over three weeks in Papua, New Guinea and Bougainville, where it collected the remains of 5,093 war dead. (The complete remains of individuals weren't collected; only portions were gathered and cremated.).

- **1950s to 1970s:** The Japanese Government sent 11 missions to the Pacific area and collected more than 230,000 remains. In New Guinea and the Solomon Islands, the remains of more than 36,000 Japanese from the nearly 300,000 killed have been collected. In addition to these official missions, Japanese veterans' groups were also extremely active in bone collecting.

In October 1969, members from the Kochi Prefecture branch of the New Guinea Veterans' Association conducted a typical search for remains. Before the war, the 144th Infantry Regiment had been based in Kochi Prefecture and more than 3,700 soldiers from Kochi died in Papua. Those 'soldiers who returned alive', wrote Nagano Tadao, president of Kochi Prefecture branch, 'never forgot their pledge to their comrades that they would collect their bones when they died'.

✔ **1970s to 1990s:** Groups of Japanese battlefield pilgrims, called *irei-dan* (literally 'groups trying to console the spirit of the dead') visited Papua New Guinea in large numbers. These groups were usually between 20 and 30 strong, made up of family members or friends of the dead. They toured various battle sites, praying for the dead at each location. When remains were found, they were cremated on the spot according to traditional Japanese customs.

# The Bone Man of Kokoda

One Japanese veteran who returned to the battlefields after the war was Nishimura Kokichi, who served as a first class private, then corporal in the infantry of the South Seas Detachment, the Japanese formation that fought its way along the Kokoda Trail in 1942 towards Port Moresby. After the war, Nishimura became known as the 'Bone Man'.

Nishimura was one of the few to survive the final battles of the campaign on the north coast of Papua at Buna, Gona and Sanananda, where the Japanese force was all but eliminated. He had a successful career in Japan after the war but retired in 1979, left his family in Japan and returned to Papua. He spent the next 25 years in Papua searching for his comrades' remains and relics. He found hundreds of remains and, in a few cases, identified them and handed them over to the next of kin.

Living alone in a house at Popondetta, Nishimura travelled to the battle sites along the track, where he camped for several weeks at a time. He had fought in many of the battles so had a good idea where he might find Japanese remains. He had a special interest in the Battle of Efogi because most of his own platoon was killed there on 8 September 1942 on Brigade Hill where Nishimura was wounded.

Nishimura cremated the remains he couldn't identify, which was the vast majority, and sent them to the Yasukini Shrine, Japan's official shrine for its war dead in Tokyo. In 2005, Nishimura, in his mid eighties and seriously ill, was forced to return to Japan. He made his most recent trip to Papua in 2010, aged 90 years and is the only surviving member of his battalion, the second battalion of 144 Regiment (2/144).

# Part II
# Australians in Retreat

*Glenn Lumsden*

*'That's close enough, sunshine.'*

## In this part ...

When the Japanese began the Pacific War (that part of World War II fought in Asia and the Pacific Ocean), they were incredibly successful for the first six months. In a series of military catastrophes, the British, Indians, Dutch, Americans and Australians were driven back. Thousands of Allied troops were killed and wounded, thousands more captured, their ships sunk and their aircraft shot down. Even the Canadians didn't escape unscathed; their troops were captured at Hong Kong.

For Australia, the greatest loss was in February 1942 when Singapore fell and 20,000 Australians were marched into captivity. Soon after, more Australians were killed or captured when the Japanese took the Dutch East Indies and landed in Rabaul. It seemed Australia was in the path of a juggernaut headed for our northern shores. The natural avenue of approach to Australia's east coast, the mainland of New Guinea, was next. The Japanese landed there and drove Allied forces back along the Kokoda Trail until the Japanese were 40 kilometres from Port Moresby.

In this part, I connect Hitler's war in Europe with the outbreak of the Pacific War, explain why the Japanese entered World War II and detail the mournful list of our military defeats that led across the western Pacific, to New Guinea and almost to Port Moresby.

# Chapter 4

# The Pacific War: Setting the Scene

*T*he fighting along the Kokoda Trail was a small event in a large war in the Pacific, itself a smaller part of the wider world war that Hitler had begun in Europe in 1939. To see why Australians and Japanese found themselves fighting in appalling conditions in the mountains of Papua in 1942 we need to link together the events that led from Blitzkrieg to Buna.

In this chapter, I connect the links, explaining how Kokoda fits into the big picture, by taking a tour. I start in Europe, then move to Japan to explain Japan's reasons for going to war and their relationship with the United States. Then I follow the Japanese advance south towards Australia, pausing here and there to explain battles, the outcomes of which led both sides to Kokoda.

## Warring in Europe

On 1 September 1939, World War II began when Germany, under Adolf Hitler, invaded Poland. Three days later, France and Britain declared war on Germany. The Soviet Union, under Joseph Stalin, had a non-aggression pact with Germany and attacked Poland from the east. Poland was defeated and in the following year Germany attacked France and the Netherlands, defeated them, and forced their British allies to evacuate their army from Europe at Dunkirk.

In 1940, and until December 1941, the British and their Commonwealth allies, including Australia, stood alone against Germany and Italy. The British, threatened with invasion, couldn't do much to assist their colonies in Asia if Japan intervened in the war, which seemed likely. Hong Kong, Malaya and the British naval base at Singapore had to fend for themselves. After the French surrendered to Germany, a pro-German (though not pro-Japanese) French government, the Vichy Government, was formed.

The Vichy Government had no power to oppose the Japanese. In September 1940, the Japanese moved into Indochina (modern-day Vietnam, Laos and Cambodia) but the Vichy Government could do nothing about it. Similarly, the Dutch government in exile in Britain was powerless to reinforce its small forces in the Dutch East Indies.

The war in Europe created great opportunities for Japan, which was intent on expanding its empire. Japan had extended its hold on China in the Second Sino–Japanese war from 1937. China had reserves of the raw materials Japan coveted, but they weren't enough. Only the resource-rich south Asian colonies of the recently defeated European countries would suffice to fuel Japan's economy and strengthen Japan's military and naval forces.

The Japanese decision to go to war in Asia and the Pacific in December 1941 was influenced by Hitler's victories in Europe against the countries that owned colonies in Asia that the Japanese wanted.

# Oiling the Wheels of War

The Japanese invaded Papua in 1942, and posed a threat to Australia, because of a war in Europe and the deteriorating relationship between Japan and the United States. As a member of the Axis, an alliance of Germany, Italy and Japan, the Japanese wanted to profit by the war Germany, under Adolf Hitler, had started in Europe in 1939.

Japan was a resource-poor country without the capacity to be a great power unless it took what it needed from others. The oil of the Netherlands' colony, the Dutch East Indies (now Indonesia), was on the top of the list, but the rubber in the British colony of Malaya and the quinine in Java were also desired.

The Imperial Headquarters in Tokyo had to make a big decision: Should they strike north into Siberia against Soviet Russia or south against the colonial possessions of France, Britain and the Netherlands? The war in Europe shaped this decision too; with Hitler in a short-term alliance with

Stalin, attacking the Soviets would've been a problem. Then, in 1940, Hitler conquered the Netherlands and France, and chased the British army out of France at Dunkirk. Japan decided that the colonies of the Netherlands, France and Britain in south-east Asia seemed ripe for the picking. Even when Hitler reneged on his agreement with the Soviet Union and invaded the Soviets in June 1941, the Japanese didn't change their mind. The decision had been made to go south.

A problem existed though. Another great power that also had interests in Asia, the United States, wouldn't stand by and let the Japanese proceed (see the sidebar 'Tensions between the United States and Japan' to find out why). The Americans had armed forces in the Philippines, a Pacific fleet in Hawaii and held strategic islands, stepping stones between the Philippines and Hawaii, across the Pacific at Midway, Wake and Guam. The Japanese taking what they wanted would mean war with the United States.

## Tensions between the United States and Japan

The determining factor for Japan going to war in the Pacific was oil. Japan is a raw materials- and resource-poor country (not the best place to start an empire). Even with synthetic methods and the extraction of oil from shale in Japanese-held Manchuria, Japan couldn't meet even 10 per cent of its oil needs, and Japan's expanding economy and large armed forces needed 20 million barrels of oil each year. Even more oil would be needed with the decision to take advantage of the war in Europe to expand the Empire.

US foreign policy at the time was to limit Japanese expansion. Oil was a useful weapon that could be used against Japan for, in the late 1930s, Japan imported 80 per cent of its oil needs from the United States.

In September 1940, the US warned the Japanese not to move on the French colony of Indochina. The Japanese did anyway. In return, the United States embargoed certain exports to Japan.

A year later in July 1941 the United States took the far more serious step of the *Export Control Act*, whereby Japanese assets and credits in the United States were frozen, and no more oil would be sold to Japan.

This decision persuaded Japanese leaders that without the oil of the Dutch East Indies, Japan couldn't survive. Japan was importing 4 million barrels of oil a year from the Dutch East Indies; however, in August 1941 the Netherlands government (in exile in London) closed that avenue by joining the United States in refusing to sell oil to Japan.

Japan had stockpiled 54 million barrels of oil, which they believed would last them 18 months — enough time, the Japanese calculated, to capture the oil they needed and get it into production.

Assuming the Japanese plan to take over most of the western Pacific in six months was successful, then the Japanese had to hold what they'd taken. The second part of their plan was to draw a defensive line around their conquests. This is where Australia and New Guinea became important, because the defensive line was to be set up north of Australia — and New Guinea was to be a part of it. (See the following section for more details about how the Japanese planned to implement this defensive line.)

Having made a decision to attack south, the Japanese turned to planning the details. Most of Japan's army was required in China to hold their possessions there, but all of Japan's navy was available.

A dozen separate and simultaneous operations were to be launched and not all were to begin in Japan. The Versailles Treaty that ended World War I had granted Japan useful territories in the Pacific as a reward for fighting on the Allied side. Some of these were close to Australia; Truk (now known as Chuuk) and the Caroline Islands, for example, were closer to Port Moresby than Port Moresby is to Brisbane.

Here is what the Japanese wanted and where they had to go to get it:

- Copper — Sumatra
- Iron ore — Indochina
- Oil — Borneo
- Quinine — Java
- Rubber — Malaya
- Tin — Burma

To obtain everything on their shopping list, the Japanese also needed to defeat the armies and navies who would oppose them. This required taking the British bases at Singapore and Hong Kong, and the American base in the Philippines, as well as Guam and Wake islands.

Once the Japanese had what they wanted, the strategic plan called for the construction of a defensive ring around those areas. The Japanese expected Germany to be victorious in Europe so the Allies, including America, wouldn't be able to devote all their attention to fighting Japan. The Japanese thought that when the Allies were unable to penetrate the defensive ring, the Allies would eventually agree to a compromise peace, allowing Japan to keep most of what it had stolen.

In the south-west Pacific, the defensive line was to run along an east to west perimeter just north of Australia. Rabaul in New Guinea was to be the major base for the defensive line in that region, one where the Japanese fleet could be based, ready to meet any Allied counterattack coming from Australia. For Rabaul to be the major base for the Japanese fleet, no enemy air bases could be within bombing range. Port Moresby was within bombing range, so Port Moresby was also included in the planned conquests.

From Port Moresby, the Japanese expected to make air attacks on Queensland but, except for a brief period in March 1942 when they toyed with the idea, they never planned to invade Australia.

# The War in the Pacific

World War II came to the Pacific Ocean on 7 December 1942 (8 December in the western Pacific), when the Japanese launched multiple sudden attacks spread across a quarter of the world's circumference, 10,000 kilometres from Malaya to Hawaii.

In the most successful series of amphibious operations ever, the Japanese mounted surprise attacks at a dozen places simultaneously. The attacks worked like a charm and, as conquest succeeded conquest in Asia and the Pacific, Japanese generals and admirals began to feel the effects of what one of them later called 'the victory disease'. Everything the Japanese touched turned to gold and they began to think of further conquests until their defeats at the naval battles of Coral Sea and Midway brought the Japanese back to reality:

- **7 December 1941:** Japanese attack Pearl Harbor, Malaya, Thailand and the Philippines
- **26 December:** Fall of Hong Kong
- **23 January 1942:** Rabaul surrenders
- **31 January:** Allied forces in Malaya retreat to Singapore Island
- **3 February:** Japanese capture Ambon
- **15 February:** Battle of Singapore ends in Allied surrender
- **19 February:** First Japanese air raid on Darwin
- **20 February:** Japanese land on Timor
- **28 February:** Japanese land in Java
- **8 March:** Japanese land on mainland New Guinea, and occupy Lae and Salamaua.
- **4 to 8 May:** Japanese sea invasion of Port Moresby turned back at the Battle of the Coral Sea
- **4 to 7 June:** Japanese invasion of Midway Island defeated

Figure 4-1 shows a map of the Pacific Ocean, with the Japanese offensive in the western Pacific marked.

**Figure 4-1:**
The
Japanese
advance in
the western
Pacific.

# *Clashing at Pearl Harbor*

To prevent the US Pacific Fleet intervening in Japan's plan to conquer south-east Asia, Admiral Yamamoto Isoroku, commander of the Imperial Japanese Navy's Combined Fleet, decided to launch a surprise attack on the United States at the same time that hostilities commenced elsewhere. Pearl Harbor was a successful surprise attack, but not in the sense usually understood. America was aware war with Japan was probably imminent and that some of the US bases (those in the Philippines, and Guam and Wake islands) would be hit. The true surprise of Pearl Harbor is the Americans considered it extremely unlikely that the Japanese would do something as risky as attack the major US Pacific base some 7,000 kilometres from Japan. The Americans thought that any Japanese fleet attempting to sneak up on them from 7,000 kilometres away would surely be spotted by reconnaissance aircraft or ships.

The Americans were wrong and on Sunday morning, 7 December 1941 (8 December in Australia) the Japanese struck. In two waves, 350 aircraft launched from six carriers, sank four US battleships and heavily damaged another four. Fourteen other warships were sunk or damaged, 187 aircraft destroyed, and 2,700 people killed. The cost to the Japanese was 29 aircraft.

Fortunately for the Americans, their two aircraft carriers, the weapon that was to prove decisive in the naval war in the Pacific, weren't in the harbour at the time. Nevertheless, the attack was a great success and severely limited the United States Navy's (USN) ability to delay or halt the Japanese advance. Not until May 1942, at the Battle of the Coral Sea, when the Japanese first attempted to take Port Moresby, was the USN able to disrupt the Japanese advance. (See the section 'Battle of the Coral Sea', later in this chapter, for more information about this battle.)

The Japanese attack wasn't preceded by a declaration of war, which came hours later, and US President Franklin Delano Roosevelt pronounced 7 December 'a date that will live in infamy'. Whether Japan intended to issue a declaration of war, or failed to do so as result of an error, is still debated.

Admiral Yamamoto Isoroku didn't want to make war on the United States because he feared it was too strong for Japan. As things turned out, he was quite right to say, as he did just after Pearl Harbor, 'I fear all we have done is to awaken a sleeping giant and fill him with a terrible resolve'.

## Pounding the Philippines

Although the Americans in the Philippines had several hours warning because of the attack on Pearl Harbor (see the preceding section), they were caught unprepared. Their air force and much of their navy was destroyed by Japanese air attack.

The Americans too were a colonial power in Asia. In 1898, they had annexed the Philippines and when the war began were in the process of handing back the country to its own government. The Americans maintained strong land, sea and air forces in the Philippines, mainly on the island of Luzon.

The Japanese 14th Army landed in northern Luzon on the same day Pearl Harbor was attacked and advanced south, linking with the main Japanese landing in Lingayen Gulf on 22 December. At the same time, the US islands of Guam and Wake were captured, the former by 144 Regiment, which was later to fight on the Kokoda Trail.

US and Philippines forces were unable to halt the Japanese and withdrew into the Bataan peninsula, which the remaining 43,000 men hoped to hold as a fortress for six months or until rescued. Quickly occupying the rest of the Philippines, the Japanese launched an attack on Bataan in mid January 1942.

The commander of all US and Philippines forces, General Douglas MacArthur, was ordered by President Roosevelt to leave for Australia in March to command the south-west Pacific theatre of war, which included Australia and New Guinea. Bataan fell on 10 April. The remaining US forces held out on the island of Corregidor until 6 May. The Japanese were now free to use the Philippines as a base to attack further south towards the islands north-west of Australia.

## Terrorising Malaya and Singapore

Ninety minutes before the attack on Pearl Harbor (refer to the section 'Clashing at Pearl Harbor') the Japanese invaded Malaya. The Japanese 25th Army, based in southern Vietnam, landed at six points along the east coast of Thailand and Malaya on 8 December 1942 (local time). The Japanese objective was Singapore, an island on the southern tip of Malaya, and the British naval base there, the centrepiece of the defence of British colonies in Asia.

No. 1 Squadron of the Royal Australian Air Force was the first into action. An aircraft of the squadron had seen the Japanese fleet on its way the day before and when the Japanese landed at Khota Baru the Lockheed Hudsons of the squadron launched 18 sorties against Japanese shipping. Two aircraft were lost and three damaged. One of the lost aircraft was flown by Flight Lieutenant John Leighton-Jones who crashed on to a Japanese barge, killing most of those aboard.

A Royal Navy battleship, HMS *Prince of Wales*, and a battlecruiser, HMS *Repulse*, sortied from Singapore to intercept the Japanese fleet but were sunk by air attack on 10 December.

Everywhere the Japanese attacked in the first month of the war they met with success. Malaya and Singapore were no exception. Tanks and aircraft made up for Japanese inferiority in numbers. At the start of the campaign, 100,000 British, Indian and Australian troops were in Malaya, and an extra 50,000 reinforcements arrived during the campaign.

The Australians, two brigades of 8th Division AIF, had their turn to stop the Japanese in January 1942, but they too failed. The Commonwealth forces withdrew onto Singapore Island having already lost 40,000 of their force, mostly captured. The Battle of Singapore lasted a week, from 8 February to 15 February 1942.

Lieutenant General Arthur Percival scored two notable firsts; he presided over the greatest ever surrender of British troops, and the worst disaster in British military history, when he capitulated to the Japanese in Singapore on 15 February 1942. More than 100,000 men, including 16,000 Australians, spent three and a half years in captivity, during which over a third died.

# Going Dutch

After Singapore fell (refer to the preceding section), and the Americans were confined to the Bataan peninsula, nothing could stop the Japanese taking their prime objective, the world's fourth largest exporter of oil, the Dutch East Indies (DEI — modern Indonesia).

One of the chief objectives of Japan's attacks was to gain access to natural resources, especially oil. Refer to the section 'Oiling the Wheels of War' to understand why oil was so important to Japan's burgeoning empire.

The Dutch government in exile declared war on Japan on 8 December 1941, and on 17 December the Japanese invasion commenced with a landing at Borneo. All key points on the DEI were in Japanese hands by 19 January 1942.

In late February, operating from Davao in the southern Philippines, two Japanese invasion forces set out for the Celebes, Java and islands east including Bali and Timor. The Imperial Japanese Navy taskforce covering the invasion fleets met with a combined Australian, American, Dutch and British fleet in the Battle of the Java Sea on 27 February 1942. The Allies were badly defeated and no longer posed any naval threat to Japanese operations in the DEI. In a subsequent naval battle, the Australian cruiser HMAS *Perth* was sunk. A third Japanese invasion fleet took Sumatra in February and March.

Japan used 50 warships, 650 aircraft and 50,000 soldiers to subdue Holland's colonial empire. The defenders were a combined group of 66,000 Dutch troops and 8,000 Americans, Britons and Australians. Two thousand of the defenders were killed in the fighting and the rest captured. On 8 March 1942, Allied forces in DEI surrendered.

# Invading Timor, Rabaul and Ambon

The Australians had placed three forces to protect the natural approaches to northern Australia. They were at

- Rabaul, 2,000 kilometres from north Queensland
- Ambon, 900 kilometres north of Darwin
- Timor, 700 kilometres north-west from Darwin

The purpose was to delay any Japanese advance toward Australia and act as patrol bases for RAAF aircraft to warn of approaching Japanese fleets. No-one believed the three bases could be held for long if the Japanese made a serious attempt to capture them and that's how it turned out.

## Rabaul

The 1,400-strong Lark Force was attacked on 23 January 1942. The attackers, 144 Regiment (known as the Nankai Shitai, the South Seas Force) who had recently captured Guam, easily defeated the Australians and captured over 1,000, executing more than 130 of them after they had surrendered. Rabaul then became the main base for Japanese operations in New Guinea and the Solomon Islands.

## Ambon

From 30 January to 3 February 1942, 1,100 Australians (Gull Force) and 2,700 Dutch troops resisted a 5,300-strong Japanese invasion. Fifty Australians were killed in battle. After the surrender, more than 300 Australian and Dutch prisoners were executed by the Japanese. The remainder spent the war as prisoners, and more than half died.

## Timor

The Japanese invaded Timor on 20 February 1942. The west of the island was Dutch, and the east was a Portuguese colony. Landing 3,000 troops in each half of the island, supported by tanks and paratroopers, the Japanese quickly overcame Australian (Sparrow Force) and Dutch resistance in the south. In Portuguese Timor, the Australians retired into mountains and conducted a guerrilla war until early 1943 when they were evacuated.

## Heading for mainland New Guinea

The first Japanese landing on mainland New Guinea was the occupation of Lae and Salamaua on 8 March 1942. The landing was unopposed because the small Australian force present withdrew inland. Two days later, before the Japanese disembarkation was complete, an air attack from US carriers Lexington and Yorktown, supported by Australian Hudson bombers, hit the Japanese ships. Three transports were sunk and 110 men were killed. The air raid persuaded the Japanese that greater air cover would be needed for any further advance south.

The Japanese hadn't yet decided how to capture Port Moresby. Three options were under consideration:

- ✔ Advancing along the coast from Lae in the Territory of New Guinea into the Territory of Papua to Buna, then a march along the Kokoda Trail.

- ✔ Making an amphibious landing at Buna, then marching along the Kokoda Trail.

- ✔ Ignoring Buna and making a direct amphibious assault on Port Moresby by sailing across the Coral Sea.

In May 1942, they attempted the third option, which resulted in the naval Battle of the Coral Sea (see following section).

## Battle of the Coral Sea

The Battle of the Coral Sea was a naval battle fought 1,000 kilometres northeast of Cairns, Queensland, from 3 to 8 May 1942.

The Battle of the Coral Sea was the first sea battle in history when the ships of either side didn't actually see each other. All the fighting was done by aircraft bombing and torpedoing enemy ships.

The Japanese set sail from Rabaul (refer to the section 'Invading Timor, Rabaul and Ambon' to find out how they got there) with transports carrying the invasion force and an escort composed of one small and two large aircraft carriers. Signals intelligence had warned the Allies, and the US fleet with two Australian ships, *Hobart* and *Australia*, sailed to intercept the Japanese.

Materially the battle was a Japanese victory, because they lost a small escort carrier, the *Shoho*, against the American loss of a much larger fleet carrier, the *Lexington*. Strategically, however, it was a victory for the Allies because the Japanese didn't achieve their main objective: To get their invasion force (the Nankai Shitai, which later advanced along the Kokoda Trail) to Port Moresby by sea. Having been surprised by the appearance of the US carriers, the Japanese deemed it wiser to turn the vulnerable troop transport vessels back to Rabaul rather than take a risk by pushing on towards Port Moresby.

The outcome of the Battle of the Coral Sea was important because, had the Japanese won then, no Kokoda campaign would've taken place; Port Moresby would've been in Japanese hands, with no need to march over the island on the Kokoda Trail.

With the failure of the Japanese seaborne attempt to take Port Moresby, the Japanese now turned to a landward approach. As soon as reinforcements arrived, in July 1942, General Hyakutake in Rabaul decided that the Nankai Shitai would land at Buna and march over the Kokoda Trail to capture Port Moresby (see Chapter 7).

# Altering the Naval Balance: Midway

In June 1942, another naval battle made its effect felt (along with the Battle of the Coral Sea — see the preceding section), even though it was far from New Guinea.

A Japanese attempt to capture the island of Midway, an American island base west of Hawaii, failed disastrously. The Imperial Japanese Navy lost four of its eight fleet carriers against the loss of one US carrier.

Both sides had discovered by now that the fleet carrier was the key to victory at sea in the Pacific. Japan's loss of four carriers altered the naval balance and forced a change of plan upon the Japanese.

Instead of completing their conquests with the leisure granted by having a superior number of fleet carriers, the Japanese now had to play a more careful game. The move from part one of their strategic plan (capturing all their objectives — refer to the section 'Oiling the Wheels of War' to discover what these objectives were) to part two (establishing a defensive ring around their conquests — refer to the section 'The War in the Pacific' for details on how they planned to achieve this) now had to be modified.

The plan to capture New Caledonia, Samoa and Fiji was cancelled so that more resources could be devoted to taking the locations that were vital to defend what they had taken so far. In the south west Pacific, Port Moresby was at the top of the list.

# Chapter 5

# The Papuan Campaign: Spies, Port Moresby and Guadalcanal

*I*t's often said that the Japanese knew nothing about the Kokoda Trail before they arrived in Papua. The story usually goes that the Japanese thought a road had been laid over the Owen Stanley Range, but this is untrue. Even before World War II in the Pacific broke out in December 1941, the Japanese were investigating the possibility of capturing Port Moresby.

In this chapter, I explain why Port Moresby was so valuable to the Japanese they were prepared to expend considerable toil, blood and treasure to obtain this harbour on the south coast of Papua. Barely had the Nankai Shitai (South Seas Force) begun landing at Buna when their plans began to unravel. The Americans landed at Guadalcanal, threatening the Japanese march on Port Moresby.

The Guadalcanal campaign was concurrent with the fighting in Papua and had a major influence on it. I cover the Guadalcanal campaign at the end of this chapter. If the Americans hadn't gone to Guadalcanal, or had been defeated there, the Japanese probably would've captured Port Moresby.

# Understanding What the Japanese Knew

In 1931, the Japanese Ministry of Foreign Affairs, in conjunction with the army and navy, began to consider the possibility of a future war in the south Pacific. The Japanese published a series of reports on islands that they considered capturing, but New Guinea was not then of special interest. (Refer to Chapter 4 for details about what outcomes the Japanese wanted to achieve by invading various nations in the Pacific.)

By 1940, this view had changed and both the Japanese Army and Navy wrote reports in which New Guinea was considered to be an outlying but necessary acquisition. The reports were based on the investigations of spies who had visited New Guinea disguised as sailors, tourists or botanists.

The Australian Commonwealth Investigation Branch noticed in 1937, when Japanese ships were visiting Papua with no commercial purpose, that the Japanese were taking a keen interest in the region. The occasional genuine Japanese tourist did appear in Papua, usually wealthy businessmen on luxury yachts, but spies were also present. They measured the depth of water at anchorages, at Buna and Milne Bay (both later used for landings), gathered grass samples to see if their horse-reliant army could operate in New Guinea, and hired aircraft and took aerial photographs.

The Imperial Japanese Army report on Papua noted all the roads there and was quite clear that no road existed over the Owen Stanley Range.

The Japanese investigation of New Guinea involved more than Japanese spies. Other sources of information involved the unlikely trio of a Japanese officer, a Swiss spy and an Australian journalist.

## Discovering information

The author of the Japanese Army report on Papua was Major Toyufuku Tetsuo, who later became the senior intelligence officer of the Nankai Shitai and was wounded at the Battle of Isurava.

On 13 March 1941, nine months before the Pacific war began, Toyufuku arrived in Port Moresby disguised as an ordinary seaman aboard the *Takachiho Maru*. He walked around asking questions, visited the land office to buy maps, and followed the road inland. He appears to have been more successful in going unnoticed in Port Moresby than in an earlier trip to Rabaul, after which the Commonwealth Investigation Branch received word that a Japanese officer dressed as a member of a ship's crew was seen carrying out reconnaissance on shore.

The most important thing Toyufuku discovered was the road network of Papua. He was well aware that the road leading north out of Port Moresby didn't go very far and certainly didn't cross the Owen Stanley Range. He also found out that 40 kilometres of driveable road led from Buna towards Kokoda.

All this information appeared in Toyufuku's report, which also contained information on food the Japanese would find in Papua: 'On average two pigs are raised by each family in a village ... they are small and thin, average weight 30kg ... wild pigs are found all over the mountains but it is difficult to catch them'. The report contained a list of local fruit and vegetables, an estimate of the numbers of eggs that might be found in a village and the types of fish in the streams. For an army whose doctrine emphasised local foraging, this was vital information.

## *Mining other sources of information*

The Japanese knew that they could find out a lot about New Guinea in the country that administered it, Australia. Books and maps about New Guinea were easily obtainable by Japanese living in Australia — 3,000 Japanese immigrants were living in Australia in 1939. The information was sent back to Japan and later distributed to the officers of the Nankai Shitai.

All of this was general information but the most important source the Japanese had on the specific route from Buna to Kokoda to Port Moresby came from a long-time resident of Papua and New Guinea, Josef Anton Hofstetter. A Swiss whose family came from Bavaria, Hofstetter arrived in Australia in 1914. He worked his way up the east coast and at one point was a cane cutter at Innisfail. In 1918, he tried to join the AIF but was rejected on medical grounds. By 1921 he was a miner in New Guinea. A number of Germans were living in New Guinea, some miners, others connected with the Lutheran church. It seems Hofstetter sympathised with the Nazi Party and was connected with a Nazi party member living in New Guinea, Hans Schmidt Burck. When Australia declared war on Germany in 1939, German citizens were rounded up but, being from Switzerland, a neutral country, Hofstetter wasn't.

Hofstetter was a shady character and his background is difficult to pin down. However, Hofstetter appears to have worked at Yodda and Bulolo, and visited Kokoda, Buna and Port Moresby several times in his 20 years of living in New Guinea. When the Japanese landed in Lae in March 1942, Hofstetter joined them and gave them the benefit of his extensive knowledge of the region.

Hofstetter's name, or the term 'the Swiss informant' appears on a number of Japanese maps of the Kokoda Trail as the sole informant. How he came by his information is unclear, but Hofstetter was able to describe the track and assist Japanese cartographers in creating maps of the route the Japanese were to follow when they invaded Papua in July 1942.

After the war, the Australians tried to find Hofstetter, unaware that they had already got their man. He was killed in action while fighting for the Japanese Army during the attack on Wau in February 1943.

## Eavesdropping on radio broadcasts

A small unit that arrived in Rabaul with the Nankai Shitai in January 1942 was designed to eavesdrop on Australian broadcasts. It proved so useful that, as the fighting began along the track, the eavesdropping unit doubled in size to 20 English language specialists. They learned some remarkable things:

- **July 1942:** When the Japanese had lost radio contact with their own advanced force marching from Buna to Kokoda, an Australian broadcast gave enough information to tell them where their force was.

- **August 1942:** An Australian broadcast mentioned that the efforts of Allied aircraft dropping supplies at Myola along the track were seriously inhibited by low clouds. The Japanese probably didn't know of Myola before and finding out a suitable supply dropping spot existed that they could use when they advanced was helpful. Finding out the Australians were also having great difficulty supplying their troops on the track was also helpful to the Japanese.

- **September 1942:** Australian politician Billy Hughes, member of the Advisory War Council and United Australia Party leader, stated that he advocated a 'flank move on the Japanese supply line ... well behind their forward forces in the Owen Stanleys', at exactly the time General MacArthur was planning such a move. This information was reported in a newspaper and, together with other sources of intelligence, may have helped to alert the Japanese to the possibility that the Allies were about to try exactly what Hughes suggested.

- **October 1942:** While the Japanese were retreating and were unaware how far behind them was the pursuing Australian force, an Australian broadcast stated that the Australian force was at Efogi. Knowing where your enemy is when he's following you is useful, because you can estimate how long your enemy will take to catch up, allowing you time to prepare.

Much of the information in the preceding list was broadcast by the war correspondent Chester Wilmot, from radio station 4QG in Brisbane. No wonder General Blamey withdrew Wilmot's accreditation and said that 'we should give thousands of pounds to have someone in your position in Japan trying to undermine the commander-in-chief there'.

# Explaining the Japanese and Allied Strategy

Strategy is the art of planning and directing military operations and movements in war to achieve the objective. Two objectives were in play during the Papuan campaign:

- ✔ The Allied objective was to prevent the Japanese from seizing Port Moresby and then to eject the Japanese from Papua.
- ✔ The Japanese objective in Papua was to seize Port Moresby.

To achieve their aims, both sides had to control the sea lanes from New Guinea to their bases and this meant controlling the air above the sea. To control the airways, both sides needed to capture or build air bases.

## Controlling sea lanes

No less in New Guinea and the Coral Sea than elsewhere (refer to Chapter 4 for details about the Battle of the Coral Sea), the war in the Pacific was strategically a sea war.

During World War II, and for many years previously, the seas and oceans of the Pacific region were highways via which the great navies of the United States and Japan exercised their power. The movement of armies to islands like New Guinea, where they could engage in land warfare, was predicated on control of the sea. Armies on Pacific islands couldn't find all that they needed there; food may be available but (in New Guinea, for example) no factory was available to manufacture arms and ammunition and no fuel could be accessed for vehicles. All this had to be brought by transport ships along the sea lanes.

During the fighting in Papua, the Japanese, who had assembled a huge store of war materials in Rabaul, had to keep the sea lane across the Solomon Sea open. They did this reasonably successfully; more than 30 ships made the trip from Rabaul to Buna during the campaign and only two were sunk.

The Australians and Americans had a similar problem. Their supplies for New Guinea had to come from the east coast of Australia; weapons and ammunition from the arms factory at Lithgow and food from Australian farms. The Allies kept their sea lane open too, but at greater cost: Seventeen Allied ships were sunk by Japanese submarines off the east coast of Australia during 1942.

## Choosing between aircraft carriers and airfields

By 1942, the aircraft carrier had replaced the battleship as the premier weapon of naval war. Fleet carriers could carry up to 80 aircraft and proved to be the decisive weapon in sea battles. But in 1942, carrier aircraft weren't as powerful as a similar number of land-based aircraft. Land bases were more efficient and couldn't be sunk, as could aircraft carriers.

To keep the sea lanes open (refer to the preceding section to understand why this was so important), both sides needed to keep enemy aircraft away from their transport ships. Aircraft carriers were simply not as good as land-based aircraft in achieving this.

Consequently, the army that held the air bases in New Guinea could dominate the sea around it, ensuring a constant supply of the necessities to keep their forces supplied.

Regardless of victories on land, armies on Pacific islands eventually starved if denied food coming by sea. The ships carrying supplies would be sunk by aircraft unless the air above them was denied to the enemy.

## Finding airfields in Papua

Before the Pacific war began, both the Australians and the Japanese had noted existing airfields and identified potential airfield sites in Papua.

Basic inland strips, such as Kokoda in Papua and Wau in New Guinea, could be used by small air units but couldn't become large concerns because an air base consumed huge amounts of fuel, bombs and spare parts, not to mention the supply requirements of the 20 to 40 men who worked on the ground to keep each aircraft aloft.

The prerequisites for a large airfield complex were that the land was bare, flat and mostly dry with a small anchorage nearby. In theory, necessities to keep the troops going could have been flown in but, in practice, that would require more than all of the air transport available to either side in 1942. Large air bases had to be supplied by sea and had to be near to the coast to exist at all. The Dobodura-Buna complex of airfields built by the Allies in 1943 illustrates the point. Such a large establishment, with six runways and a capacity to handle several hundred aircraft a day, was only possible because sea supply was available from nearby Oro Bay.

As well as being near the coast, a square kilometre of suitable land was needed for each runway of an airfield complex, to contain a dispersal area, repair facilities, fuel farm, accommodation and storage space. This type of land wasn't easily found on south-west Pacific islands, which tended to be mountainous with lowlands prone to flooding and swampy coasts. Coral reefs severely limited coastal navigation and land communications were poor.

In Papua, just four good locations were available with a functioning airfield, or the potential to develop one or more airstrips. They were

- ✔ Buna
- ✔ Kokoda
- ✔ Milne Bay
- ✔ Port Moresby

That these airfields are also where land battles took place is no surprise.

Neither side wanted any natural resources or raw materials in Papua; what they wanted was control of the four sites in the preceding list.

Yodda and Wanigela were second-rate abandoned airstrips, and neither side considered using them in the early stage of the campaign. Samarai Island, near Milne Bay, was considered a possible site for airfield construction by the Japanese until they discovered Allied airfields in Milne Bay that could be taken.

# Appreciating Why Port Moresby Was Important

Armies need a base to conduct their operations. Port Moresby was the best one in all of Papua and New Guinea. By 1942 it had

- ✔ Airfields
- ✔ Buildings to store supplies
- ✔ Dock facilities in a respectable harbour
- ✔ Reliable supplies of fresh water
- ✔ Roads linking all these elements

No other place in Papua was as suitable as a base of operations for an army of tens of thousands of men. Other bases, such as Milne Bay, could be made useful with the expenditure of a great deal of effort, but with Port Moresby much of what an army required was already there. The main Japanese base in Papua at Buna came a poor third; virtually nothing an army needed was there to begin with. Everything, from bores to sink wells, sheds for storage, concrete for bridge footings and gravel for roads had to be brought to Buna from Rabaul.

Two words explain the importance of Port Moresby: Facilities and location. Port Moresby already had many of the facilities armies need and was located in a useful place, either for the Japanese on their way to Australia or for the Allies on their way to Rabaul. Figure 5-1 shows a map of Papua New Guinea and surrounds, and the Japanese operations there from January to August 1942.

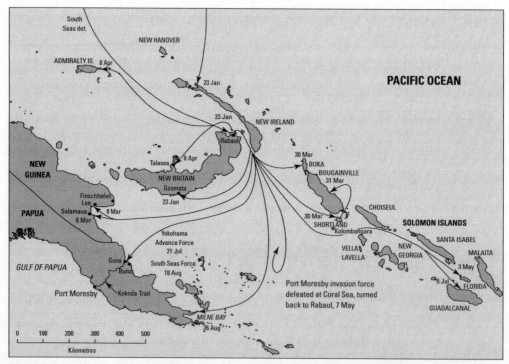

**Figure 5-1:** Japanese operations in New Guinea and the Solomon Islands from January to August 1942.

*Source: http://kokoda.commemoration.gov.au. Reproduced with permission of Department of Veterans' Affairs.*

## A storage and supply area

A useful military base required a harbour and docks, airfields, and critical infrastructure like storage sheds and a guaranteed water supply. Some of this didn't exist when the Australians first arrived in Port Moresby early in 1941, but within a year the town was transformed into the only suitable site in Papua capable of supporting a large Allied army. It was, therefore, vital for the Australians to hold it if they were to advance northwards.

The scale of Australia's operation in Port Moresby was truly vast. In 1942, one ship a day from Australia arrived in Port Moresby, with either 500 men or 4,000 tonnes of cargo. All had to be unloaded, the men sent to barracks or tented camps and the cargo stored. A battalion of 500 or so men required 10 tonnes of supplies — not only for their daily rations but also to build up a several-month reserve, in case the sea lane from Australia was cut. Tens of thousands of square metres of storage space was required, most of which had to be brought from Australia and assembled by a workforce of more than 10,000 Australians, Papuans and Americans. Losing Port Moresby to the Japanese would've ended all Allied operations in New Guinea.

## Location, location

The location of Port Moresby in relation to Australia further increased its strategic value.

Military historians now know that the Japanese didn't intend to invade Queensland but that wasn't known in Australia in 1942. Figure 5-2 shows an example of the wartime propaganda that was used in this period.

The importance of Port Moresby was that if the Japanese captured it, they could and might decide to invade Australia. Without Port Moresby, they couldn't. This was because amphibious operations — sending armies across the sea to invade another land mass — require a base from which to prepare and launch the operation.

Source:
Unknown Artist
He's coming south, 1942
Off-set lithograph on paper
75.9 × 50.4 cm
Australian War Memorial ARTV09225

**Figure 5-2:**
The Australians felt threatened by the Japanese advance, as this wartime poster shows.

The closer the base is to the objective, the better. If the base is too far away, the operation is likely to fall short in two key requirements:

- **Fighter aircraft are required to protect an invasion force at sea.** Aircraft had a relatively short range in 1942, so airfields needed to be close to the objective.

- **Transport ships must, after the invasion has occurred, constantly shuttle back and forth from the base to the landing point to provide supplies, equipment and reinforcements.** If the base is too far from the landing point, the turnaround time is too great and an impossible number of ships are required to ensure the invasion force builds up its strength more rapidly than the defenders can build up theirs.

In 1942, the Japanese were capable of launching amphibious operations in the south-west Pacific to a maximum of 800 kilometres away from their base. This is also the distance from Port Moresby to a suitable invasion site in north Queensland: Cairns. Even if the Japanese didn't intend to invade the eastern coast of Australia in mid 1942, holding Port Moresby allowed them to threaten to do so one day. Without Port Moresby, the threat was a hollow one.

# Taking Aim at Port Moresby

The Japanese bombed Port Moresby more than 100 times from January 1942 to September 1943. The Japanese air raids were launched from their bases at Rabaul and Gasmata on New Britain, and from Lae in New Guinea and Buna in Papua.

At first, no Allied fighters defended Port Moresby, but on 21 March 1942, 75 Squadron RAAF arrived. Within two hours, pilot officers Wacket and Cox had shot down the squadron's first kill, a Mitsubishi 4GM Betty bomber. In 44 days operating at Port Moresby, 75 Squadron claimed 18 Japanese aircraft shot down and lost 12 pilots killed.

Some notable air raids on Port Moresby include the following:

- **14 May 1942:** In the heaviest raid thus far, 13 fighters and 37 bombers attacked. Most of 75 Squadron were refuelling after an earlier raid and were unable to intercept.

- **16 June 1942:** An inexperienced US 8th Pursuit Group flying Airacobras replaced 75 Squadron. In their first combat, they lost five fighters to the Zeros escorting the bombers.

✔ **17 August 1942:** Four out of six Australian transport aircraft were destroyed. They had been airdropping supplies at Myola on the track and their loss caused severe supply shortages to the Australians holding Isurava.

# Considering the Role of Guadalcanal

Two Allied areas of command were side by side in the southern Pacific:

✔ General Douglas MacArthur commanded the south-west Pacific theatre, based on Australia and with responsibility for New Guinea.

✔ Vice Admiral Robert Ghormley (from the United States) commanded the south-Pacific area including New Zealand, New Caledonia and the New Hebrides.

As the Japanese began their advance on the Kokoda Trail, both American area commanders were planning a counteroffensive. Ghormley's offensive, directed north along the Solomon Island chain towards Bougainville, began on 7 August 1942, when 11,000 US Marines landed on Guadalcanal, capturing an airfield the Japanese were constructing. The second offensive would begin when, after halting the Japanese advance on Port Moresby, MacArthur's troops would advance from there in September.

Imperial Headquarters in Tokyo decided that recapturing Guadalcanal was more important than taking Port Moresby. (This was a big shift in the Japanese thinking — refer to the sections 'Appreciating Why Port Moresby Was Important' and 'Taking Aim at Port Moresby' for background reading.)

Reinforcements intended to aid Major General Horii Tomitaro, commander of the Nankai Shitai (South Seas Force) in Papua were sent to Guadalcanal instead. The six-month-long Guadalcanal campaign drew in the major naval, air and land resources of both the Americans and the Japanese, overshadowing the fighting in Papua and significantly influencing its course and its outcome.

## Sinking ships and shooting down aircraft

The fighting at Guadalcanal turned out to be a nightmare for the Japanese. They made five attempts to retake the island and failed each time, giving up and evacuating in February 1943.

Each attempt to recapture Henderson Field, the airbase that made the island a key objective, required the successful delivery of thousands of army troops in transport ships. In turn, this required a major fleet action to prevent the US fleet interfering.

What followed was a series of intense naval battles, the likes of which weren't seen again in the Pacific war. In six major battles and 30 smaller surface actions, the Japanese lost two battleships, an aircraft carrier, four cruisers, 11 destroyers, six submarines and numerous transports — or one-seventh of their navy at the time. The US Navy lost two aircraft carriers, seven cruisers (and the Australian cruiser HMAS *Australia*), 14 destroyers and 14 transports in attempts to land troops on Guadalcanal.

In four major land battles and at sea, the Japanese lost 31,000 dead against 7,000 Americans. This was even worse than it appears, because the Japanese couldn't replace their losses as well as the Americans: Among the Japanese losses were 1,200 highly trained and irreplaceable prewar aircrew.

An indication of the relative industrial capacity of Japan and the United States can be seen in the production of aircraft carriers and aircraft. During World War II, the Imperial Japanese Navy built eight large and small aircraft carriers. The United States built more than 100 (though many were sent to the European theatre of war). Even in 1942, US aircraft production was 49,000 aircraft, compared with just 9,000 aircraft produced by the Japanese.

The Battle of Guadalcanal, which was fought at the same time as the Kokoda campaign, was a larger conflict and more important to the outcome of the war. Many of the 40,000 Japanese troops that went to Guadalcanal would've otherwise been used in Papua, which may have brought about a different outcome there.

## Changing Japanese plans

At first, 17th Army commander Hyakutake, who commanded the forces in both Guadalcanal and Papua, thought Guadalcanal would be easily recaptured and shouldn't much affect his plans in Papua. He simply postponed the attack on Port Moresby in August 1942, while allowing a small Japanese force to advance along the Kokoda Trail, with the aim of seizing a forward position from which the attack on Port Moresby would later be mounted.

Meanwhile, he, and his naval counterpart Admiral Mikawa, saw no reason the attack on Milne Bay shouldn't go ahead. However, by September that year, things were going so badly in Guadalcanal that Hyakutake had to order

Horii to pull this advanced force back north along the track. This was the Japanese retreat from Ioribaiwa.

In October 1942, Guadalcanal caused yet another Japanese retreat in Papua. By November, Imperial Headquarters in Tokyo had still not given up the idea of recovering Guadalcanal, but realised that they must now abandon the offensive towards Port Moresby.

The great Australian victory at Oivi–Gorari and the Australian–American advance along the coast towards Buna in November confirmed what Imperial Headquarters had already decided: If any chance remained for the Japanese to retake Guadalcanal, then all that could be done in Papua was to hold their base on the coast between Gona and Buna.

It was not until the Japanese decided, in December 1942, to evacuate Guadalcanal that significant land and air reinforcements were once again sent to Papua. It proved to be too little, too late.

## Connecting Guadalcanal and Kokoda

Whether Hyakutake made the correct choice in deciding Guadalcanal was more important than Papua is open to debate. What can be said is that had he decided otherwise, the Australians along the track and at Milne Bay would've faced far larger Japanese forces with strong air support.

The ongoing influence of the fighting on Guadalcanal on the fighting in Papua can be seen in the following list:

- **7 August 1942:** US Marines land on Guadalcanal. The Japanese began to consider limiting or halting the planned attack along the Kokoda Trail.

- **8 to 9 August 1942:** Naval Battle of Savo Island. The destruction of the US and Australian cruiser squadron seemed to the Japanese to present an opportunity to capture Milne Bay because without cruiser cover they correctly believed the US carriers wouldn't venture into the Coral Sea.

- **21 August 1942:** Battle of Tenaru River and the destruction of the Ichiki Detachment, the first Japanese attempt to recover Guadalcanal. Hyakutake decided to lengthen his postponement of the Port Moresby attack from a few weeks to a few months because further reinforcements coming from the Philippines, slated for Papua, would now be needed in Guadalcanal.

✔ **23 to 25 August 1942:** Naval Battle of the Solomon Islands. The Japanese transports for the next attempt to retake Guadalcanal were destroyed at sea. The Imperial Japanese Navy decided more air cover would be needed for the next attempt, so Horii's air support in Papua was withdrawn.

✔ **12 to 15 September 1942:** The Battle of Edson's Ridge. The defeat of the Kawaguchi Detachment on Guadalcanal persuaded Hyakutake that a more cautious approach was called for in Papua. He ordered Horii to withdraw from Ioribaiwa Ridge, only 40 kilometres from the Allied airfields at Port Moresby.

✔ **23 to 25 October 1942:** Battle of Henderson Field. The last and largest Japanese attempt to recapture Guadalcanal was defeated. Hyakutake ordered Horii to retreat from Eora (15 kilometres south of Kokoda), abandon Kokoda and retire to the Kumusi River.

✔ **12 to 13 November:** The first (naval) Battle of Guadalcanal. Another Japanese reinforcement convoy took heavy losses. Hyakutake ordered Horii to retreat from Oivi–Gorari, unaware that Horii's force had already been defeated there by the Australians.

# Chapter 6

# Building Up Troops and Assembling the Armies

The war in Papua wasn't just a contest between Australians and Japanese. Both sides fielded what we now call multinational forces. The Australian allies were from Papua itself and from the United States. Other Papuans chose to fight on the Japanese side which also included Koreans, Taiwanese, Chinese and New Guineans from the island of New Britain.

Of the Australians, the infantry did most of the fighting in the rugged mountains where the armies clashed, but air and sea forces were also important to the Allied victory in Papua. The United States Army Air Force fielded the mass of the aircraft on the Allied side, ably supported by the Royal Australian Air Force. At sea, the Royal Australian Navy and the United States Navy escorted transport ships carrying supplies by sea from Australia.

On land, the Allies were up against the Imperial Japanese Army as well as land forces from the Imperial Japanese Navy (IJN). As with the Allies, the IJN's ships ensured the safe arrival by sea to Papua of the army's men and equipment, and also provided aircraft for the Japanese forces.

The weaponry used by the protagonists differed in vital areas — for example, on the Kokoda Trail, the Japanese had the advantage of artillery against an opponent with none, whereas later, at Buna, the Allies had tanks but the Japanese had none.

In this chapter, I cover how Australia made use of both its militia and the AIF in Papua, the contribution made by the local Papuans and by forces from the United States, and the make-up of the Japanese forces the Allies faced. I also look at the weaponry the Allies and the Japanese had access to, and how this influenced the fighting.

# Mobilising Australians and Local Allies

When the Japanese launched their attack in Asia and the Pacific on 7 December 1941, Australia had been at war for two years, with the majority of its troops based in the Middle East.

From mid 1940, military strategists in Britain and Australia suspected Japan would make a move in Asia and the Pacific. With the bulk of Australian troops far from home, some plans and measures were put in place to prepare for this eventuality. These plans and measures included

✔ Making use of the Citizen Military Force militia on threatened Australian territory

✔ Raising and training a new 8th AIF division

✔ Placing a screen of Australian bases, using troops from the 8th Division, across the northern approaches at Timor, Ambon and Rabaul

✔ Increasing the production of all war material, from ships to aircraft

When Japan did indeed attack, the bulk of the new 8th Division was captured at Singapore. Use was made of the militia, but the main focus was to bring home most of the Australian forces in the Middle East.

The following sections cover the build up of Australia's militia and AIF in Papua, the role played by the Allied Air Force and the Australian and US navies, and the help received from local Papuans.

## Installing the militia

Australia's Citizen Military Force, the *militia,* was a part-time force created for the sole purpose of defending Australian soil. Under the Defence Act, the militia were only permitted to serve on the Australian mainland or Australian territories, including Papua and New Guinea.

In the early years of World War II, the Australian militia were looked on with derision, particularly by members of the AIF who called them koalas — not to be exported or shot at.

Because Papua and eastern New Guinea was Australian mandated territory, the militia could be sent there (refer to Chapter 5 for more on why Australia considered it important to defend Papua and Port Moresby). So, in 1941, 30th Militia Brigade sailed for Port Moresby. Composed of three battalions — 39th, 49th and 53rd — they were soon engaged in the labouring duties required to build Port Moresby into an important base. The militia, as a consequence, didn't receive the further training that was planned and needed. The militia in Port Moresby had many problems because a large minority didn't want to be there. The theft of stores was rife and disciplinary issues arose due to alcohol.

From the beginning of World War II in Europe, the militia had been called up for intensive periods of training in Australia. However, the commander of the 30th Brigade in New Guinea, Brigadier Selwyn Porter, didn't think his troops were fit for battle. In April 1942, when the Japanese were already in New Guinea north of Papua, Major-General Vasey wrote to Porter to find out how combat efficient the brigade was. At the time, a ratings system was used to rank the battle-readiness of brigades, from A (efficient and experienced for mobile offensive operations) to F (the worst rating). Porter gave the 30th Brigade an F. Possibly the worst trained infantry brigade in the Australian armed forces was in the position of greatest danger. But when the Japanese landed in Papua in July 1942 the militia were all that was available. Porter selected his least troublesome battalion, the 39th, and sent it up the Kokoda Trail. They were the first Australian battalion to engage the Japanese in Papua.

# Arrival of the AIF (Australian Imperial Force)

As part of Australia's preparation for what was seen as a likely Japanese attack in Asia and the Pacific, the newly created 8th Division of the AIF was stationed closer to home. Two-thirds of the division was in Malaya and was captured when Singapore fell to the Japanese on 15 February 1942. The other third was in battalion groups forming a screen of Australian bases on Timor, Ambon and Rabaul. All were easy meat for much larger Japanese forces well supported by sea and by air. The Australian garrisons fell one after another in January and February 1942. (Refer to Chapter 4 for more on these battles and the strategic importance of the bases to the Japanese.)

Despite previous assurances from Prime Minister Churchill in Britain and President Roosevelt in the United States that they would send troops to protect Australia from the Japanese, in January 1942, Australian Prime Minister Curtin decided he wanted the AIF stationed in the Middle East to return. Neither Churchill nor Roosevelt liked the idea because it would require the use of all too rare shipping. A deal was struck: Two-thirds of the remaining AIF, the 6th and 7th divisions, would return to Australia while 9th Division would stay in Africa.

The AIF nearly didn't get home from the Middle East. Churchill's plan was that the returning AIF should be landed on Java and Burma in February 1942, where it would've been rapidly swallowed up in the as yet unstoppable Japanese advance. Churchill and Curtin exchanged blunt cablegrams; neither would give way. Churchill asked Roosevelt to intervene but that didn't work and eventually Curtin had his way. The AIF continued on to Australia, but not before 3,000 men landed on Java. They were captured and spent the rest of the war as prisoners.

The returning AIF arrived in Australia in March and April 1942. After rest and retraining, they were deployed to Papua, with the first AIF units arriving on the track in August 1942.

## Flying in the squadrons

The Royal Australian Air Force (RAAF), formed in 1921, was one of the earliest independent air forces (that is, independent from the army and the navy) in history. In 1942, the RAAF combined with the Dutch East Indies Air Force and the United States Army Air Force to form the Allied Air Force. This force would provide the air support for the Papua and New Guinea campaigns, with all Australian and American air assets in the Queensland–New Guinea theatre of operations placed under the command of US General George Kenney.

The Americans hadn't gotten around to forming an independent air force by 1942 so the United States Army Air Force represented the nation in the Allied Air Force's contest with the Japanese in the sky over New Guinea.

Port Moresby was an important air base, but vulnerable to Japanese air attack so General Kenney decided to keep most of his 400 aircraft in far north Queensland. The main north Queensland air bases were Horn Island, Iron Range, Cooktown, Mareeba and Townsville. The American and Australian aircraft operated against the Japanese by flying forward to Port Moresby, refuelling there, striking the enemy, then returning to Queensland. Sometimes a second refuelling at Port Moresby was necessary on the return leg. Initially, only fighter aircraft were kept at Port Moresby to defend against frequent Japanese air raids. The Allies also flew long-range reconnaissance missions far out into the Coral and Solomon seas.

## Calling in the navy

The Royal Australian Navy had 15 fighting ships in December 1941, more than half of them in the Middle East. Those nearer home were committed to supporting the defence of Singapore and the Dutch East Indies. HMAS *Perth*, *Yarra* and *Vampire* were lost in the first few months of the Pacific war and Japanese submarines began to *interdict* (deny the use of) shipping routes along Australia's coast. Similar to efforts in the air (refer to the preceding section), the Americans helped beef up Australian numbers, and a United States Navy fleet, under Vice-Admiral Herbert Leary, reinforced the Royal Australian Navy.

The sea war in support Papua was not, apart from the Battle of the Coral Sea (refer to Chapter 4), one of the mighty naval clashes. Rather, off the coast of Queensland and the eastern tail of Papua, the Australian and American ships supporting the fighting in Papua had a more mundane, though vital, task. They hunted Japanese submarines and escorted the material of war from Queensland ports to Port Moresby and Milne Bay.

## Preparing the Papuans

Trained and officered by Australians, 800 Papuans fought in defence of their homeland against Japanese invasion. The Papuan troops were grouped in two organisations, as follows:

✔ **The Papuan Infantry Battalion (PIB):** Raised in 1940, this battalion's privates were Papuan, its corporals and sergeants were both Papuan and Australian, and it was commanded by a New Zealander, Major William Watson. The PIB were the first to engage the Japanese in Papua on 23 July 1942 at Awala when 38 of them ambushed the Japanese advanced guard. Half of the then available 300 PIB were cut off when the Japanese landed. They conducted a guerilla war behind Japanese lines until October 1942, when they were withdrawn to Port Moresby.

The PIB acquired the nickname 'green shadows' when a Japanese soldier's diary was captured and translated. The diary recorded that fighting the Papuans in the jungle was like fighting green shadows which appeared, fired on the Japanese, then disappeared.

✔ **The Royal Papuan Constabulary (RPC):** Less well known than the PIB, the RPC was an armed police force established in 1895. Unlike the PIB, the RPC didn't fight in large conventional formations. Rather, small groups were attached to Australian and American forces to act as guides and scouts. By end of the war in Papua, the RPC had 1,127 members.

## Sending in the Americans

President Roosevelt promised American troops would be available to help in the defence of Australia against Japanese invasion. True to his promise, Roosevelt sent a large force and, by the time the Japanese landed in Papua in July 1942, 80,000 US troops were training on the east coast of Australia, under the command of US General Douglas MacArthur, commander of the newly created South West Pacific Area.

## *Enter: MacArthur*

When the Japanese landed in the Philippines (then under US control) in December 1941, the Philippine Army was under the command of General MacArthur. The Japanese quickly forced MacArthur's second-rate army to retreat to the fastness of the mountainous Bataan peninsula. After it was apparent the US was unable to rescue the force trapped in Bataan, MacArthur was ordered to leave. MacArthur made a dramatic escape by torpedo boat and aircraft, arriving in Australia on 17 March 1942. As Japanese successes after Pearl Harbor multiplied, the Allies created a new theatre of war — the south-west Pacific theatre. It stretched from the Philippines to Australia and MacArthur was chosen to command it.

After MacArthur arrived in Australia, he reorganised the command arrangements. An American admiral, Vice Admiral Herbert Leary, took over the combined Australian and American navies, and an American Lieutenant General, George Brett, commanded the Allied air forces, including American, Dutch and Australian squadrons. An Australian, General Sir Thomas Blamey, became the Allied land forces commander. Figure 6-1 shows MacArthur and Blamey together in Papua.

**Figure 6-1:** General MacArthur and General Blamey on their tour of the Papuan battle area.

*Source: Australian War Memorial Archive, AWM 013424*

## Combining arrogance and charm: General MacArthur

General Douglas MacArthur's name isn't a popular one in Australia. He was seen as talented, arrogant and egotistical, and charming when he wished to be. Blamey said of MacArthur that the best and the worst things people heard about him were both true.

MacArthur was from a military family. His father, Lieutenant General Arthur MacArthur, was awarded the Medal of Honor in the American Civil War. Douglas followed his father into the army and also won a Medal of Honor. MacArthur rose to command a division at the end of World War I and then served as the superintendent of the United States Military Academy at West Point. He served in the Philippines and rose to become a major general and US army chief of staff in 1930. When MacArthur retired from the United States Army, the President of the Philippines, Manuel Quezon, offered him command of his army. MacArthur accepted, but when President Roosevelt federalised the Philippine Army in 1941, MacArthur once again became a major general in the US army. In 1942 MacArthur was ordered to leave the Philippines and take command in Australia.

At first seen as a saviour, MacArthur later sullied his reputation in Australia. Australian generals, admirals and air marshals felt ignored as MacArthur gave most of the important command posts to Americans. Many of these had come with him from Bataan and were known as 'the Bataan gang'. Then MacArthur criticised the Australians for being beaten and forced back down the Kokoda Trail. Australian commanders were sacked by Blamey at MacArthur's insistence. In October 1942, when the Australians were advancing back along the track, MacArthur felt they were too slow. Again, popular Australian commanders were relieved as a result. Australians to this day haven't forgiven MacArthur.

## *Training in Toowoomba: Yanks Down Under*

American soldiers, sailors and airmen were transiting through Australia from January 1942 on their way to the Dutch East Indies (Indonesia) and the Philippines, where an American army had been trapped by the Japanese. When the strategic decision-making body of the Allies, the Combined Chiefs of Staff, decided that the Philippines couldn't be saved, the Americans in Australia were retained there. MacArthur was told to use the Americans, and the Australians, in a counteroffensive north toward Rabaul via Papua. The counteroffensive didn't take place until September 1942, and its main thrust was the Australian advance along the Kokoda Trail. The mass of the American infantry in Australia wasn't committed to Papua until the Battle of Buna–Gona from November 1942.

The main unit was 1st Corps, 45,000 men under Lieutenant General Robert Eichelberger. He commanded men from around the United States. The Corps wasn't of the best quality; as National Guard, they resembled the Australian militia in that they were part-time soldiers. They weren't prepared for war and spent almost a year training in Australia before they were committed to Papua at the Battle of Buna–Gona.

The Americans had already done a little fighting before Buna, but in Australia! American servicemen were popular among Australian civilians but Australian soldiers said that the Americans were 'oversexed, overpaid and over here'. Tensions came to a head with the 'Battle of Brisbane' on 26 and 27 November 1942. One thousand servicemen rioted in the streets of the city. Shots were exchanged between the Americans and the Australians. One Australian was killed and hundreds from both countries were injured.

## Engineering victory

From January 1942, thousands of US army engineers began arriving in Australia. The war required a huge construction effort and Australia didn't have enough specialised trained men. US engineers built roads, constructed and maintained wharves — and served as wharfies when the Australian wharfies went on strike — and built camps and bridges. But the main contribution of the American engineers in Papua was building airfields, without which the Battle of the Coral Sea may have turned out differently.

On 18 March 1942, 46th Engineer Regiment arrived in Townsville to build three airfields. Four days later the first aircraft landed on one and within a month, only weeks before the Battle of the Coral Sea commenced, the three airfields were complete and 100 aircraft were operating from them. The American engineers didn't stop there. Before the Japanese had landed in Papua, the engineers built airfields all along the coast of Queensland; at Horn Island at the tip of Cape York, at Iron Range, Mareeba and Cooktown. By June 1942, 7,000 United States Army engineers were working on Australia's east coast. Several thousand more were sent on to Port Moresby and Milne Bay. At Milne Bay, they again can claim some part of the credit for the Allied victory because the airfields they built enabled RAAF aircraft to give strong support to the Australian ground troops there. Like their infantry and artillery, the American engineers were absent from the Kokoda Trail fighting, but they again came to the fore at the end of 1942. They constructed six airstrips at Dobodura so that the Australian and American infantry could be supplied by air during the Battle of Buna–Gona.

## Engaging the Japanese Army

In contrast to the Australians (refer to the section 'Mobilising Australians and Local Allies', earlier in this chapter), the Japanese maintained a large permanent regular army with proud traditions stretching back to 1873. The Japanese Army also had a strong record of victory. It had won all its wars, the samurai rebellion of 1877, the Sino–Japanese war of 1891 and the Russo–Japanese war of 1904 to 1905. Japan's war against the Germans in China in 1914 was successful and, in 1942, Japan was well on the way to victory in the second Sino–Japanese war. Even the AIF's victories in the Middle East couldn't match this impressive record. In 1942, the Imperial Japanese Army was a highly skilled, well-trained, battle-hardened force and the Nankai Shitai (South Seas Force) contained some of its best troops.

The Nankai Shitai, which fought along the track, wasn't the enormous force that Australians have believed. It was a specially organised light division with six infantry battalions, an artillery battalion, several combat engineer battalions and supporting troops. The huge Japanese base on the island of Truk supplied the Nankai Shitai. The Nankai Shitai had already fought Australian, British and Americans in Malaya, Singapore, the Philippines, Guam and Rabaul by the time it arrived in Papua. The men of the Nankai Shitai believed the Allies they had beaten so far lacked 'fighting spirit' and were confident the Australians in Papua would be the same.

## *Drawing on experience gained in China*

The Japanese Army and Navy that fought the Allies in the Pacific in World War II had learned their trade fighting in China. Since 1931, more than one million Japanese had served in China. Intermittent fighting began in 1931 and the second Sino–Japanese war broke out in 1937. Most Japanese were conscripts; many had served several tours of duty in China. Consequently, when World War II began, Japan was able to call upon a large reserve of battle-hardened troops. Of the Japanese who fought on the track, more than half had some experience of war in China. Their junior leaders tended to be long service veterans. The average non-commissioned officer had been in the army at least five years and senior NCOs (non-commissioned officers) in Papua usually had ten, or even 20, years' army service.

## Learning the trade of war

Lieutenant Abe Hideo recalls fighting in China before going to New Guinea.

Before we went to New Guinea we learned our trade in China. My first battle there was Xuzhou in 1938. I was a lieutenant in command of an infantry company. There were thousands of us in the division and we sang the song 'To Xuzhou, soldiers and horses are marching'. The battle was a shock to me, you cannot describe the noise of the bullets and the confusion unless you have witnessed it. One bullet went through my water bottle. We fought for a month and I lost a lot of my men there. After Xuzhou, the following year, we went to fight the Russians in northern China at Nomonhan, so you see we were very experienced soldiers by the time we went to the south seas.

The 144 Regiment, which led the attack along the Kokoda Trail, had served in China more than most. It was known in Japan for its amphibious landing at Shanghai in 1937. The Regiment took the city in several weeks of hard fighting, then marched up the Yellow River and seized Nanking, the capital of the Chinese Republic. 41 Regiment, the other major Nankai Shitai formation, had also served in China, spending most of its time in Manchuria.

## Counting up the Japanese

After the early Australian defeats on the Kokoda Trail (see Chapter 7), the legend grew of overwhelming Japanese numbers. The front-line troops believed the legend to be true, but figuring out in the jungle how many enemy were out there was difficult and the natural tendency was to imagine the enemy was everywhere. Japanese veterans also report that they were convinced that they were outnumbered on the track (see Chapter 17 for more about this myth).

In fact, the Japanese rarely outnumbered the Australians during the Australian retreat, and during the later Australian advance on the track the Australians outnumbered the Japanese by at least two to one. Of the almost 20,000 Japanese who landed on the north coast of Papua, only 4,000 of them ever went up the track and not all of those participated in the battles there. The senior Australian and American commanders knew this because they had received accurate intelligence about the strength of the Japanese forces engaged, but the 'front-line view' — that the jungle was full of Japanese — has a stronger hold on the public imagination today.

## From Kyoto to Kokoda: Getting supplies to the Japanese on the track

The Allies in Papua were fortunate to be fighting just 2,000 kilometres from their nearest major supply base, Brisbane in Queensland. The Japanese home base in Kyoto was three times this distance — 6,000 kilometres from Kyoto to Kokoda.

The distance from the battlefield to the place where the weapons are made and the food for the troops is produced is important. In war, no nation ever has enough ships to transport its war materials, so the closer you are to where you want do battle, the fewer the number of transport ships you require to shuttle back and forth between the fighting and your base.

## Understanding the Japanese soldier: Bushido vs 'Banzai'

'Bushi' is warrior (or samurai) in Japanese and 'do' is 'the way'. Bushido is the way of the warrior, a code stressing honour, bravery, self-discipline and simple living. The Japanese Army and Navy embraced Bushido as a way to increase the morale of their men. The Japanese soldiers' shorthand description of Bushido was 'the warrior's search for a place to die'. By this they meant that, having joined the armed forces, they had handed over their life to the Emperor and didn't expect to return home. However, this didn't mean that they would sacrifice their lives pointlessly.

The comic book description of the Japanese soldier of World War II has him throwing his life away in a massed bayonet change, called a 'banzai charge'. Later in World War II, poorly trained Japanese infantry sometimes did this, but the army of 1942 that landed in Papua and marched along the track was composed of well-trained soldiers. Their officers were instructed not to throw away the lives of their men senselessly with bayonet charges. They preferred, if possible, to use another characteristic of Bushido, that of winning by cunning and guile, with few battle casualties.

Australian veterans often report that Japanese soldiers would try to trick them by calling out in English at night 'Corporal Jones are you there?' This was Bushido on the battlefield, the attempt to kill the enemy by trickery.

Fortunately for the Japanese, getting supplies wasn't as bad as these distances imply. The 144 Regiment, which led the advance down the Kokoda Trail in July 1942, came all the way from Japan, leaving the regiment's home base, Kochi, on the island of Shikoku, in November 1941. The regiment stopped at Iwo Jima, then invaded the US-held island of Guam. In January 1942, the regiment took Rabaul, capturing the Australian 2/22nd Battalion there. But 144 Regiment's war materials didn't have to come from Japan because the Japanese had a major base as close to Port Moresby as Brisbane.

Truk Island (now Chuuk) had been a part of the Japanese Empire since the end of World War I. The Japanese, who were on the Allies side in World War I, had taken Truk from the Germans in 1914 and the postwar settlement allowed them to keep it, something that displeased the Australian government of the time. By the outbreak of the Pacific war, enough materials were stockpiled in Truk to keep Japanese operations in the south Pacific going for a year. When Rabaul fell to the Japanese, much of these supplies were moved there and Rabaul, as close to Kokoda as Cooktown in Queensland, became the base from which all Japanese operation in Papua — the Kokoda Trail, Milne Bay and Buna–Gona — were conducted.

## The Emperor's Navy

The Imperial Japanese Navy (IJN) was more interested in Guadalcanal than New Guinea, but played an important part there nevertheless. All the Japanese aircraft that fought in Papua were navy aircraft and all the transport ships that went to New Guinea were escorted and organised by the IJN. The IJN also had its own army, marines who fought on land. The marines never fought on the track. They weren't renowned for their ability to fight on land and at Milne Bay they lived up to their reputation by losing badly to the Australians. The Imperial Japanese Army and IJN had their base of operations at Rabaul, where their south Pacific fleet was located. Rabaul was equidistant from Guadalcanal and Port Moresby, so the IJN was easily able to launch an air attack against Guadalcanal on one day and against Port Moresby the next.

# Fighting Advantages: Arming Each Side

The weapons the two sides used gave the advantage to one or the other, depending on the nature of the fighting. When the fighting was very close, the Australians held the advantage: Their Thompson submachine gun offered rapid firepower if the enemy were only tens of metres away. Japanese grenades weren't as good as Australian grenades, another advantage for the Australians. But at longer ranges, the Japanese held all the cards. Their heavy machine gun was effective at more than 1,000 metres and the Australians had no weapon to match it. The Japanese also had artillery able to fire beyond 2,000 metres, though the close jungle terrain meant the enemy could rarely be seen at that distance.

Over the battlefields of Papua, the Allies had the greater number of aircraft, but when the Japanese did appear their Zero fighter proved to be qualitatively superior to anything the Allies had. Table 6-1 outlines the weaponry used by both sides.

| Table 6-1 | Weaponry Used by Allied and Japanese Forces in Papua | |
|---|---|---|
| **Weaponry** | **Allies** | **Japanese** |
| Rifle | Australian and Papuan infantry used the .303 Lee Enfield, a heavy bolt-action weapon used by the Australians in WWI; American troops used the M1 Garand, a semi-automatic rifle | The Japanese used the Arisaka, also a bolt-action WWI vintage weapon, but of poor quality compared to the Allied infantry rifles. |
| Submachine gun | Allies used the Thompson submachine gun, a superb jungle fighting weapon. Having access to submachine guns while the Japanese infantry had none gave the Allies a considerable advantage in the close fighting common in the jungle conditions. | The Japanese infantry weren't equipped with a submachine gun. The IJN's marines did have a submachine gun, the Type 100 Nambu. |
| Light machine gun | One Bren gun was carried per section of a dozen men. The Australians liked the Bren gun so much they carried two per section when possible. It had a 30-round magazine and was very accurate. | The section weapon was a type 96 Nambu, which had a 30-round magazine and was similar in performance to the Australian Bren. |
| Grenades | The Australians used the Mills bomb and the Americans the MkII fragmentation grenade. | The unusual feature of the type 91 hand grenade used by the Japanese was that the fuse was ignited by striking it on a hard object, usually the soldier's own helmet. |
| Medium machine gun | The Vickers .303 was belt fed and weighed 23 kilograms. The Vickers wasn't taken up the track until later in the campaign because of the weight of the gun and the additional weight of the ammunition. | The Japanese didn't have a medium machine gun. |
| Heavy machine gun | The Allies didn't have a heavy machine gun. | More robust and with a larger calibre round than the Allies' Vickers gun, the Type 3 Juki heavy machine gun used a 30-round strip magazine. The Juki was fitted with a telescopic sight and could fire accurately to 1,000 metres. |

*(continued)*

**Table 6-1** *(continued)*

| Weaponry | Allies | Japanese |
|---|---|---|
| Mortars | The Australians used 2-inch and 3-inch mortars. Each Australian infantry platoon had a 2-inch mortar that could fire up to 400 metres. The 3-inch mortar was the infantryman's artillery, with three times the range and explosive power of the 2-inch. Without artillery on the track, the 3-inch mortar was the only weapon capable of reaching the Japanese artillery. | The only mortar used by the Japanese on the track was the Type 89, called a 'knee mortar' by the Allies (although if you rested this mortar on your knee you would break your leg when the round was fired). The Type 89 was a close-range weapon and three were carried with each platoon. Weighing less than 5 kilograms, the Type 89 had an effective range of 120 metres and could fire smoke grenades to create a screen to mask infantry movement from the enemy. |
| Artillery | The Australians had no artillery on the track, but a battery of 25-pounder field artillery came in handy at Milne Bay. At Buna–Gona, the Australians and Americans used 25 pounders, mountain guns and 75-millimetre pack howitzers. | On the track, the Japanese had three kinds of artillery: A 37-millimetre anti-tank and anti-personnel gun, a 70-millimetre infantry gun and a 75-millimetre mountain gun. The gunners usually couldn't see the target in the jungle artillery, so fire was called down by forward observers. |
| Tanks | The Australian 2/6th Armoured Regiment, with the American-designed M3 Stuart light tank, turned the tide at the Battle of Buna–Gona. | The Japanese used tanks only once in Papua, at Milne Bay, where they had two Type 98 light tanks. The Type 98s were effective against Australian infantry, but couldn't cope with the Milne Bay mud in which they became bogged. |
| Aircraft | P-40 Kittyhawk and the Bell Airacobra were the standard fighters. The most common Allied medium bombers used were B25 Mitchells and B26 Marauders. Their heavy bomber was the B17 Flying Fortress. The Australian and American fighters weren't as good as those of the Japanese, and the Allied aircrew hadn't had the experience of combat that many Japanese aircrew had. | The most famous aircraft of the Pacific war was the Japanese A6M Zero fighter. Light, fast and nimble, the A6M Zero could outmanoeuvre any Allied fighter, but was prone to catch fire if hit. The Japanese used two types of medium bomber, the Mitsubishi G3M (called 'Nell' by the Allies) and the Mitsubishi G4M ('Betty'). They didn't have any heavy bombers. |

Bombers are divided into light, medium and heavy, which tells you something about the weight of the aircraft, the number of crew and the tonnage of bombs the aircraft might drop.

# Chapter 7

# Making a Fighting Retreat: Kokoda and Deniki

The Japanese landing in Papua came as a surprise. For a month from 21 July 1942, the Australians and Papuans scrambled to halt, or at least delay, the Japanese advance from the north coast of Papua, along the Sanananda track and across the Kumusi River to Kokoda and Isurava. Marching on Port Moresby via the Kokoda Trail was not the only Japanese objective. They also planned to

✔ Conquer all of Papua, including Milne Bay

✔ Build a major base in the Buna–Gona area capable of maintaining up to 20,000 troops

✔ Construct an airfield at Buna

✔ Investigate approaches to Port Moresby apart from the track

✔ Establish a supply line to Kokoda that would become the forward base for the thrust over the Owen Stanley Range

✔ Fly in supplies and ammunition to the Kokoda airstrip

In this chapter, I tell the story of the first month of the campaign, from the Japanese landing in Papua to the Battle of Deniki.

# Watching the Japanese Advance

On 21 July 1942, two Japanese transport vessels with escorting warships were seen by Australian aircraft crossing the Solomon Sea from Rabaul, heading for the north coast of Papua. The transport vessels and warships dropped anchor at Basabua, near Buna, which Japanese spies had examined before the war (refer to Chapter 5). The ships were attacked by Allied aircraft and one, the *Ayatosan Maru*, was sunk after its cargo had been unloaded. A week later, two more transports arrived, completing the concentration of the Japanese advanced force.

Though the timing of the Japanese landing was unexpected, the place they chose was not. An old airstrip was at Buna and enough dry flat land nearby where other runways could be built. This was unusual on the coast of Papua and both sides were well aware of the importance of Buna. (Refer to Chapter 5 to understand how both sides had looked for potential air bases in Papua before the fighting began.) The Australians and Papuans had 400 men in the region and were concentrating their forces to occupy Buna, but were a week too late.

Speed was important to the Japanese at this stage. A small force moved rapidly along the track from the coast to Kokoda, driving back the Papuans and Australians every time they tried to stop the Japanese.

## Yokoyama Force

The advanced guard of the Nankai Shitai (South Seas Force) was known as *Yokoyama Force*, after the commander of 15 Independent Engineer Regiment, Colonel Yokoyama Yosuke.

Yokoyama had 4,200 men, but only one-third were fighting troops, because Yokoyama's task was one of preparation for the main body of the Nankai Shitai, which was to arrive in August (see the section 'Arrival of the Nankai Shitai', later in this chapter). Yokoyama had 2,300 naval pioneers, engineers and labourers from New Britain to build what was to be a large Japanese base in the Gona to Buna area, including two runways, an administrative and storage area, and a hospital. Chapter 5 explains how the Japanese knew where to build their base.

## Marching to Kokoda

As soon as trucks were unloaded from the Japanese ships, in July 1942, a small force set off towards Kokoda. Captain Ogawa Tetsuo commanded it and his task was to clear aside all Australian and Papuan opposition as far as Kokoda. With Kokoda airstrip in their hands, the Japanese could land supplies and reinforcements there instead of carrying them 100 kilometres from the coast. Ogawa took his own infantry company and some other attachments. The company travelled the first 40 kilometres by truck, then marched.

The troops would've made quite a sight: They carried not only their food and ammunition but also rubber boats for river crossings — all on bicycles and two-wheeled carts.

On 23 July, a day after they set off, Ogawa's men walked into an ambush set at Awala by the Papuan Infantry Battalion (PIB). The Papuans didn't have the strength to hold on for long, and once Ogawa's single light howitzer (a small artillery piece) opened fire, the Papuans fell back. The Australians didn't have a weapon similar to the light howitzer in Papua (see Chapter 9 for more about the weapons the Japanese and Australians used).

Later the same day, a platoon of the Australian 39th Battalion ambushed the Japanese again. Further brief stands were made by the 39th and the Papuans at the crossing of the Kumusi River on 24 July, where the Australians destroyed the bridge to further slow the Japanese, and again the next day at Gorari. The Australian plan was to delay the Japanese on each occasion, because to stand and fight would invite destruction.

---

### Dinner postponed

Ogawa's advance caught a number of Australians unawares. Lt John Chalk of the PIB was cooking a roast of vegetables at Sangara Mission while he awaited the return of Captain Harold Jesser on 22 July. Jesser later told the story to his son Peter:

At the end of the day I was just coming back, walking down the track, and I see these fellows standing at the gate. The house was about 200 yards back from the track and I see these fellows ... about eight or ten of them ... All of a sudden it dawned on me — they were bloomin' Japs. The house was surrounded by a hedge. I don't know if I went through it or over this great big hedge ... I ran across into the back of the house and sang out to John, 'For Christ's sake get out, the Japs are at the front gate.' And he left the tea cooking. We left it for the Japs.

## Escaping from Oivi

The Australians and Papuans had been caught out by the rapid Japanese advance and tried to gather as many troops as they could for a serious attempt to stop the Japanese getting to Kokoda. By the time they got to Oivi, 16 kilometres east of Kokoda, they had collected 140 men of the 39th Battalion, the Royal Papuan Constabulary, a few men of the Australian New Guinea Administrative Unit and the PIB.

Major William Watson, commander of the PIB, had arrived and he was joined by the 39th's Captain Sam Templeton, a World War I veteran after whom Templeton's Crossing is named (you can read more about Templeton's Crossing in Chapters 3 and 8). The Japanese were held up for several hours at Oivi, but then threatened to encircle the Australians.

Templeton went along the track, which took him further back behind the Australian position, to investigate reports of Japanese blocking the track to Kokoda and wasn't seen again. At the time, a mystery surrounded just what happened to him, but we now know he was wounded, captured, interrogated then executed — a fate suffered by as many as 110 Australians who were captured during the fighting in Papua. Not one survived in Japanese captivity.

The Australians were saved by the local knowledge of Corporal Sanopa, a member of the Royal Papuan Constabulary then serving with the PIB. Sanopa found a track not guarded by the Japanese and led the force out to Deniki. Sanopa was later awarded the Loyal Service Medal for saving the Australian and Papuan force.

The Japanese didn't pursue so Watson decided to move his men from Deniki to Kokoda. Figure 7-1 gives a closer look at the northern end of the Kokoda Trail.

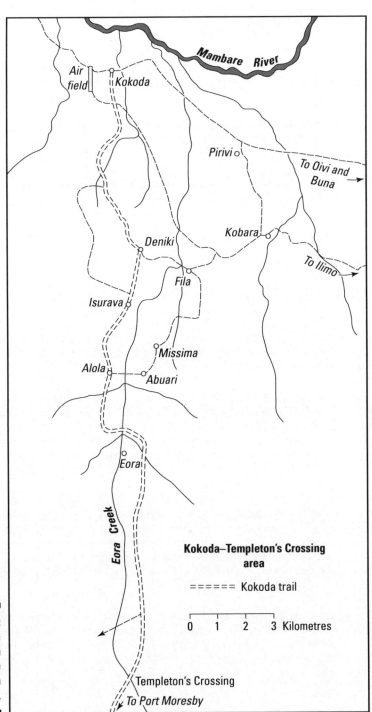

Mambare River

Air field

Kokoda

Pirivi

To Oivi and Buna

Kobara

Deniki

To Ilimo

Fila

Isurava

Missima

Alola

Abuari

Eora

Eora Creek

**Kokoda–Templeton's Crossing area**

====== Kokoda trail

0   1   2   3 Kilometres

Templeton's Crossing

To Port Moresby

**Figure 7-1:**
The northern end of the Kokoda Trail.

*Source: C F Cornelius*

# Standing at Kokoda

The most important piece of ground from the beaches where the Japanese landed to Port Moresby was Kokoda airstrip, about halfway between the two, and where the Kokoda Trail began.

The army that held Kokoda could fly in reinforcements and supplies. The army that didn't hold Kokoda would have to carry everything on the backs of men. (Chapter 5 looks at the importance of secure air fields.)

Two fights took place for Kokoda: One when the Australians lost it to the Japanese on the night of 29 July 1942, and the second when the Australians retook Kokoda, temporarily, two weeks later.

## Losing Kokoda: The death of Colonel Owen

Colonel William Owen, a survivor of the Australian defeat at Rabaul (refer to Chapter 4), flew into Kokoda on 23 July and took command of Maroubra Force. Ten metres above the surrounding land is a flat-topped plateau jutting north to the east of Kokoda airstrip.

This is where Colonel William Owen chose to stand on 28 July. He had 130 men from his own battalion, the 39th, the PIB under Watson, and a few men each from the Royal Papuan Constabulary and the Australian New Guinea Administrative Unit. Owen was hoping reinforcements would arrive by air from Port Moresby. They did; two aircraft circled the field but, unsure who was holding it, the aircraft returned to Port Moresby without landing.

Deploying his force in a semicircle around the northern end of the plateau, Watson awaited the Japanese attack. After midnight, Ogawa, with his one artillery piece and just over 200 men, launched his attack. He came from the north and sent one platoon out to the east and another to the west looking for a way into the Australian position. The Japanese attack wasn't initially successful, but within an hour the Japanese gun found the range and began inflicting serious casualties on the defenders.

The Australians began to waver. Owen was moving among the forward positions steadying the men, when he was shot in the head. The mortal wounding of Owen further shook the morale of the Australians and Papuans. Major Watson (still in command of the PIB) took command and ordered a retreat.

In the dark, the Australians and Papuans escaped without the Japanese, whose own commander had also been killed, realising they had gone.

## *Retaking Kokoda temporarily*

After the Australians were ejected from Kokoda, they retreated once more to Deniki. A lull occurred in the fighting because the Japanese main force hadn't yet landed and the Japanese fighting troops that had come with Yokoyama's advanced force, 1/144 Battalion, were still marching up from the coast.

Colonel Allen Cameron, who had also escaped from Rabaul after the Japanese captured it in January, arrived from Port Moresby to take over Maroubra Force. Now with 500 men, he decided that, because the Japanese had halted their advance, an opportunity existed to retake Kokoda. A company of 49th battalion in Port Moresby was standing by to fly into Kokoda if Cameron held the strip. If the plan worked, a company per day (more than a battalion per week) could fly in and tip the balance in Australia's favour.

Unfortunately for Cameron, the Japanese 1/144 Infantry Battalion had arrived at Kokoda and the Japanese made their move the very same day Cameron made his.

Cameron split his force and attacked along three tracks:

- ✔ On his right, at Pirivi, the Australians were to block any Japanese coming from the coast to Kokoda. No Japanese were actually coming that way, but the Australians at Pirivi encountered two platoons of Japanese engineers. The engineers' main job was to improve the route from the north coast to Kokoda but they were combat trained and could fight well when called upon. The Australians fought them all day with no advantage gained by either side. When it got dark, the Australians retired to Deniki.

- ✔ On the left, Cameron, with the strongest of his three forces, bumped headlong into Colonel Tsukamoto Hiroshi with his battalion of 144 Regiment coming the other way. Both commanders were surprised and eventually Cameron, seeing no way through, also withdrew to Deniki.

- ✔ The third Australian force, using a track somewhere in the middle of those on the left and the right, arrived at Kokoda without any contact with the Japanese. They dug in and awaited reinforcement from the air, but Cameron was unable to communicate with Port Moresby so no reinforcement came.

## Recalling the skirmish at Pirivi

Arnold Forrester, from Australia's 39th Battalion, tells of his experiences at Pirivi:

We met up with the rest of the boys at Deniki, which is three-quarters of a day's walk out of Kokoda, overlooking the strip. We had a bird's eye view of the Japs cooking their meals down near the strip. Colonel Cameron arrived to take charge after Colonel Owen was killed. Cameron decided to split the troops to retake Kokoda. He sent two companies down from two different directions and my company was sent way out towards Pirivi to stop the Japs advancing.

We came across a very strong force of Japanese. My skipper, Captain Bidstrup, sent a section forward to take a track junction, the Japs got between us and them. He sent two runners to tell the section to retreat. Tommy Freestone and Bill Joss. We never saw them again. By this time, it was dark. Captain Bidstrup decided to retire for the day. We went back to Deniki carrying the wounded. We expected the Japs to follow us.

Because the Australian forces had retired to Deniki, Tsukamoto (144 Regiment) followed them up to Deniki, which he intended to attack. There he learned that an Australian force was behind him, who were holding Kokoda. He sent a company back to retake Kokoda, but they failed. After a day and a half, the Australians at Kokoda, who were running low on food and ammunition and unable to communicate with Cameron (who didn't know where they were), withdrew from Kokoda. Within three days of the beginning of Cameron's attack, all his men were back at Deniki — exactly where they had begun.

## *Digging in at Deniki*

With no prospect of having another go at Kokoda, Maroubra Force (which was the name given to the Australian force fighting on the Kokoda Trail) dug in at Deniki.

Deniki was of importance because it commanded a good view of Kokoda. If the Japanese were reinforced, or tried to outflank Deniki, the Australians would see what the Japanese were up to. Tsukamoto was well aware of this and now proceeded with his attack on Deniki, which had been delayed several days by Cameron's retaking of Kokoda on 9 August.

Cameron and Tsukamoto each had about 450 men, but Tsukamoto also had an *artillery piece*, a weapon with which he could bombard the Australians (and they had nothing with which to reply).

The fighting at Deniki took place over three days:

- **12 August 1942:** The Japanese probed the Deniki position until they found the exact deployment of an Australian platoon. Their gun was then directed onto the location and accurate artillery fire fell on the Australians.

- **13 August 1942:** The Japanese repeated their performance and again the Australians lost men due to their lack of artillery.

- **14 August 1942:** Cameron decided he couldn't stay and prepared to withdraw early in the morning. Tsukamoto thought that his gun had softened up the Australians enough and organised an assault on the same morning. Cameron's men moved out just in time and the Japanese assaulted an empty position.

After withdrawing from Deniki, the Australians retired to Isurava where another lull in the fighting occurred as both sides awaited reinforcements.

## A Japanese soldier comments on the fighting at Deniki

Ueda Kameji, from Japan's 144 Regiment, spoke about what happened at Deniki and Kokoda in August 1942:

The Australians around Kokoda caused us some problems. We had not found them so difficult at Rabaul, they surrendered quickly there. And the move forward from the coast of Papua was easy. The Australians kept falling back and we thought it would be just like Guam, where the Americans did not fight hard. When they surrendered they expected us to give them cigarettes! We were thinking that if this kept up we would be in Australia pretty soon. But at Kokoda and Deniki all that changed. The Australians even retook Kokoda from us for a while. That gave us a shock. But eventually we recaptured it and advanced on towards Port Moresby. But it was there, at Kokoda, and at Deniki, that we first realised that this was not going to be easy.

# Considering the Next Moves

In the first month from the Japanese landing on 21 July 1942, only relatively small forces had fought one another in Papua. But from mid August, as the main bodies of both armies began to arrive, the Allies and the Japanese had to reconsider their respective plans.

## Sending in the Australian Imperial Forces

The 2nd AIF was a special force raised in 1939 for overseas service. By 1942, the force was well trained and battle hardened, having had experience of war in Africa, Syria, Greece and Crete. The 2nd AIF was much better quality than the Australian militia that had been fighting in Papua until then.

General MacArthur, who commanded all Allied land, sea and air forces in the south-west Pacific theatre of war, wasn't yet convinced that the Japanese meant to advance along the track all the way to Port Moresby. He believed they may only have intended to establish a large base at Buna and to secure that base by pushing the Australians back beyond Kokoda.

If this was the Japanese plan, MacArthur also thought a possibility existed that the Japanese wished to lure more Australians out of Port Moresby along the track to Kokoda. He knew they hadn't yet landed their main force at Buna, and considered that they might use it for another amphibious landing on the beaches of Port Moresby, as the Japanese had intended during the Battle of the Coral Sea in May.

But when, in mid August 1942, the main body of the Nankai Shitai was seen by reconnaissance aircraft at sea headed for Buna, MacArthur realised that the Japanese did intend a major move by land on Port Moresby along the track. It was then clear that Papua had to be reinforced by troops from Australia. New Guinea Force Headquarters in Port Moresby controlled two bodies of troops in Papua: Two militia brigades in Port Moresby and one at Milne Bay.

General MacArthur directed General Blamey, who commanded all land forces under MacArthur, to send the 7th Division, under Major General Arthur (Tubby) Allen, to Papua. The troops were split as follows:

- 18th Brigade was sent to Milne Bay.
- 21st Brigade went to Port Moresby:
  - Two of the brigade's battalions, 2/14th and 2/16th, were sent up the track.
  - One battalion, 2/27th was kept in reserve in Port Moresby.

Enlarging the Australian force in Papua also required an extra level of command. 1st Australian Corps, under Lieutenant General Sydney Rowell, went to replace Major General Basil Morris, who had commanded in Papua since the Japanese landing of 21 July 1942.

## Arrival of the Nankai Shitai

Like the Allies (refer to the preceding section), the Japanese too were momentarily unsure of what to do next.

Cameron's retaking of Kokoda on 9 August had prompted a discussion in Rabaul among the staff of General Hyakutake Harakuchi, commander of 17th Army. The Japanese hadn't expected serious Australian resistance until they were much closer to Port Moresby and Hyakutake's plan was that the Nankai Shitai would make a rapid advance along the track.

But now it appeared that a more measured approach might be called for. While considering this, Hyakutake had more unwelcome news. The Americans had landed at Guadalcanal on 7 August and retaken the airstrip the Japanese were constructing there. For a few days, Hyakutake wasn't sure if the American attack was only a small raid or a major move. His superiors in Imperial Headquarters in Tokyo were convinced that the Allies didn't have enough strength to mount two counteroffensives and that the one they expected would come via New Guinea and be based from Port Moresby — which was the reason the Japanese wanted to get there first.

The origins of the *MO operation* (the Japanese plan to capture Port Moresby) were in an attempt to forestall this counterattack by taking the base it would be mounted from. Now it was apparent that the Imperial Headquarters had it wrong; the Allies did have the resources for two counterattacks, one from Australia via New Guinea and the other up the Solomon Islands chain from Guadalcanal.

Was it necessary, the Japanese pondered, to postpone MO, and not send the Nankai Shitai to Papua? The force could be kept in Rabaul for use against Guadalcanal if necessary. After discussion with Tokyo, Hyakutake adopted a middle course. Reinforcements were coming from the Philippines and he would use them to retake Guadalcanal. Meanwhile, he would send the Nankai Shitai to Papua. The commander of the Nankai Shitai, General Horii, was told he could advance part way along the track but he was forbidden to attack Port Moresby. After Guadalcanal was retaken, Horii would be reinforced and the attack on Port Moresby would commence.

At the same time the Allies began to reinforce Papua with a large number of first rate troops, the Japanese decided to put the Papua operation on hold until they had recaptured Guadalcanal. Refer to Chapter 5 for information about Guadalcanal and the action that took place there.

# Counting Casualties up to Deniki

From the Japanese landing in Papua to the end of the Deniki engagement, the Australians and Papuans had suffered defeat after defeat, but as the whole period, from 21 July to 14 August 1942, can be seen as a series of attempts to delay the Japanese, it had been reasonably successful for the Australian side. Another measure of how well the Australians were doing was how many of the enemy they had killed or wounded, against how many they lost themselves.

Both sides were fighting in the jungle, where the enemy aren't often seen. Working out whether one side is inflicting heavier casualties than the other can be difficult.

Both the Japanese and the Australians made extraordinary claims of enemy casualties. At the fight at Pirivi, a part of the second Kokoda engagement, the claims were that

✔ The Australians killed 50 Japanese

✔ The Japanese killed 74 Australians

In fact, the actual number of casualties (killed and wounded) was as follows:

✔ The Japanese lost six killed and had 16 wounded.

✔ The Australians lost five killed and had six wounded.

Since the Japanese landed, the Australians and Papuans had generally been successful in inflicting more casualties than they lost. From the first ambush at Awala to Deniki, they had killed 50 Japanese and wounded 87 while losing 42 dead and 34 wounded.

Only 500 men on each side had so far been engaged, so these were serious casualties relative to the size of the forces.

# Chapter 8

# Entering the Mountains

- - - - - - - - - - - - - - - - - - - - - - - - -

## In This Chapter

▶ Trying to halt the Japanese at Isurava

▶ Retreating again

▶ Sacking the commander at Efogi

▶ Halting the retreat on Imita Ridge

- - - - - - - - - - - - - - - - - - - - - - - - -

After Deniki, the scene of conflict switched to the Owen Stanley Range through which the Kokoda Trail winds.

For the next three months, from August to October 1942, the Australians, Papuans and Japanese fought in this unpleasant, exhausting and hostile terrain, the likes of which few of them had seen before. The mud, living exposed to the rain, and the cold nights at altitude conspired to wear down the Allies and their enemy.

In this chapter, I cover the series of failed attempts by the Australians to halt the Japanese advance: Isurava, the retreat to Efogi and the Australian disaster there, and the final Australian defeat on Ioribaiwa Ridge. Again, the Australians fell back, to Imita, but there the retreat halted.

## Standing at Isurava

The Battle of Isurava was the first test between the major Australian and Japanese forces. Now commanded by Brigadier Arnold Potts, the Australian objective was to prevent further Japanese penetration into the Owen Stanley Range towards Port Moresby.

Potts had 2,300 men, the remains of 39th battalion and the Papuans, now reinforced by 53rd militia battalion and two experienced AIF battalions, the 2/14th from Victoria and the 2/16th from Western Australia (both 21st Brigade Battalions).

The Japanese commander, Major General Horii Tomitaro, had about 4,000 men available. Because Imperial Headquarters had decided to postpone the advance on Port Moresby, Horii had been instructed not to advance to the southern side of the Owen Stanley Range with his main force.

However, Isurava was on the north side of the range. From Horii's perspective, the Australian force blocking the Kokoda Trail at Isurava presented him with the opportunity to destroy them before, as he feared they might, they retreated beyond the point where he was allowed to pursue them.

The story of Isurava is told in three parts. First the Australians and the Japanese had to assemble their forces. Then the Japanese attacked and drove the Australians back from Isurava. Finally the defeated Australians made their escape.

## *Massing the forces*

Brigadier Arnold Potts was careful not to tire out his men by marching them too quickly up the track or burdening them with extremely heavy loads. The Australians marching to Isurava to join the force already there along the track advanced at 10 to 15 kilometres a day and carried 20 kilograms per man. As a result, they arrived fresh and ready to fight.

Not so with the Japanese. Horii's main body, three infantry battalions and his artillery, a dozen light howitzers, began arriving at Buna on 19 August, each carrying more than 30 kilograms of equipment, ammunition and food. They were immediately sent to Isurava at breakneck speed. Marching 20 kilometres a day was too much for the Japanese infantry; hundreds fell out along the way and didn't arrive in time to participate in the battle.

Unworried by the loss of strength and very confident of victory, Horii didn't even use all the troops that did arrive. Horii kept one of his battalions from Buna out of the fight, to be used to pursue the broken Australians. For these reasons, he only had about 2,300 men engaged at Isurava, about the same number the Australians had. His big advantage was his artillery; the Australians had none.

The pursuit of a defeated enemy is as important as the battle in annihilating an enemy. Soldiers who have fought in a battle are too tired to pursue the broken enemy effectively, which is why Horii kept one battalion back in reserve from the fighting in Isurava.

## Describing the battlefield

The Battle of Isurava was fought on both sides of a steep-sided gorge through which runs Eora Creek.

Eora Creek is a constant companion of the track as it rises at Myola, and follows the track north through Templeton's Crossing to Eora Village, past Isurava and down to the lowlands, flowing into the Mambare River just east of Kokoda village.

On the left slope of the gorge as the Australians looked north towards Kokoda was Isurava, held by 39th and 2/14th Battalions. On the right slope of the gorge, only two kilometres away as the crow flies but a tough four-hour walk to get there, was 53rd Battalion, later reinforced by half of 2/16th Battalion, the last battalion to arrive. A second track ran along the right of the gorge parallel, to the track on the left.

The Japanese attacked down both tracks. Horii's plan was to pin the Australians at Isurava with a frontal attack by 1/144 while another battalion, 2/144, attacked along the track east of the gorge, then crossed Eora Creek to cut the track in the Australian rear at Alola. As this was occurring, a third battalion, 3/144, would sweep around the Australian left and meet up with 2/144, surrounding the Australians.

The Australian plan was much simpler: To hold on like grim death.

## Losing Isurava

The Japanese 1/144 Battalion had arrived in Papua with Yokoyama's advanced force (you can read about them in Chapter 7) in July 1942. While Yokoyoma's force waited for the Japanese main body to arrive, the force investigated the position of the Australians at Isurava, to discover the location and length of the Australians' position.

By 27 August, the rest of Horii's force had arrived and the attack took place over the following days:

✔ **27 August 1942:** 1/144 Battalion attacked Isurava with the support of the artillery and a company of 3/144. Across the gorge to the east, 2/144 advanced against 53rd Battalion. Neither attack was successful, though 53rd, a poorly trained Australian militia battalion, showed signs of being unable to hold up the Japanese.

✔ **28 August 1942:** The 2/16th battalion arrived to stiffen Australian defences east of the gorge. Until the end of the battle, the Japanese battalion to the east, 2/144, was unable to break through the Australians there and cross the gorge to Alola. Australian counterattacks against the Japanese also failed. On this day, the Battle of Isurava was decided on the west side of the gorge. Here the 3/144 Battalion slipped around the Australian left and the following day Potts's battalion commanders on this front told him that they couldn't hold on much longer.

✔ **29 August 1942:** During the night, Potts retreated his force to Isurava Rest House, one kilometre to his rear. The Japanese were unaware of the Australian move and launched an attack on Isurava in the morning to find the Australians gone.

## Heading back to the rest house

Potts's attempt to hold on at Isurava Rest House wasn't successful. The Japanese 3/144 Battalion again slipped around his left and attacked down on to the rest house from higher ground. In addition, the Japanese artillery bombardment on the rest house increased as more guns arrived on the battlefield. Seven Japanese guns were situated on a ridge north of Isurava and the Australians had no weapon with the range to engage them.

Potts again planned a retreat. He had no time to bring the Australian force across the gorge to join the Australians on the western side so they were directed to head south on the east side and rejoin the main body at Eora village, seven kilometres away along the track. West of the gorge, Potts planned a series of rearguard actions to hold back the Japanese to allow time for the wounded to be evacuated.

## Getting away from Isurava

As Maroubra Force (which was what the Australian force on the Kokoda Trail was called) was extracting itself from Isurava Rest House, the Japanese 3/144 Battalion launched a new attack from the high ground west of the rest house.

The Japanese fire scattered the Australians who were formed up along the track waiting for the order to withdraw. So great was the confusion that one Australian company accidentally attacked towards another, causing casualties and scattering the headquarters of 2/14th Battalion into the jungle. On the east side of the gorge, where neither side had gained an advantage, the remainder of 53rd and 2/16th battalions were able to slip away south as Potts had ordered.

IN THEIR OWN WORDS

# A Japanese soldier at Isurava

Imanishi Sadaharu, a Japanese soldier, tells of what it was like, fighting in Isurava:

I heard that Australia was where the British sent the criminals and that the Australians were scared of dying in battle. But I must say that, though they were different to us, I was impressed with the Australians I fought at Isurava. They were very tenacious.

My company fought right through the whole battle. We were there at the start and I was ordered to scout to find the Australian position. The order was to go up the main track at night and be back by ten o'clock the next day. My company commander told me to be careful, to take off my shoes and socks, not step on twigs and not make any sound. He advised me not to walk around a track corner, but to go through the jungle at the side. He added unhelpfully that our scouts were often killed. We left and soon came across a log bridge over a small stream and Matsuo, who accompanied me, saw an Australian asleep there and shot him. So as it turned out we made quite a lot of noise. The enemy responded with fire. We thought we had found their main line so we could go back and report now, but we had lost Ohama. When we found him, he was wounded. We carried him back to the medical tent but he was bleeding a lot. The hospital orderly told us that it was too late to help Ohama. He died.

A couple of days later our big attack at Isurava began. My company was on the right trying to get around the end of the Australian line. I led the company as I knew the way. Matsuo was with me again and after a while he said that he thought we had come too far up the hill so we went back a little and there was the enemy position. We looked down and saw five or six Australians with their rifles on their shoulders talking to each other. I thought it was a good chance to shoot them. We fired and they fired back but I do not know if we got any of them as we were 100 metres away. I remember one of them had a submachine gun and he just sprayed the jungle with bullets. He didn't know where we were.

There was a man under my command who had joined up at the same time as me. He was the son of a farmer and was very brave. I told him to sneak up closer to the Australians to see if they were still there. I told him not to fight, just to see what they were doing and come back and tell me. But he did not come back and I sent a second soldier who came back and said that the farmer's son was dead.

Then we were ordered to attack. I led the platoon but we did not do too well. The next morning we tried a different approach and showered them with grenades before advancing. Nothing happened, we thought they had gone. I called 'forward' and as I did so I felt something hot on my face. I was shot in the face. I had not realised that the Australians were only a few metres away hidden by the jungle.

The fighting at Isurava resulted in a Japanese victory, but the Australian force wasn't completely destroyed as Horii had planned. The main reason for the Japanese victory was their artillery, which Australian forces sorely lacked. In fact, no further attempt to halt the Japanese was possible unless the Australians were reinforced. The wash-up of the casualties was as follows:

- The Australians lost 99 dead and 111 wounded. The surviving Australians were disorganised and some were demoralised.

- The Japanese lost 130 dead and 226 wounded.

# Rearguards and Vanguards: Struggling for Possession

The Australian force leaving Isurava needed a *rearguard* whose job was to delay the Japanese and keep them from ruining the retreat. The Japanese had a *vanguard* whose job was to break through the Australian rearguard and get at the main force, disrupting the Australian retreat. The contest, between the Australian rearguard and the Japanese vanguard as the Australians retreated from Isurava to Efogi, was won by the Australians. In six days of trying (31 August to 5 September), the Japanese didn't manage to overcome the Australians who, in each of three engagements, delayed the Japanese, then slipped away.

The Japanese vanguard was the elements of 41 Regiment that had been kept in reserve during Isurava for just this moment — the pursuit of a defeated enemy. The regiment wasn't at full strength but it did have 1,305 men and several guns. The Australian rearguard was about half the Japanese strength.

Colonel Key of 2/14th would normally have been in command but he was still missing after the Battle of Isurava (we now know that he was captured by the Japanese and killed), so Colonel Caro of 2/16th took command of the two battalion rearguard. Weakened by casualties and with some lost men still to rejoin their unit, the rearguard was no stronger than 700 men. Three times, at Eora, Templeton's Crossing and at Myola Ridge, the Japanese tried and failed to wipe out the Australian rearguard.

## Entering Eora

The first Australian position after Isurava was a little south of Alola. The Japanese didn't attack so the Australians retreated to the high ground above and south of Eora Village on 31 August. There they dug in and came under a Japanese artillery bombardment.

After dark, the Japanese 41 Regiment came across the creek and attacked, trying to get around the Australian flanks to cut the track in the Australian rear. By dawn, it looked like they were about to achieve their aim so Caro ordered 2/16th to fall back through 2/14th, then 2/14th passed through 2/16th and so on until contact with the Japanese was broken.

## Reaching Templeton's Crossing

By 2 September, the Australian rearguard was a kilometre north of Templeton's Crossing.

The 41st Regiment's commander, Colonel Yazawa, was unhappy with his men's progress. Again he ordered a force to pin the Australians to the front then another to slip around the flank. This time the Australians didn't wait but retreated before the fighting became intense.

In an attempt to speed up the retreat, Caro sent one of his battalions down the Kokoda Trail and the other on a side track that joined the Kokoda Trail further south. Caro calculated that if the Japanese were already on the main track behind him, the battalion on the other track would be able to bypass them. In the end, the Japanese didn't interfere with either battalion and the whole force was able to cross to the west side of Eora Creek and dig in on Myola Ridge (see following section).

## Making it to Myola Ridge

The third Japanese attack on the Australian rearguard took place on the north end of Myola Ridge on 4 September. The Japanese had only one artillery piece forward but they made good use of it. Watching the Australian positions in the afternoon, they determined where the fire of the gun would be most effective. Then, after dark, the gun opened fire in support of the Japanese attack.

Once more a Japanese flanking force of two infantry companies tried to block the track behind the Australian troops. This time the Japanese were successful but didn't realise it. Several tracks existed and in the dark the small Japanese force that had blocked the Kokoda Trail didn't know which track it was on so didn't call to be reinforced. The Australians were forced to do what they had been able to avoid so far in the retreat since 31 August — on the morning of 5 September they cut their way out to the rear through the Japanese blocking force and retreated to Efogi.

In the contest between the Japanese 41st Regiment and the Australian rearguard from 31 August to 5 September, the Australians were once again able to inflict more casualties than they lost. The Japanese had 43 killed and 58 wounded, against 21 Australians killed and 54 wounded.

# Being Blindsided at Efogi

The Australian rearguard (refer to the preceding section) caught up with the main force at Efogi. The 2/27th Battalion had arrived as a reinforcement and 3rd Militia Battalion was on its way so Rowell, in Port Moresby, ordered Potts to try once more to halt the Japanese advance with the 1,500 men he now had.

Potts chose the heights of Brigade Hill and Mission Ridge, a boomerang-shaped feature that offers unusually good views in the direction of the Japanese approach. This was just what Potts wanted because he could call for air strikes from US and Australian aircraft. Normally air strikes weren't successful because the aircrew couldn't see soldiers in the jungle and, if they did, they weren't sure if they were friendly or enemy because ground to air communication was poor.

But at Efogi the bombers found the Japanese in the open and on 6 and 7 September bombed and strafed them, inflicting more than 30 casualties. This was an unusually good result. A week earlier, the same bombers had accidentally attacked the Australian 39th Battalion but had hit no-one.

Maroubra Force held the northern arm of the hills, called Mission Ridge. Here Potts drew up his new arrivals, 2/27th Battalion. Behind them on Brigade Hill, he rested 2/16th and 2/14th, who were exhausted after the rearguard action they had fought the previous week.

Horii was unhappy with the efforts of 41 Regiment in the pursuit of the Australians so he replaced them with a force drawn from 144 Regiment. The regiment had won the battle at Isurava and been rested for a week. Now under Colonel Kusunose Masao with a two-battalion force and six artillery pieces, in total only 100 men more than the Australians, the regiment was sent forward to attack the Australians near Efogi.

# Fighting back at Mission Ridge

In a by now predictable pattern, half of the Japanese, 3/144 Battalion, attacked the Australians' 2/27th on Mission Ridge, while the other half, 2/144 Battalion, went through the jungle in a half circle to cut the Kokoda Trail behind the Australians. This resulted in two separate but related fights, one on Mission Ridge and the other on Brigade Hill.

With artillery support, 3/144 advanced on Mission Ridge on 7 September but made little progress. So far on the track, the Australians had possessed no weapon to counter the Japanese guns, which, at Isurava and Eora, had sat back out of range and pounded the Australian infantry, who could do nothing about it.

At Efogi that changed. The Australians had several three-inch mortars that fired on the Japanese gunners, killing four and wounding 14.

The Japanese infantry could make no impression on the 2/27th. The Battalion held Mission Ridge until 8 September when, as a result of an Australian disaster on Brigade Hill, they were ordered to retreat.

# Being defeated at Brigade Hill

On 7 September, as 3/144 attacked Mission Ridge, the Japanese commander Kusunose and Major Horie, commander of 2/144 Battalion, were examining Brigade Hill with binoculars. Kusunose pointed out a distinct lone tree shaped like a fork. He told Horie that he wanted 2/144 Battalion deployed near that tree by dawn the next day.

Marching at night along the Fagume River on the Australians' left, and led by Papuan guides familiar with the area, Horie's battalion arrived on Brigade Hill at dawn. The Australians were unaware of the movement until then.

By accident or design (more likely the former), 2/144 was now placed between Potts's headquarters to its south and the three Australian infantry battalions to the north. Ejecting the Japanese force from their position blocking the track was essential. From the south, Potts directed an attack by headquarters personnel which failed. From the north 2/14th and 2/16th battalions made a larger assault.

IN THEIR OWN WORDS

# Australian mortars in action

Bob Iskov, a member of the 2/14 Battalion, gives an impression of what it was like during the fighting at Efogi:

We got up as far as Myola, initially we were told the mortars would not be going but after a few days we were sent off up the Kokoda track. We took one mortar and 39 rounds of ammo, the bombs were carried in a pannier of three rounds, three ten-pound bombs in individual cylinders and handled like a suitcase. The mortar was in three pieces, each weighing roughly 32 pounds, ugly things to carry. The infantry still had their little two-inch mortars but ours was three inch, with a much longer range.

Then we went back to Efogi and took up another defensive position. Normally mortars, especially the two-inch ones, were of limited use in New Guinea but at Efogi we had a bit of open ground to the front with a clear view for several hundred yards. The Japanese opened up on us with their mountain gun and machine guns, the one we called the woodpecker, and we fired at them. The Japs had a lot of rounds for their guns, must have fired at least 20 or 30 just at us. Until our three-inch mortars arrived, the Japanese artillery outranged anything we had. We could see where our bombs were landing and one bloke claimed he saw a mortar bomb land on a Japanese officer's head. I could have had 20 bombs in the air at once I reckon, but we didn't waste them. We fired one, watched where it landed, waited for correction, then fired another. We had good targets, could easily have fired all 39 rounds in two minutes but we took two hours.

We drew a lot of their fire as they were trying to knock us out. We drew some comment from our own infantry nearby too, as they didn't like the extra attention they were getting from the Jap guns because of us and were losing casualties. Eventually the Japanese got a shot close to the mortar and it blew the mortar askew and wounded two of the crew. I was standing back a bit taking a breather at the time. Bob Mitchell got a bit in the cheek and Bill got it in the buttock. We got an order to withdraw down the track and, having fired the last of our ammunition, we dismantled the mortar, took the firing pin out and threw everything away down a cliff.

Though they broke into 2/144's position and wiped out a Japanese platoon, this attack was also a failure and cost more than 100 Australian casualties, two-thirds of all their losses for the battle.

# Escaping to Menari

With the failure of his efforts to eject the Japanese (refer to the preceding section), Potts decided to retreat. The force with him (the headquarters, a composite company that had arrived late and one company of 2/16th Battalion) had no trouble following the track to Menari.

On the other side of the Japanese blocking force, the Australian retreat didn't go so well. Cutting a path through the jungle to the south east, the 2/14th and 2/16th battalions managed to join Potts at Menari on 9 September just before the Japanese arrived.

However, the 2/27th on Mission Ridge was the last battalion to leave. Burdened with wounded soldiers on stretchers, the battalion didn't get to Menari in time and was cut off when the Japanese got there first.

# Losing the 2/27th Infantry Battalion

The advantage Potts had at Efogi was the experienced 2/27th Infantry Battalion. Newly arrived, fit and with high morale, the Battalion had shown its quality on Mission Ridge (see the section 'Fighting back at Mission Ridge', earlier in this chapter). Unfortunately for Potts, the battalion was cut off during the retreat from Efogi and failed to rejoin Maroubra Force.

Spilt into several groups, the battalion spent between two and four weeks marching south to the east of the track. Each time they approached the track, they encountered Japanese. Hungry and still carrying their wounded, they were helped by some Papuans, but attacked by others and by Japanese patrols sent to hunt them.

By the time the survivors found their way to Australian lines, the battalion was no longer fit for battle. Rested and reformed, it was sent to fight at the Battle of Buna–Gona in November 1942.

# Sacking Brigadier Potts

Even before the disaster at Efogi, Blamey and MacArthur were unhappy with the Australian performance on the Kokoda Trail.

MacArthur complained to US President Franklin Roosevelt that the Australians were unable to match the Japanese in jungle fighting. Brigadier Potts was in command on the track so he was responsible for the failure. He was relieved of command by New Guinea Force commander Lieutenant General Sydney Rowell.

Some see this as unjust and Potts remains a hero to those who fought under him. Some argue that no-one else could have done a better job because the Japanese were in greatly superior numbers, and Potts and his men certainly believed this.

However, Potts's superiors had access to intelligence reports that showed the Japanese on the track weren't in such large numbers as the men in the front-line thought so they weren't inclined to accept Potts's explanation for defeat.

Simply put, Potts was replaced by Brigadier Selwyn Porter because Potts had been sent up the track to stop the Japanese and he had failed.

# Defending Ioribaiwa Ridge

After Efogi (refer to preceding sections), their rearguard harassed by the Japanese, the Australians fell back over the Maguli Range to Ioribaiwa Ridge. Porter's force there was composed of the remaining soldiers from the Australian defeat at Efogi and 3rd Battalion. Brigadier Ken Eather arrived from Port Moresby with the last of the three brigades of 7th Division, 25th Brigade, comprising 1,800 men in three well-trained, battle-experienced battalions, giving the Australians a total of almost 3,000 men.

Australian firepower was increased by the addition of Vickers medium machine guns and ten three-inch mortars. It appeared that Maroubra Force was at last strong enough to stop anything that the Japanese could throw at them.

The Japanese campaign against the Americans on Guadalcanal was still going badly (refer to Chapter 5) and until the Japanese recaptured the island they had no reinforcements to send to Horii to make an attack on Port Moresby viable. Meanwhile, Horii's superior, Hyakutake, didn't want Horii sticking his neck out too far and had forbidden Horii from sending forward the majority of his fighting troops. Hyakutake also insisted that the advance be halted on Ioribaiwa Ridge, once the Australians on it had been driven off.

For these reasons, except for the arrival of three mountain guns, Kusunose's pursuit group hadn't been reinforced since Efogi. Kusunose had no idea that he was about to attack an Australian force now almost twice as large as his, just as Eather, who commanded the defence of the ridge, was unaware the Japanese force was so small.

From 14 to 16 September, Kusunose drove Eather's force from Ioribaiwa Ridge. This was the last Japanese attack and the closest the Japanese came to Port Moresby.

## Flanking the flankers

Brigadier Eather had an ambitious plan. The Australians had been on the defensive since July 1942 (and it was now September 1942), always worried about a Japanese force appearing out of the jungle behind them. Now Eather wanted to do the same thing to them. While Porter's force held Ioribaiwa Ridge, Eather ordered one battalion from his 25th Brigade to swing wide to the west and another to the east with a view to capturing Nauro Village in the Japanese rear. His third battalion was left as a reserve behind the ridge in case Porter got into difficulties.

Kusunose planned a re-run of Efogi. His 3/144 would attack the Australians directly, supported now by eight guns, while 2/144 went around the Australian left. His attack commenced on 14 September.

The Australian centre was held by a composite battalion that combined the tired and depleted remnants of 2/16th and 2/14th battalions. Under the bombardment of the largest number of guns the Japanese had assembled so far in Papua, the Australians gave some ground but still held the ridge.

On the Australian left, Eather's flanking 2/31st Battalion encountered the Japanese 2/144. On the Australian right, the other flanking battalion, 2/33rd, had found the going too tough, cutting their way through the jungle. Eather directed that they give up their move on Nauro and instead deploy on the right of Porter on Ioribaiwa Ridge. There, on 15 September, they encountered another Japanese flanking move. Kusunose felt his attack in the Australian centre wasn't making enough progress, and his move around the Australian left had also failed, so he had sent his only reserve, half of 3/144 Battalion, to try to find its way around the Australian right.

There they encountered the 2/33rd and inserted themselves between that battalion and the 3rd militia battalion. Australian attacks on 15 and 16 September failed to eject them.

## The brigadier blunders

By 16 September, the Battle of Ioribaiwa Ridge could be considered a draw. Both sides had executed their respective plans (refer to the preceding section) but neither had worked as intended.

At the end of three days' fighting, the Japanese had failed to capture the ridge, but the Australians had failed to push them off the parts they did hold. Kusunose had all his troops committed and by now realised he was facing a much larger Australian force.

Eather's situation was much better. He had twice as many troops, half of them were fresh, he had not lost many men and he had one battalion still in reserve. Had he persevered, it's hard to see how the Australians wouldn't have been victorious.

Unfortunately, Eather didn't know of his advantage and still believed himself outnumbered. He told his divisional commander, Major-General Arthur 'Tubby' Allen, that he couldn't hold the ridge and asked to withdraw to the next ridge to the south, Imita Ridge. Allen gave his permission and by the afternoon of 16 September the Australians were on Imita Ridge. Lieutenant General Sydney Rowell confirmed Allen's order to Eather but warned 'Further withdrawal is out of the question and Eather must fight it out [on Imita Ridge]'.

## Seeing the lights of Port Moresby

On the night of 16 September, Japanese soldiers holding Ioribaiwa Ridge celebrated when they saw what they thought were the lights of Port Moresby just 50 kilometres away. In fact, they probably saw searchlights, not the lights of the town itself.

The ordinary soldiers believed that their trial on the track was nearly over and soon they would be swimming in the harbour, eating their fill and sleeping in houses. They weren't told that the reinforcements for the final attack on Port Moresby weren't coming and that soon they'd be ordered to turn around and march back the way they had come.

Ioribaiwa Ridge marked the limit of the Japanese advance and the end of the first phase of the fighting along the track. In the second phase, it was to be the Australians' turn to be on the offensive.

Chapter 11 explains what happened when Australia went on the offensive. You can read more about the specifics of jungle warfare in Chapters 9 and 10.

# Part III
# Fighting In the Jungle

*Glenn Lumsden*

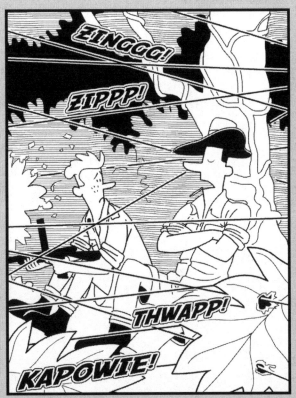

*'Don't worry mate ... those are
just the mozzies.'*

# In this part ...

Fighting in the mountainous jungle on the Kokoda Trail was different from any other kind of warfare. Movement was slow, visibility poor, and the supply of food and ammunition and evacuation of the wounded caused constant and complex problems. Neither side was familiar with the jungle and found it an unnerving and disorienting environment, adding yet another layer of difficulty to fighting in what has been described as the worst terrain in the world.

In this part, I explain the peculiarities of fighting on the Kokoda Trail. With almost no flat ground on the track, movement, fighting, evacuating wounded and supplying the troops was many times more difficult than in open countryside. The lack of visibility and tropical disease also caused almost insurmountable problems.

# Chapter 9

# Understanding Jungle Warfare

Fighting in the mountainous jungle of Papua was more difficult than fighting in the open. Many of the AIF in Papua had experience in the north African desert from 1940 to 1942; however, the open desert was very different to the mountainous jungle terrain they now found themselves in.

The attacker, moving through the jungle, often can't find his way and becomes lost. The men can't see each other so can't easily coordinate fire and movement. The defender, unseen in his fighting pit, can hear the attacker coming but can't see him, nor can he direct his fire on targets hidden by thick foliage. His weapons, which in other circumstances can fire accurately for hundreds of metres, are much less useful when he can see only short distances.

If the jungle is also mountainous with frequent mist and heavy rain, as the terrain is in the Owen Stanley Range on the Kokoda Trail, these problems are compounded because all movement is greatly slowed and visibility further restricted.

World War II infantry doctrine stressed that the infantryman can't expect to succeed in attack without a great deal of support. In the war in Europe, aircraft and artillery bombarded the target before the infantry attacked and tanks went in with the attack. Little of this was available in Papua, which is best understood as a foot soldier's war.

In this chapter, I explain how the Papuans, Australians and Japanese moved and fought in an environment that was alien to all but the Papuans.

# Defining the Tactics of Jungle War

Tactics is the combination of firepower and movement to achieve a military objective. Mountains and jungle make the cooperation of large formations like brigades and battalions difficult, if not impossible. The terrain, difficulty with communications and the weather made even the coordination of a company-sized attack difficult.

Tactics, as the average soldier saw it on the track, revolved around *platoons* (30 to 40 troops) and *sections* (12 troops) fighting to achieve their objective in isolation from the other platoons and sections, which they couldn't see.

The tactics of infantry fighting are built upon fire and movement. When attacking, one group moves towards the enemy while the other fires to keep enemy heads down. The former was called the rifle group, armed with rifles, submachine guns and grenades. The latter was the gun group and had at least one light machine gun.

A submachine gun, like the Thompson or the Owen, is a close range automatic weapon that combines the firepower of a machine gun with the small bullet of a pistol. A light machine gun, like the Bren or the Nambu, is a longer range weapon with a crew of two and is an infantry section's main source of firepower.

Tactics are also influenced by ground. In open terrain, holding the high ground allowed the defender to see the attack coming and gave time to respond to it. In the jungle, high ground only rarely offered a useful view, as occurred at Mission Ridge, though it was still an advantage to make the attacker climb a steep slope to get at the defender. The dominant terrain feature that influenced the fighting was, however, the track itself.

## Moving in the jungle

Everything about jungle fighting is slow (much slower than fighting in open, flat country); even just getting to the battlefield or, if you're defeated, getting away from it, is slow.

Armies expect their infantry to march at four kilometres per hour along a road over normal countryside. Along the track, soldiers averaged one or two kilometres per hour. Most people today finish the track in 50 hours of actual walking, but that's because they're not being shot at! Current-day trekkers travel in small groups, whereas armies move by battalions of 500 men or more and large groups always move slower than small groups.

A force on a mountain track must move in single file, allowing about four metres per person. After Isurava, the Japanese had 4,000 men in the mountains. This force would've stretched over 16 kilometres of track if they were all moving in one group. This was more than the average day's march on the track, so those leaving camp first would've reached their destination before those at the tail of the column had left the previous night's camp.

Off the track, or off any of the network of tracks in the Owen Stanley Range, movement slowed again. At Ioribaiwa, the Australian 2/33rd Battalion, with five days rations, was tasked to march through the jungle around the Japanese flank to Nauro, a distance of 10 kilometres. After a day, the battalion commander reported that progress was so slow he would run out of rations before he got there. The move was cancelled.

Things slowed when the enemy were near. On the track, the lead scout, knowing that at any moment a hidden enemy might open fire on him, would proceed with the utmost caution, perhaps just a few hundred metres each hour if he wanted to stay alive.

## Owning the track

The key terrain feature in all the battles along the Kokoda Trail was the track itself. It was the best route over the mountains.

Armies can't carry everything they need; they require constant resupply, so the track was the route by which all supplies came from a base in the rear. The sick and wounded were carried back along the track. (Refer to Chapter 5 for more information about setting up bases in Papua.)

The main tactic, used by the attacker in all battles along the track, was to keep the defender holding the track busy with a frontal attack, while another force slipped through the jungle on one or both flanks and tried to block the track in the enemy rear. The defender, who was now cut off from supply and communication, felt isolated, often forcing him to retreat. He could only retreat by cutting a new track through the jungle to one side to reach a point on the main track beyond the furthermost enemy.

After the Battle of Efogi, the Australians had the problem of being cut off from their supply. One particular battalion didn't manage to outpace the Japanese advance and remained lost in the jungle for weeks. Each time the Australians came to the main track, they found the advancing Japanese were there before them.

The threat of being cut off, or the reality of it at Efogi (refer to Chapter 8), persuaded the Australians to retreat in all the battles along the track during the Japanese advance from July to September 1942. After that, when the Australians advanced, they tried the same trick of cutting off the Japanese at Templeton's Crossing and Oivi–Gorari (see Chapter 11). This tactic worked there too.

A force that sneaks through the jungle on a flank to get behind the enemy and cut the track behind the enemy is, of course, bluffing because the force will itself become cut off. But the bluff usually worked. The track is the source of all supplies, such as ammunition and food coming forward, and the way to get the wounded and messages back. The trick to the game is to find out who's willing to stay cut off the longest and persuade the other side that his supply situation is worse, so the enemy would retreat, hopefully just before your own force starved or ran out of ammunition.

---

# Winkle's War

Lieutenant Frederick Winkle was second in command of a 30-man patrol that left Port Moresby on 6 September 1942. Proceeding by coastal lugger to Yule Island, the patrol marched inland along the Vanapa River and established a patrol base on the Mambare River 20 kilometres north-west of Kokoda.

For two months, resupplied by the same track they had used but always short of food, the patrol, from far behind enemy lines, reported by radio the activity of the Japanese.

On 25 October, Winkle, leading two men, attempted to enter Kokoda taking advantage of a fog. The village was unguarded, and Winkle and his men saw Japanese cooking food and taking their ease. Unseen, they made their way back to base to send a report. The presence of the patrol was revealed when they killed a Japanese soldier near Yodda and the Japanese began hunting for them.

On 30 October, the Japanese found the patrol base. Winkle was washing his clothes and, clad only in a towel, grabbed his weapon and fled. Winkle spent four days alone in the bush before he was reunited with his men and was able to obtain more dignified military attire.

## Masters of camouflage

The Australian soldiers on the track were convinced that the Japanese were masters of camouflage. Veterans say that you couldn't see the Japanese in the jungle because they were expert at the art of concealment. But Japanese veterans also say that the Australians were clever fellows because they hid themselves so well.

Neither side had any special training in the art of concealment in the jungle and both felt themselves in a strange environment unlike any they had seen before. Both jumped to the conclusion that the enemy were very skilled at hiding themselves. The average veteran rarely saw any live enemy. Typically, they fired into a patch of jungle where they thought the enemy were and later, if they won, they might find a dead enemy. But seeing live ones wasn't so common and many veterans admit that they never saw a live enemy — though they had participated in several battles.

## Getting lost in the dark

One of the very curious aspects of fighting in the mountainous jungle on the track was that when both sides tried to move off the track to attack their enemy in the flank or rear they usually got lost. The reasons for this were

- ✔ Compasses weren't as common as was desirable
- ✔ Many of the manoeuvres were made at night so the soldiers wouldn't be seen by the enemy
- ✔ Maps were poor

Getting lost had a major influence on the fighting. Generally speaking, the defender became lost less often because he had time to become familiar with his surroundings and in battle he manoeuvred less often. Here are some examples of the dangers of getting lost:

- ✔ At Isurava, the Japanese 2/144 battalion lost a whole day trying to outflank Australians east of Eora Gorge. They got lost and achieved nothing. At first Eora, another Japanese battalion, 2/41, also got lost.
- ✔ When the Australians were on the attack at Oivi–Gorari, one battalion lost a whole day trying to get around behind the Japanese in daylight. They missed the track junction they were looking for and had to retrace their steps.

# An infantryman's war

The experience of the infantryman, Japanese or Australian, on the track was fighting in a section divided into two small groups, a six-man rifle group and a gun group of similar size. This is what a typical encounter would've been like:

1. **The defenders in their camouflaged fighting pit weren't seen until the attacker's lead scout was suddenly fired on by the hidden enemy.**

   Even if the scout was able to discern the *muzzle flash* (the flash of light a weapon makes when fired), he may not have been in a position to report where the fire was coming from, or even be aware of the enemy's firing position. Unable to determine the direction of fire, the gun group, further back, wouldn't have known where to fire or *manoeuvre* (the military term for moving bodies of troops).

2. **When the scout located the enemy, the gun group with a light machine gun, sometimes two, *brought fire to bear on them*. The NCO of the section coordinates the attack and directs the fire of the gun group.**

   While under cover of the fire, the rifle group crawled carefully closer to try to lob grenades into the enemy's fighting pit.

3. **Suddenly another enemy opened up.**

   Where he was or if more than one was present, was unclear. The whole *movement* halted while the problem was reassessed. (The movement in this case was the manoeuvre of the rifle group towards the enemy.)

4. **The platoon leader committed another of his sections to tackle the new threat.**

   Slowly, usually by crawling and using every scrap of cover, and with long periods where no-one could see the enemy and the enemy couldn't see the attacker, the attack proceeded.

   Behind the platoon commander is his company commander, who may have 100 men spread over a front of more than 100 metres. In the thick jungle, he could see few of them. The company commander and his platoon commanders were often unsure where they were in relation to each other or other platoons.

5. **A great deal of firing occurred.**

   Officers and sergeants had to control how many shots were fired, but often couldn't see the enemy. Most of the fire was directed by section commanders at where they thought the enemy was. Probably half the men in the fight wouldn't see live enemy at all during an engagement.

6. **Eventually one enemy was grenaded in his pit and a gap in the enemy defences was made.**

   Taking advantage of this gap in the enemy line, the attackers continued edging forward and gradually killed the defenders or forced them back.

Such engagements required a great deal of patience and skill; to kill a few enemy troops may have taken several hours. This was how the campaign along the track was fought. The popular image of *serried ranks* making heroic bayonet charges wasn't the experience of war for the ordinary soldier on the Kokoda Trail.

 Tactics is about fire and movement. The jungle makes coordination of large bodies so difficult that a battle actually consists of dozens of small fights between platoons. When you look at a map, the Battle of Kokoda may seem like one whole battle, but it didn't appear that way to the soldiers.

# Patrolling the Jungle

The jungle could easily conceal large numbers of men, so knowing where the enemy was and what he was up to was vital. However, in the Battle of Kokoda, most of the patrolling didn't take place on the track.

 For 50 kilometres on either side of the track, small groups of Japanese, Papuans and Australians searched the jungle. The purpose was to check that the enemy weren't sending a large force along one of the other tracks that crossed the Owen Stanley Range from north to south and to look for alternative routes friendly troops might use if required. Patrols were also sent deep into the enemy rear via these alternative routes over the mountains. (Refer to the sidebar 'Winkle's War' for a true story of some action that took place behind enemy lines.)

 In the vast, jungle-covered and rugged mountains of the Owen Stanley Range, these patrols rarely encountered one another. Most returned with no contact nor any sign of the enemy — though this wasn't, in any sense, a failure because sometimes confirming where the enemy *aren't* located is almost as useful as knowing where they are.

 Some notable examples of patrols during the Battle of Kokoda include these events:

✔ **Looking for a way to Port Moresby**. In September 1942, during the Japanese advance, the 41st Regiment was based at Nauro. Extensive Japanese patrols were made west to the Brown River then south along the Goldie and Laloki rivers. These patrols were looking for alternative routes to Port Moresby apart from the Kokoda Trail. The most southern patrol was to Hombrun Bluff, only 10 kilometres from the Allied airfields at Port Moresby and only a few kilometres from the 2/9th Australian General Hospital. The Japanese made plans to raid the Allied airfields, but owing to their retreat at the end of September this didn't occur. The Japanese patrols were being hunted by 2/1st Pioneer Battalion, but they found the Japanese just twice. On one of these occasions, they clashed, firing on Japanese crossing the Goldie River in a canoe just a few kilometres from the Allied airfields.

✔ **Watching the Kumusi crossings**. Patrols of 2/6th Independent Company made deep patrols into the Japanese rear via the Kumusi River. As the Japanese retreated from Ioribaiwa Ridge in late September, these patrols increased in intensity. For several weeks in October, as the Battle of Second Eora was fought, an Australian 2/6th patrol sat concealed on a hill near Assisi overlooking the Japanese supply line. In radio contact with New Guinea Force headquarters in Port Moresby, they were able to count every Japanese crossing the Kumusi River, and provide details of what was being carried and which direction they were going. The Australian patrol also reported on the effect of Allied air attack on the Kumusi crossings.

## The green shadows

Waging a war of patrols behind Japanese lines was the Papuan Infantry Battalion (PIB), known to the Japanese as 'the green shadows' for their ability to appear and disappear suddenly in the jungle. The swift Japanese advance from the coast in July cut off a company of PIB in the Buna region.

Ordered by New Guinea Force (NGF), the body charged with running the war in Papua and the Territory of New Guinea, to maintain contact with the Japanese and report on their activities, these men waged their own small war 100 kilometres behind the front-line.

Under pressure from Japanese patrols hunting them, the Papuans were reinforced in October by another PIB company, which marched into the region along a track far to the east of the track.

During the Japanese retreat from the Battle of Oivi–Gorari in November, PIB patrols cut off and killed many small parties of Japanese dispersed by the battle and heading for their base at Buna. In January 1943, as the Japanese attempted to escape north from Buna after their defeat there, PIB patrols killed an estimated 150 Japanese.

# Using Weapons in the Jungle

The weapons of World War II had long ranges and a high rate of fire. Those Australians in AIF units who had fought in north Africa were used to being able to see up to five kilometres in the desert and to using a great deal of ammunition in the knowledge that resupply was usually not a problem.

Conditions in Papua were different, with visibility restricted to short distances and resupply of ammunition tenuous — if no airdrop of supply was possible, every round had to be carried up the track. The Australians had to adopt new methods for the use of their weapons while they were in a strange environment.

## Artillery

The Australians didn't have artillery that could be taken apart and carried along the track as the Japanese did. However, for a short period in the Kokoda campaign, the Australians had artillery support. When the Japanese took Ioribaiwa Ridge, they came within range of Australian artillery 10 kilometres away. In September, 14th Field Regiment had dragged three 25-pounder field guns to Owers' Corner. There, the track fell away into the Goldie River so the guns couldn't be brought further forward. From 21 September, the Australians fired 700 rounds at Japanese positions on Ioribaiwa Ridge. On 27 September, the Japanese retreated and no more Australian artillery was used until the Battle of Buna–Gona in November.

The most important weapon used on the track was the Japanese artillery, precisely because the Australians usually had none. The Japanese guns were of three types:

- 37-mm gun, which could fire anti-tank and anti-personnel rounds

- 70-mm light howitzers in each battalion's gun platoon

- 75-mm mountain guns brought to Papua by the 55th Mountain Artillery Regiment

All of these guns could be taken apart and carried by horse or man. At least six were used in most of the battles along the track.

The great advantage of the Japanese guns was that they could be placed out of range of the Australian weapons to bombard the Australians, who couldn't return fire. The problems were ammunition consumption and the difficulty of seeing the enemy. One gun might fire two tonnes of ammunition in a day's firing, which was the equivalent of 100 man loads. The visibility problem was solved by forward artillery observers who lay hidden close to the Australians. In field telephone contact with their gunners, they adjusted the fall of shot on to the target.

## Machine guns

Although the Australians didn't have much in the way of artillery (refer to preceding section), they did have the Thompson submachine gun.

With one or two per infantry section, an effective range of 50 metres, 30 or 50 round magazines and a high rate of fire, the Thompson submachine gun was very useful in a close range fire fight.

The Japanese Army had no submachine guns in 1942. Japanese after-battle reports often mention the effectiveness of the Thompson and their desire to be equipped with a similar weapon.

The infantry's most important weapon was the light machine gun. Neither side had an advantage here, because the Japanese Nambu and the Australia Bren were quite similar weapons.

## Using different weapons in Kokoda

Corporal Des Moran remembers his experiences in Kokoda:

I was impressed that the Japs got their guns up over the mountains. That must have been a stupendous effort. Our battalion had the Vickers, only one or two of them. For automatic weapons, though, you relied most on your Brens. You work on hearing because you want to know the difference between ours and theirs. You can pick the difference between a Bren and a Nambu as easy as bloody wink. Now the Thompson, they were such rapid firers. We trained with them in Middle East.

The kids would come around with bags of oranges: 'Oranjee George, oranjee George'. 'Give us the whole bag,' I said. So what you done was you got a bag of these big Jaffa oranges, they were rippers, and took them down the wadi [dry river bed] and your mates stood behind you with the bag of oranges and threw them up on top of the sand dunes. You had to shoot them rolling down. On automatic [the Thompson could be fired on both automatic or single shot], we could cut an orange in half.

The back site was ranged up to 600 yards but you would never see that far in the Owen Stanleys. Anyway, I was determined not to use automatic fire, I just fired one shot at a time because I carried 250 rounds over the mountains and I didn't want to waste them. I saw the Yanks firing on burst later at Buna but that wasn't good. Sometimes they would accidentally kill one another.

The situation was different with the larger medium and heavy machine gun class. The Japanese Juki, called the 'woodpecker' by the Australians because it had a slower than normal rate of fire and sounded like the slow tap-tap noise a woodpecker bird makes when tapping into the trunk of a tree, had telescopic sights and an effective range of more than 1 kilometre. The Australians at first believed their Vickers medium machine gun would be of no value in close terrain, so didn't take any along the track. When they saw the Juki in battle, they changed their minds. The first Vickers guns went into action on Ioribaiwa Ridge in mid September.

## Mortars

Both sides used small mortars which were organic to their infantry units, meaning the weapon was normally in the unit, unlike other kinds of weapons that might only be temporarily attached to the unit.

A *mortar* is an indirect fire weapon, meaning that the projectile that emerges from the barrel of the weapon follows an arc that might almost be a half circle from the firing point to the target point. The projectiles of direct fire weapons travel almost in a straight line, such as the bullet from a pistol.

Soldiers found that the mortar rounds were often deflected by the jungle canopy.

When the Australians brought forward larger three-inch mortars, the problem was the same. However, this weapon, with a range of one kilometre, was sometimes able to counter the Japanese artillery by firing on the gunners.

## Rifles

The standard infantryman's weapon was his bolt action rifle:

- ✔ The Australians used the sturdy .303 Lee Enfield, with a ten-round magazine.
- ✔ The Japanese Arisaka was a poorly designed weapon with a five-round magazine.

# Grenades

Like their rifles (refer to the preceding section), Japanese grenades were less effective than Australian ones because the design of the Japanese grenade was inferior.

A *grenade* is a handheld explosive thrown at the enemy. The Australians used the Mills bomb, a British design and a very effective grenade. The Japanese used several grenades, ranging from the type 91 to the type 99. The Japanese design was inferior. The distinction between the British and Japanese grenades represents two design philosophies. The British approach produced a heavier grenade to throw, resulting in a shorter throw distance, but with a greater effect on the target. The Japanese produced a grenade that was lighter and cheaper to manufacture that had a greater throw range. Combat in World War II proved that the Allied approach to grenade design was the most effective.

The grenade was an extremely important weapon in jungle war when the enemy was in a trench or fighting pit and couldn't be seen or fired on with a direct fire weapon.

At night, the grenade was also useful because, unlike a rifle that flashed when fired, it wouldn't reveal the location of the thrower when it exploded.

# Bayonet

World War II bayonets were fearsome weapons with 12-inch blades. Bayonet fighting was more common in the jungle because the two sides were often quite close to each other before they were aware of the others' presence.

Even so, bayonets weren't used as often as is commonly thought. In the end, the main effect of the bayonet was psychological. Soldiers often fled when confronted with a determined-looking bayonet attack, before bayonets could be crossed.

# Flying Over the Jungle

Not a great deal of air combat occurred over the Owen Stanley Range because one of the air combatants was often not present. From late August, at the time of the Battle of Isurava (refer to Chapter 8), the Japanese had decided that their major effort would go towards recapturing the island of Guadalcanal from the Americans (refer to Chapter 5). All their aircraft based at Lae and Buna were withdrawn.

## Shooting down Zeros

One of the few air-to-air combats in the Kokoda to Buna region occurred on 25 August 1942 when American P-40 fighters caught Japanese Zeros while taking off from Buna strip. Fighter ace Tsunoda Kazuo was there:

Our squadron was soon moved to the newly constructed airfield at Buna. On the morning following our arrival, nine planes were taxiing to take off for another raid on Milne Bay. Our first aircraft was ready to go when the lookout reported the enemy. P-40s appeared out of nowhere. The strip was narrow so only one plane at a time could take off. Our first three Zeros off the ground were immediately shot down, two becoming fireballs when barely a few metres up. Once a Zero is seriously hit it is likely to catch fire. This was a dangerous feature of an otherwise excellent aircraft.

I was next off. I stayed close to the edge of the jungle to avoid being spotted. Once airborne, it took some time to get the plane into fighting condition. I had to adjust the flaps, prime the guns and drop my long-range fuel tank. I was attacked before I was ready. I could hear the bullets hitting my plane. There was fuel in the cockpit and white smoke. I looked down and saw another Zero falling into the jungle, a mass of flames. However, I was not deterred and turned to attack them. I was determined not to return to base without a good result. By this time, the enemy were departing. I caught one, diving down on him and shooting with all my guns. I am fairly sure I shot him down. I came back to the airfield to land. This was difficult as the aircraft was badly damaged but on my second try I managed it.

Thereafter, Japanese aircraft appeared in Papua only on certain occasions: To support the landing at Milne Bay, and to provide air cover for raids on Port Moresby and shipping supplies from Rabaul to Buna. The Allies had air superiority, which meant the Japanese couldn't prevent most of what the Allies wanted to do in the air.

## Bombing the Japanese

The Allied Air Force was a combination of the air forces of the United States, Australia and the Netherlands. It was commanded by an American, General George Kenney.

Kenney had 400 aircraft, most of which were based in Queensland, out of range of Japanese bombing raids. Kenney feared that if he based large numbers of aircraft at Port Moresby or Milne Bay, they could be destroyed on the ground.

To fly to attack Japanese ships at sea, north of Buna, or to bomb the track, most of the aircraft needed to refuel at Port Moresby, either on the outward or homeward leg. This was time consuming and resulted in far fewer sorties being flown than might otherwise have been achieved.

Kenney was also worried that small Japanese patrols approaching Port Moresby from the mountains might suddenly appear on his airfields and destroy parked aircraft. He once said that if a single Japanese patrol crossed the Goldie River, he would pull all his aircraft back to Queensland.

For these reasons, as well as the great difficulty the aircrew had in spotting targets in the jungle, the Allied air attack on the Japanese on the track was quite limited. It's doubtful that they killed as many Japanese on the ground as the 320 Allied aircrew lost from July 1942 to January 1943.

## Interfering with Japanese supplies

General George Kenney was commanding the Allied air force in Papua (he's introduced in the preceding section). The centrepiece of his air offensive in Papua was his attempt to interrupt the Japanese supply line.

Kenney chose the crossing of the Kumusi River, halfway between Kokoda and Buna, as his focus. From August to October 1942, his bombers destroyed at least six Japanese bridges over the river.

However, as fast as the AAF knocked the bridges down, the Japanese rebuilt them. The smaller wire suspension bridges were easily rebuilt, but the main achievement of the AAF attack was in knocking down a large wooden bridge capable of bearing trucks.

Since the Japanese had arrived in Papua, they had been extending a vehicular road from Buna towards Kokoda in an attempt to ease their supply difficulties. The AAF knocked down this bridge twice and the Japanese rebuilt it. When it was knocked down a third time, the Japanese gave up.

# Chapter 10

# Feeling Hungry and Sick in the Jungle

*W*hen soldiers march out of their barracks to go to war, they tend to be fit and well fed. As the days go by, they slowly and steadily deteriorate; less food and medical attention is available, even if the soldiers are only bivouacking in the bush at Bonegilla. The problem increases if they move to a less healthy climate in a war zone such as Papua. Problems are compounded when the soldiers head off up a mountain track far from roads by which their requirements are delivered. Then the shooting starts, they need more ammunition and have the added burden of evacuating their wounded. Delivering all that's needed to their fighting units after a period in a hostile climate is a huge problem for armies. The Kokoda Trail was without doubt the most hostile climate Australians were to encounter in World War II.

The Australians, Americans and Japanese all studied the war in Papua after the campaign concluded. One of the things they looked at was just how long they might expect their troops to stay well and fit enough for battle in such a situation. They all concluded that, after three months in Papua, their men weren't fit for hard marching or offensive operations, but they could still be effective defending. The studies concluded that after four or five months on a poor diet and with exposure to tropical diseases, their troops became ineffective and should be replaced.

In this chapter, I describe how both armies sent forward into the mountains the beans and bullets to keep their fighting men supplied, and what medical problems arose, either as a result of the harsh conditions, or when the supply of food and medicine failed.

# Addressing Problems of Supply

Soldiers in action are great consumers of goods. Fighting forces require an amazing variety of things, not all of them needed by the front-line rifleman, but some by others who sustain, direct and support him. Apart from food and ammunition, troops also needed things such as medicines and bandages, telephone wire, tents, timber and spare bootlaces. All of these supplies had to be delivered to battle in the Owen Stanley Range. For every Australian soldier at the front, an average of 20 kilograms of supplies arrived by sea at Port Moresby each day in 1942.

To deliver provisions to the front-line, supplies went by truck from Port Moresby to Owers' Corner, then were carried on the backs of men. When reinforcements went up the track, they carried some of these objects, but thousands of Papuan carriers were needed. Each of the 15,000 Papuan carriers (sometimes known as Fuzzy Wuzzy Angels) who worked on the track carried a load of 20 to 25 kilograms. Dumps were established at the end of each day's march, spaced about 10 kilometres apart. Early in the campaign, a carrier was given a load to deliver all the way from Owers' Corner to the front-line, but as the system became more efficient, men would live at a base dump, carry goods to the next dump, then return. Several hundred man loads a day had to arrive at the front to keep the Australians on the track supplied in the period before regular airdrops took over part of the problem. Figure 10-1 shows engineers building a bridge to help ferry supplies to the front-line.

**Figure 10-1:**
Engineers built bridges so that supplies could be sent along the track.

*Source: Australian War Memorial Archive, AWM 013598*

## Voluntary and conscripted labour

Not all the thousands of Papuans, called Fuzzy Wuzzy Angels (see the sidebar 'The Fuzzy Wuzzy Angels lend a hand'), who carried supplies to the front-line or wounded back to Port Moresby, gave their services freely. Figure 10-2 shows a group of carriers with Australian officers on the track.

A system of indentured labour existed on plantations in Papua and when the Japanese landed the plantation owners were ordered to send their labourers, and their white overseers, to the track as carriers. This didn't provide enough men so a system of conscription began.

General Basil Morris invoked National Security Regulations, providing whatever number of labourers the army might require. Civil administration had been suspended during the war, so the Australian New Guinea Administrative Unit conscripted thousands of men from Papua, who were paid up to 10 shillings per month with contracts from one to three years. Many stayed on but others simply deserted. Lieutenant Bert Kienzle of ANGAU (Australian New Guinea Administrative Unit; refer to Chapter 3) found in July that the Papuan labourers were 'sullen and unhappy' and frequent desertions occurred. A further problem was that the carriers would refuse to get close to the fighting.

**Figure 10-2:** Papuan carriers meet Australian officers at a rest spot on the Kokoda Trail.

*Source: Australian War Memorial Archive, AWM 150655*

The Japanese too brought labour to Papua, some voluntary, some forced. Several thousand Korean and Taiwanese civilians came as specialist labouring units and 2,300 men from New Britain were employed to carry supplies. They were treated badly and within three months two-thirds had deserted.

## Sourcing beans and bullets

The two armies had differing doctrines when it came to providing rations:

- ✔ The Australians tried to supply their men well, and attempted to deliver food of acceptable quality and quantity to the front-line. When the Australians went hungry, and they often did, they foraged for wild animals and vegetables, and, when attacking, ate any captured Japanese food. The 2/33rd Battalion reported in October 1942 that captured rice was the staple diet of the battalion.

- ✔ The Japanese intended their men to get by on as little as possible, and sent forward a bare minimum of provisions. Their philosophy was that the ration should be supplemented by local forage and capturing enemy food. This worked to a degree, more so when the Japanese were on the offensive. Japanese soldiers' diaries often make reference to shooting pigs and raiding taro gardens.

Virtue can be found in both approaches in the preceding list. Where roads are available, the army that delivers more keeps its troops healthy and combat ready for longer. Until the Australians had to fight in Papua, they were accustomed to trucks delivering their considerable requirements to the front-line. But when no roads are available, as in the Owen Stanley Range, the frugal Japanese Army adapted faster and managed better.

The different approach of the two armies can be illustrated by looking at what the ordinary soldier's ration pack contained (see the sidebar 'What's for dinner?' to get the specifics). Australian ration packs contained many more items, most of which the Japanese would've considered luxuries. Lieutenant General Sydney Rowell, commander of New Guinea Force, recorded that 'the Japanese soldier could march for days on just rice and fish; no European troops could march and fight on such a spare diet'.

Australian packaging was also cumbersome, another legacy from fighting in North Africa where the troops were never too far from a road and supplies were always delivered by vehicle. This strained the Australian supply line in Papua more than that of the Japanese. General Rowell also noted that 'we were behind the enemy who had reduced these matters to extreme simplicity'. However, the Australians learned their lesson and streamlined their supply arrangements in 1943, and by 1944 they had completely changed the content, packaging and delivery of goods to meet the requirements of jungle warfare.

# What's for dinner?

In 1942, a soldier's daily ration weighed up to one kilogram. Australian ration packs in 1942 varied but usually contained 16 of the following items. The equivalent Japanese front-line ration contained just six items. A soldier's daily ration, when he was being fed as planned, contained the following items.

## Ration Packs of the Australian and Japanese Armies, 1942

| Australian | Japanese |
|---|---|
| Arnotts plain biscuits | bean paste |
| baked beans | green tea |
| blackcurrant spread | rice |
| caramel bar | soy sauce |
| cheese | sugar |
| condensed milk (1 tin) | tinned fish |
| corned beef (bully beef) | |
| fruit and nut chocolate | |
| peanut butter (1 packet) | |
| salt | |
| skim milk powder | |
| Steamrollers (mints) | |
| sugar (2 tablets) | |
| tea | |
| tinned meat and vegetables | |
| tinned tuna | |
| Weet Bix cereal | |

## Playing airdrop roulette

The Japanese planned to use airdrops to supply their troops on the track. A transport squadron in Rabaul had experience of airdropping supplies by parachute in Sumatra.

However, because the Japanese fighter aircraft that would've escorted the transport squadron aircraft were withdrawn from New Guinea for use in Guadalcanal (refer to Chapter 5), the squadron was not used in Papua.

During the Japanese supply crisis in September and October 1942 (see the section 'Building bridges'), however, the Japanese did fly several emergency airdrop missions near Kokoda. (Why they didn't use the runway, then in their hands and which would've allowed more supplies to be delivered, is a mystery.) Each two engine bomber dropped a tonne of food. Parachutes were used and the food arrived in good condition. When the escorting Japanese fighter pilots heard of the purpose of the mission, they filled their cockpits with tinned food and cigarettes. The pilots flew low over Kokoda, pulled back their canopies and threw out the supplies.

From a chaotic start the Australians developed a superior airdropping system on the track. Initially no parachutes were available, and food and ammunition arrived in poor condition or went astray. The front-line complained that much of what was dropped fell in the jungle and couldn't be found, or that what was promised was never sent. Port Moresby replied that this wasn't so, and all supplies that should've been sent were.

Clearly, some communication problems occurred between those who organised the flights from Port Moresby and those awaiting the delivery. George Batts, who flew on the first airdrop, said 'we were told to look out for a white flag, but there were white things all over the place, tents and I don't know what, as we flew over Myola, so we didn't know where to drop'. The dispute is still not resolved, though the Japanese (had anyone consulted them) could've pointed out that hundreds of their men spent several weeks in September gathering Australian airdropped food from the area surrounding Myola.

By the time of the Australian advance in October, airdrop techniques were improved. Drops could be made at any suitable spot just behind the front-line to minimise the manpower required for carriage. One favoured place was a rare piece of flat ground along the Brown River north of Nauro. From an average of five tonnes per day dropped during the Australian retreat, at least ten tonnes per day (which is six or seven aircraft loads) were dropped in the advance. Once the Australians reached Kokoda, the airstrip was used and airdropping became less common.

Without airdropped supplies, the 3,000 Australian fighting troops advancing on the track in October probably wouldn't have taken Kokoda.

## Harnessing horses

Using local mules and horses, some captured wild and then broken in, 1st Australian Independent Transport Troop commenced transporting supplies up the track in July 1942. The organisation soon grew in size and 75-kilogram loads were standard.

When the horses reached as far as it was practical to go, Papuan carriers took over the load (refer to 'Voluntary and conscripted labour', earlier in this chapter), which was then broken into three 25-kilogram packs for three men.

For the Australians, the use of horses in Papua was an expedient. The Australians didn't normally use horses to bring forward supplies but were forced to do so because no roads ran through the Owen Stanley Range. However, for the Japanese using horses was commonplace. The Nankai Shitai (South Sea Forces) brought more than 2,400 horses to Papua, where they became an important part of the supply line from Buna to Kokoda. As combat engineers improved the track south of Kokoda, the range of horse transport was extended as far as Ioribaiwa Ridge.

Veterinary stations were placed a day's march apart from Buna to the front-line in an attempt to maintain the health of the horses. Sadly, this wasn't very successful and by the Battle of Oivi–Gorari in November more than half of the Japanese horses had died.

## Weathering the Wet

The fighting on the track took place towards the end of the so-called dry season. This just meant that it rained less than in the wet and 1942 was a notoriously wet year.

Australian army meteorologists estimated that more than 400 millimetres of rain fell in September 1942 alone. For short periods, tracks became impassable and streams uncrossable.

The rain made it colder too. At well over 1,000 metres above sea level, where much of the track was, the temperature would fall to 5° Celsius at night, though it felt colder than that to the soldiers sitting in the open in a hole in the ground in soaking rain. Low clouds were common above 1,000 metres, giving the impression of walking or fighting in a thick mist. The poor weather seriously affected military operations, and movement of supplies and wounded soldiers, not to mention morale. The weather also severely affected the Japanese-built bridges, leading to disastrous consequences for their supply line.

## Getting the wounded out

The rain-soaked slippery slopes of the Owen Stanley Range were hard enough work for a soldier or a carrier with a load of 20 kilograms or more, but it was near to impossible carrying a wounded or sick man on a stretcher. At some points on the track (for example, the aptly named 'wall', between Menari and Nauro), imagining how carrying a stretcher was done at all is hard. The man and his personal gear and the stretcher together weighed at least 80 kilograms. Stretchers required eight men over long distance (four or six men carrying and four or two men resting) and carrying a man from the front-line to Owers' Corner could take as long as ten days.

### The Fuzzy Wuzzy Angels lend a hand

An Australian soldier, Athol Geare, told me about his encounter with the Papuans, also known as the Fuzzy Wuzzy Angels:

Some of them were in the trees when I got shot. Others were killed and there were bullets flying everywhere so I could have got dead. A bullet, an ordinary rifle bullet hit me, not a machine gun.

The fuzzy wuzzies had to carry me out. So I don't know how many days it took them. I know they made a timber stretcher and I had a blanket and we stopped each night. They kept the rain off me. They got me on the stretcher and sedated me and I don't know how many days it took. I'd be laying there and I looked up at them, those fuzzy angels, walking up the main track in case we encountered any Japanese. I was lucky to get back like that. I don't know how many days it was, just laying about, gangrene setting into my wounded leg.

Then at Port Moresby they flew me to Toowoomba 'cos I had malaria as well.

Toowoomba was the place for malaria cases. Some of us had already had malaria when we went up the track. Then that sort of finished my campaign, with the benefit of getting sent home to Tasmania for a rest. When I come back I got malaria fever again and that's when I met some of the others. We still meet up. We go to Melbourne on Anzac day and have a drink and go to the races. They come from all over but every year there is one or two less.

I don't know how many months later, maybe six months and I had to go back again and go through training again. I got well and then I trained. I didn't know where I was going. I got malaria again later. I think I had malaria four or five times in the war. Once you got it you don't get rid of it easy.

The following figure shows Fuzzy Wuzzy Angels carrying a wounded Australian soldier across a stream on the Kokoda Trail.

*Source: Australian War Memorial archive, AWM 013641*

On some days, 50 stretchers left the front-line for the rear, depleting manpower for fighting and other tasks by up to 400 soldiers or Papuan carriers. On other days, especially during the Australian retreat, no men were spare to carry the wounded.

Corporal John Metson of the 2/14th Battalion was badly wounded in the ankle at Isurava. He couldn't walk and wouldn't let his mates carry him. He began to crawl back towards Port Moresby. After two weeks crawling, just a kilometre or two a day, he could go no further. The Japanese caught up with Metson and killed him. (See Chapter 14 to read more about Metson's courage and how he has inspired other Australians.)

## *Building bridges*

Some people think that the Japanese on the track were defeated by their inability to supply their men at the front-line. This is partly true. They did bring enough food to Papua, they did set up a fair supply system from their base at Buna, but they were temporarily defeated by the weather.

In September 1942, unusually high rainfall in the Owen Stanley Range caused flooding along the Japanese supply line in the lowlands from Buna to Kokoda. The Japanese supply line was swept away. The road became a sea of mud and the bridges disappeared.

For two weeks little movement could occur, except that of Japanese engineers desperately rebuilding the road and at least 30 bridges. The supply crisis lasted a month and during this time those Japanese at the front-line, then at Ioribaiwa, ran out of food. A few starved to death and a few others resorted to cannibalism. By October, the Japanese supply line had recovered.

# Catching Tropical Diseases

Both armies were aware that maintaining the health of the troops in Papua would be difficult, but both were still surprised by the level of the problem. Both armies suffered many more casualties to disease than to battle wounds. The list of diseases was long: Scrub typhus, dengue fever, diarrhoea and various skin diseases. For both sides, however, the main problems were malaria and dysentery.

For the Australians, dysentery was their worst enemy when they were in the mountains on the Kokoda Trail, and malaria when on the coast at Milne Bay and Buna-Gona. For the Japanese, malaria caused the greatest medical problem; towards the end of the campaign the fatal cerebral malaria became common. I look at these diseases and their effects on both armies in the following sections.

Generally, Japanese medical arrangements were more successful during their advance than in their later retreat. At first, they managed to keep medical evacuations to a third or half of those of the Australians. But during the subsequent Australian advance the situation turned around and the Japanese began to suffer most from disease. By the time the Australians began to surround the Japanese base at Buna, in November 1942, both sides on the Kokoda front alone had evacuated 6,000 men each for medical reasons.

## Managing malaria

The spread of malaria depends on two main factors:

- **Mosquitoes.** Female anopheles mosquitoes bite infected humans and when extracting their blood the insect becomes the primary host of the parasite. The mosquito then transmits the disease to an uninfected human when the insect takes another bite.

Anopheles mosquitoes usually bite at night so a soldier taking maximum precautions might live in a *hyperendemic* area (a place with a very high incidence of a particular disease) for many months without contracting the disease.

✔ **A population of infected human hosts.** Low population densities inhibit the spread of the disease. Troops suffered from malaria far more in heavily populated areas.

The Australians started taking malaria seriously after Milne Bay, where they had taken few precautions. Australian and American battle casualties at Milne Bay in ten days of fighting were 377 killed and wounded. But for the period from June 1942 to the end in Papua in January 1943, Milne Bay recorded 6,000 cases of malaria, about the same number of personnel that were there at any given time over the period.

Atebrin and quinine (which could either suppress or cure malaria) were used to immunise soldiers and to treat them after they contracted the disease, but not regularly. Some of the men were convinced that taking the atebrin tablet would render them impotent. Mosquito nets weren't issued to all and many didn't bother even to roll down their sleeves at night to minimise the chance of a bite.

The Australians who fought on the track came from Port Moresby, where the incidence of malaria was relatively low. On the track, at heights over 1,000 metres, no malaria occurred. However, once the Australians entered the hyperendemic lowlands around Buna, they began to lose up to 100 men a day to malaria. The American 32nd Division, new to Papua and as ignorant of prevention of disease as the Australians were in Milne Bay, lost over half of the division to illness, mainly malaria.

The situation of their enemy was worse. In the last month of the Japanese occupation of Papua, their supply system broke down once again (refer to the section 'Building bridges' for more). Ships stopped coming and quinine ran out. A Japanese post-campaign study estimated that six-sevenths of the troops holding Buna were debilitated by malaria.

## Running from dysentery

Dysentery is a bacterial disease. You must swallow the microorganism to contract dysentery. Oro-faecal contamination occurs most commonly when contaminated food is eaten or water drunk, or the bacteria is picked up on the hand which then touches the mouth.

An outbreak of dysentery began among the Papuan carriers working on the track at Ioribiawa in late August. The disease rapidly spread up and down the track, arriving at the Australian front-line just as the Battle of Isurava began. The effect was significant. From perhaps ten medical evacuations from Maroubra Force each day before dysentery struck, the rate soared to 80 per day throughout September. This was one man in every 30 each day. Without constant reinforcements, Maroubra Force would've ceased to exist in a month. By the end of September, 1,700 Australian medical evacuations had taken place, almost entirely from dysentery.

Dr Geoffrey Vernon, who had lived and worked in New Guinea for many years, was present. He wrote that 'the whole length of track from Ioribawia to Uberi is seriously fouled and undoubtedly a dysentery focus. During the retreat in darkness the men were compelled to relieve themselves anywhere and the whole route literally stank. By this means the dysentery which had established itself at Ioribaiwa was spread'. Another medical officer thought 'the standard of hygiene was a disgrace for a modern army'.

Major General Frank Norris, senior medical officer of 7th Division, set about solving the problem of dysentery by increasing the numbers of medical staff, obtaining from Australia specialists in hygiene and making recommendations that the army adopted for the control of dysentery. In October, the dysentery epidemic ended and medical evacuations returned to a bearable level.

# Infecting the enemy

In an early, and accidental, example of biological warfare, the Australians gave the Japanese dysentery on the track.

As the Nankai Shitai advanced along the track towards Ioribaiwa, they entered the area where the Australians were suffering from an epidemic of dysentery. Healthy troops moving into a contaminated area can quickly become infected and that's what happened in early September. From a loss by evacuation of fewer than five men per day to illness of all kinds, the Japanese rate shot up to 20 per day.

The Japanese repaid the Australians in kind. In November 1942, the Australians entered the hyperendemic malarial area of Buna–Gona to attack the Japanese base there. Malaria-carrying mosquitoes, having bitten Japanese soldiers, began biting the Australians, thus transferring malaria from one army to the other.

# Part IV
# Chasing the Japanese Out of Papua

*Glenn Lumsden*

*'Advance? We haven't finished retreating yet!'*

## In this part ...

The fighting along the Kokoda Trail falls naturally into two parts: The Japanese advance towards Port Moresby and the Japanese retreat to their starting point at Buna. In this part, I tell the story of the Japanese retreat. I also include the Battle of Milne Bay.

The Japanese invasion of Milne Bay was thrown back and they evacuated the reminder of their force. It was a defeat, but at the time the Japanese saw it as only a setback. The Japanese intended to return to take Milne Bay a second time, just as they fully intended that, once they were victorious at Guadalcanal, they would reinforce the Nankai Shitai and again march on Port Moresby. For the Australians, getting to Buna quickly while the Japanese were still overcommitted at Guadalcanal was important.

# Chapter 11

# Turning the Tide Against the Japanese

The first Australian victory in Papua took place at Milne Bay in September 1942, at a time when the Australians were still being driven back along the Kokoda Trail. From late September to early November 1942, it was the Australians' turn to be on the offensive. The Australians attacked along the track, driving the Japanese through the scenes of their earlier victories. Kokoda was recaptured on 2 November and the Japanese were decisively defeated at the Battle of Oivi–Gorari in mid November.

In this chapter, I tell a story of retribution, how first at Milne Bay in September and on the Kokoda Trail in October, the Australians had their turn to build success upon success.

## Defeating the Japanese For the First Time

The Japanese weren't defeated on the ground in the Pacific War until the Battle of Milne Bay in September 1942, and this wasn't a small defeat.

Milne Bay wasn't just any land battle: The Japanese mounted an amphibious invasion, a large and complex operation, as part of a much larger plan to conquer all of Papua. They were defeated, throwing Japan's broader plan into disarray.

The Japanese plan to take Port Moresby required that they capture Milne Bay so that

- ✔ Japanese aircraft operating from an airbase in Milne Bay could support the attack on Port Moresby
- ✔ The Nankai Shitai, arriving along the track to the north of Port Moresby, could be aided by a simultaneous seaward attack overnight from Milne Bay on fast destroyers, therefore avoiding an air attack from north Queensland

The Japanese attack on Milne Bay went wrong from the start. Not only did the Japanese grossly underestimate the size of the defending force, they landed in the wrong place, and the Australians were able to keep them away from the vital airfields. Outnumbered, outclassed by the AIF and outmatched in the air, the Japanese gave up and evacuated ten days after their landing.

## Landing on the wrong beach

At Gallipoli, in World War I, the Australians and New Zealanders famously landed on the wrong beach on the coast of Turkey, leading to a botched invasion of Turkey and many unnecessary deaths. The Japanese did the same thing at Milne Bay.

With an escort of cruisers and destroyers, the first Japanese landing, of 1,170 naval infantry and pioneers, took place between Waga Waga and Wandula on the northern coast of Milne Bay on the night of 25 August 1942. This was seven kilometres east of where they intended to land (worse than the Anzac error in Gallipoli by five kilometres), and a fact that had important consequences.

If flat land by the sea could be worse terrain for fighting than the Kokoda Trail, then Milne Bay was such a place. The Japanese landed on a narrow coastal strip between the bay and rugged mountains. The Australians were able to block Japanese access to the airfields by keeping hold of the only practical approach, along the coastal flats.

Almost constant rain throughout the operation did more than just turn all tracks into mud wallows and much of the area into a swamp, slowing movement. The heavy rain and banks of low cloud also affected Japanese air support. The Royal Australian Air Force, with an airstrip only minutes away, could quickly attack Japanese ground troops during a break in the weather. Japanese aircraft, in contrast, had to come from Buna, Lae and Rabaul. Communications with their own troops at Milne Bay often failed so the Japanese had no way of knowing when breaks in the cloud might occur there. As a result, most Imperial Japanese Navy (IJN) air sorties over Milne Bay failed to find any targets.

# Failing to seize Allied airfields

Incomplete intelligence led to the Japanese grossly underestimating the defending force, with disastrous consequences.

Admiral Mikawa Gunichi, who ordered the operation, believed probably less than a battalion of Allied troops was present. He decided to attack without waiting for Imperial Japanese Army infantry because he expected that the 2,200 IJN personnel he could call upon would be adequate for the task. Two light tanks, two 37-millimetre guns and two 70-millimetre howitzers accompanied the force. In fact, almost 10,000 defenders were at Milne Bay, commanded by Gallipoli veteran Lieutenant General Cyril Clowes, including 1,300 American engineers and 4,500 Australian infantry, as well as a battery of field artillery.

The events of 26 to 30 August 1942 at Milne Bay were crucial in the Battle of Milne Bay, as follows:

- ✓ **26 August, 1942:** While the Japanese Naval Pioneers established a base, the marines advanced west towards the Allied base. The Japanese drove back the Australian 61st Battalion at KB Mission.

- ✓ **27 August, 1942:** In the evening, the 61st Battalion and elements of 25th Australian Battalion were driven back to the Gama River. There they were relieved by the 2/10th, an AIF Battalion who advanced to KB Mission because the Japanese, fearing a counterattack and awaiting more marines arriving the next night, had withdrawn.

- ✓ **28 August, 1942:** The 2/10th Battalion felt the full weight of the reinforced Japanese. Spearheading the marines, tanks split the battalion in two and drove it back.

- ✓ **29 August, 1942:** The Australians prepared their next defensive position along the line of the newly constructed number three airstrip. The roads remained rivers of mud. The Australians were unable to get anti-tank guns to the forward troops, but the Japanese were also unable to bring up their tanks, which bogged short of the airstrip.

- ✓ **30 August, 1942:** The Japanese launched a major attack across the airstrip after midnight. The assault was bloodily repulsed by 25th and 61st battalions, together with Australian artillery and American engineers. The IJN marines lost two-thirds of all their casualties for Milne Bay in this night-time disaster.

## Japanese fighter pilot at Milne Bay

Honda Minoru told me about what it was like to be a fighter pilot at Milne Bay:

> Japanese pilots were so aggressive, brave and strong. There was no-one who was scared of going on any mission. Even when they knew that they wouldn't win in impossible situations. They never gave up. You will see what I mean when you hear my story.

> One day I was escorting our dive bombers when we attacked enemy ships. I saw the dive-bombers missing targets. The bombs were exploding in the ocean. I was flying well above them watching this and I was so frustrated. So, when I returned to the base, I complained to one of the senior pilots of the dive bombing squadron, Sergeant Kato. He looked extremely upset at my criticism of his squadron, but didn't say anything.

> Some time later Sergeant Kato came to me to discuss another dive bomber attack which my fighter squadron would escort. He said 'We will soon attack Milne Bay and, please, keep an eye on us and see how well we attack the enemy targets'. My squadron took off with his. As we approached Milne Bay, he soon found some ground targets through the clouds. Kato's dive-bomber started diving very sharply. I tried to keep up with him, but the Zero fighter was too light to keep up. Right in front of me, Kato dropped a bomb, but then he also dove his plane directly into one of the enemy ground facilities. There was a big explosion.

> After that, I regretted so much what I had said to him. Kato must have felt dishonoured by what I had said before and decided to prove his skill and his spirit to me. I still feel that I killed him, and I regret it even today.

## Trouncing the Japanese

The failure of the Japanese attack across number three strip was the turning point at Milne Bay, though this wasn't yet clear to Major General Cyril Clowes, commander of Milne Force, which comprised all the Australian and Amercian troops at Milne Bay.

Clowes had a lot more soldiers than the Japanese, but was focused on his main task, which was to hold the airstrips in Milne Bay. The presence of Japanese ships in Milne Bay most nights reminded Clowes that the Japanese might land elsewhere in the bay or at Wedau, Mullins Harbour or Taupota.

Now Clowes went on the offensive, cautiously:

- ✔ **1 September:** The 2/12th Battalion drove forward east along the north coast of Milne Bay to find the Japanese were evacuating.

- ✔ **4 September 1942:** Clowes passed 2/9th Battalion through 2/12th (that is, 2/12th stopped so that 2/9th could pass through to continue the pursuit), but still didn't throw his main weight behind the advance. He had again been advised that the Japanese ships in the bay at night indicated a new landing was being made.

- ✔ **6 September 1942:** The Japanese ships were in fact evacuating their men and completed the task by this date.

The Allies lost 170 servicemen killed and 210 wounded. Included in these figures were seven RAAF pilots, and three Americans killed and four wounded at the defence of number three strip and in the sinking of the transport ship *Anshun*.

The Japanese landed 1,943 men at Milne Bay. Of these, 625 died and 311 were evacuated wounded. An additional 21 Japanese aircrew were lost.

While the Japanese had occasionally been temporarily pushed back in attacks in Malaya and the Philippines (refer to Chapter 4), this was the first time a major Japanese amphibious operation had been definitively defeated.

---

# Goodenough Island — or was it?

The Japanese attack on Milne Bay would've been 353 men stronger but for the Royal Australian Air Force.

On 25 August, the same day as the main Japanese landing, the 5th Sasebo Special Naval Landing Party was moving by barge down the coast of Papua from Buna to Taupota, where they intended to advance on Milne Bay over the mountains. The force had stopped on Goodenough Island when it was spotted by Australian P-40 fighters from 75 and 76 squadrons. The Australians strafed and sank the barges, stranding the Japanese on the island. The following day, the RAAF struck the Japanese supply base on the beach in Milne Bay and destroyed most of their food and ammunition.

In October, the Australian 2/12th Battalion, which had fought in the Battle of Milne Bay, was sent to Goodenough Island to capture or kill the stranded Japanese marines.

Landed from destroyers at two points, the Australians had difficulty finding their enemy. This was because, unknown to the Australians, the Japanese were evacuating by submarine. Most were taken to nearby Fergusson Island where they were subsequently rescued by a cruiser. The opportunity to eliminate more than 300 Japanese was missed.

# Advancing to Eora

General MacArthur (who first appears in Chapter 6) decided to mount an offensive to eject the Japanese from Papua at the end of September.

MacArthur devised a two-pronged attack:

- The Australian 7th Division under General Arthur 'Tubby' Allen was given the task of driving the Japanese back along the track, recapturing Kokoda, then pushing on along the Kokoda to Sanananda route to the north coast.

- Another offensive, on a smaller scale, was begun from Milne Bay. There, an advance by sea and air was to approach the Japanese base at Buna from the south. Apart from US engineers who found themselves in a battle when the Japanese landed at Milne Bay, this was to be the first time American ground troops, from 32nd Division, were committed to battle in Papua.

The two Allied offensives were conducted slowly and carefully because the Allies still feared the Japanese might reinforce Papua in great strength, but by mid November both Allied offensives were approaching the Japanese stronghold at Buna.

# Chasing the Japanese

The Australian 25th Brigade under Brigadier Ken Eather, almost 2,000 men, led the advance on the track. On 28 September, it moved forward to Ioribaiwa Ridge to find that the Japanese had gone. The pursuit was slow and careful, and the brigade had little contact with the Japanese for two weeks. (Refer to Chapter 8 for more on Eather and the advance on Ioribaiwa Ridge.)

The Japanese had retreated under orders from the 17th Army commander Hyakutake, who told Horii to go back as far as Templeton's Crossing. As Hyakutake's force at Guadalcanal (he commanded both the Papua and Guadalcanal fronts; refer to Chapter 5 for more information about the fighting in Guadalcanal) was still unsuccessful, he was even more inclined to play a cautious game in Papua. Hyakutake knew he couldn't spare troops for Horii if Horii got into serious trouble. Hyakutake didn't regard the retreat as a permanent move. He still intended to order Horii to attack Port Moresby once the Guadalcanal problem was solved.

# Defeating the Stanley Detachment

The next serious fighting occurred in front of Templeton's Crossing when the Australians caught up with a new formation created by Horii: The Stanley Detachment. From Efogi north to Templeton's were two tracks: the old mail track over Mount Bellamy and, further to the east (close to Myola), the Kokoda Trail. Initially a 600-man force, the detachment was placed in two blocking positions, with one Japanese position on each track.

If the Australians advanced, and Horii wasn't sure that they would, the two forces on the two tracks to Templeton's Crossing were to hold them up for a few days while the main Japanese position was prepared at Templeton's.

From 12 October, three Australian battalions attacked, but were unable to make any progress until they threatened to outflank the Japanese on the track and cut them off from Templeton's Crossing (see the following section). The threat worked and by the morning of 15 October the Japanese were gone.

# Taking Templeton's Crossing

In the time purchased by the Stanley Detachment holding the two outer positions, the main Japanese defence at Templeton's Crossing was reinforced; it now held 800 men and 4 guns.

For the Australians, fresh troops were available. Brigadier John Lloyd's 16th Brigade had arrived and, with Eather's 25th Brigade, seven infantry battalions — more than 3,000 troops — were under Allen, commander of 7th Australian Division. Allen directed the operation from Efogi while Lloyd and Eather manoeuvred their brigades in battle.

By this stage, Australian supply was improving and firepower was enhanced by the addition of Vickers medium machine guns and three-inch mortars, two useful weapons the Australians had had few or none of in earlier fighting on the track (Chapters 9 and 10 look at supply and ammunition problems that Australia had during this campaign).

From 17 to 19 October 1942, the Australians attacked slowly, driving the Japanese back. Meanwhile, 2/2nd Battalion worked its way through the bush to the high ground on the Japanese left (east). On 20 October, 2/2nd attacked while 2/1st Battalion assaulted frontally. The attack was a remarkable success. This was the first time on the track that the Australians had swept aside the opposition and stormed into the midst of their defences. The Japanese position collapsed and some were seen to flee, though they did manage to get their artillery away.

Part of the reason for the Australian success at Templeton's Crossing was that it was achieved by 16th Brigade, who were battle experienced, had received jungle training in Ceylon, and were healthy because they had only just arrived in Papua. They opposed the Japanese 144 Regiment, which had been there since July and August and were showing clear signs of wear.

## Capturing Eora

The Australian success at Templeton's Crossing was a shock to Horii. In a week he had lost his first position in front of Templeton's Crossing and his main position at Templeton's Crossing, and now he found he wasn't ready to defend his third and last position on the track at Eora Village.

Japanese troops resting around Kokoda and Oivi were rushed forward to occupy Eora. When Allen's two brigades attacked on 22 October, 600 defenders (and five guns) were in place, but four times as many Australians. However, the first Australian attacks, frontally across Eora Creek, failed at great cost. Within days, an additional 500 Japanese had arrived to further bolster the defence.

On 26 October, the Australians tried something different. The 2/3rd Battalion from Lloyd's brigade were sent west through the jungle to attack the heights north-west of Eora where the Japanese guns were dug in, overlooking the Australians and pinning them down with heavy fire. On 28 October, the Australian battalion attacked the heights and, as at Templeton's, swept through the Japanese position.

The Australians had had some luck because another Japanese disaster at Guadalcanal, the Battle of Lunga Point, prompted Hyakuate to order Horii to withdraw his forces from Eora. The Japanese had removed their wounded and their guns and were assembling their infantry to retreat when the Australians struck. The 3/144 Battalion, which had been holding the heights and protecting the guns, were caught out and scattered, losing a quarter of the men. The battalion fled and weren't able to re-assemble until they reached Isurava. The withdrawal of the rest of the Japanese force at Eora went smoothly.

The two and a half weeks of fighting from 12 October, known as the Second Eora–Templeton's action, had involved a series of Australian attacks on well dug-in defenders. The action proved very expensive for the attackers: The Australians lost 412 battle casualties, killed and wounded, against 244 Japanese casualties.

# *Sacking the commander — again*

The day after 7th Division's victory at Second Eora–Templeton's, the division's commander, Major General Arthur ('Tubby') Allen, was replaced by General George Vasey, who led the division until the end of the fighting in Papua.

Like Brigadier Potts being sacked after Efogi (refer to Chapter 8), many said Allen was unjustly removed. He had beaten the Japanese out of a series of positions and cleared the way for the recapture of Kokoda; but Potts was removed because, from the perspective of his superiors, he had been much too slow in beating the Japanese.

Allen's superiors in ascending order were

- Lieutenant General Edmund Herring, Allen's corps commander who had replaced the previous corps commander General Sydney Rowell

- General Sir Thomas Blamey, who was Land Forces Commander over Herring (see the sidebar 'An unpopular leader' for more about Blamey)

- General Douglas MacArthur, who commanded land, sea and air forces in the south-west Pacific theatre (refer to Chapter 6 for more about MacArthur)

## An unpopular leader

Field Marshal Sir Thomas Blamey fought in World War I and World War II and is the only Australian to be promoted to Field Marshal. He was Chief Commissioner of the Victoria Police in the 1920s and 1930s. During this time, he was involved in a scandal when his police badge was found in a brothel.

During World War II, Blamey commanded the 2nd AIF and 1st Australian Corps in the Middle East. In 1942, he returned to Australia as Commander in Chief of the Australian Military Forces and Commander of Allied Land Forces in the south-west Pacific (including the Australians and Americans who fought in Papua) under the theatre commander American General Douglas MacArthur. Blamey was an unpopular and controversial leader — few veterans have a good thing to say about him — because of incidents such as the rabbit speech (refer to Chapter 3 for more about this controversy). However, Blamey satisfied the most important selection criterion for a general's job: He won battles.

All three men argued that Allen had fresher troops than the enemy and lots more of them, his supply was much better than that of the Japanese, and that the several pronged Allied counteroffensive to capture Buna was being delayed by Allen's over-careful advance. Allen's superiors feared that time was their enemy. If the Australians didn't get to Buna quickly, the Japanese would reinforce, and Buna would be a much tougher nut to crack.

# Retaking Kokoda

The Nankai Shitai, badly defeated at Eora, retreated in a disorganised manner, making no effort to hold Kokoda. On 2 November, a patrol of 2/31st Battalion entered unopposed to find the Japanese had left two days before. By the afternoon, the whole battalion had arrived and secured the area, also capturing Kokoda Village, two kilometres away to the east on the track leading to Buna.

Taking Kokoda was a moment full of symbolism for those taking part in the battle and for their families in Australia. By November, Kokoda was a household word and even those who understood little about the course of the fighting could see that a corner had been turned. The *West Australian* newspaper announced appropriately that 'the reoccupation of Kokoda and the continuing advance of our troops towards Buna have set the Japanese back to where they were at the end of July in Papua. They now have nothing to show for their considerable expenditure of men and material in their short lived thrust over the Owen Stanley Range towards Port Moresby'.

The recapture of Kokoda signified an important step in ejecting the Japanese from Papua.

# Raising the flag and handing out medals

On 3 November, General Vasey arrived in Kokoda for a flag-raising ceremony. The 25th Brigade gathered around a flagpole on Kokoda Plateau. The same flag used that day was kept with the brigade and later raised to mark Australian victories at Buna–Gona, Sattleberg and Wareo.

At Kokoda airstrip, Vasey held another ceremony to recognise the Papuan contribution. He awarded 55 Loyal Service Medals to Papuan carriers, members of the Papuan Infantry Battalion and the Royal Papuan Constabulary.

## Cooking at Kokoda

Des Moran remembers:

I remember when we took back Kokoda. I remember very distinctly walking in to Kokoda and taking a break there to do some cooking. I had turned 21 and my dear old mum had baked a huge birthday cake, you know how mothers are. This thing would have been a full load for a biscuit bomber. She got a really good friend of ours to make a special case to send it in. I wanted some sugar to add. After a long time without salt or sugar you would kill to get it. No bloody shadow of doubt. I found some sugar, I said Jesus Christ, sugar! I filled my tin hat with it, my pockets, everywhere I could and it's raining its guts out and the sugar was washing out.

So I pulled the lining of a pocket out and sucked on it. It was bloody great. I found some salt and I found some sugar and [when] I got back the cake had arrived by aircraft. It was battered and busted to buggery and wet as a cow pad. But we were determined to get into it. Got this Jap cooking pot, kind of a big bowl. Tipped it all in there, got the powdered milk and sugar and made a big burgoo with the cake. A real pudding, and Christ didn't we get a gigantic dose of [diarrhoea]. It went straight through us. I think that's why I had to go back to the doctor the next day. Maybe mum's cake was the start of it because my gut problems from New Guinea are everlasting.

The third day of November is now known as Kokoda Day. The day is intended to be a day to honour not only the Australians but also the Papuans (the Fuzzy Wuzzy Angels) who assisted them by carrying supplies in and wounded men out.

## *Flying in burgoo, bombs and bullets*

The practical importance of capturing Kokoda lay in the value of its airstrip, the only one in the 200-kilometre trip from Port Moresby on the south coast to Buna on the north coast.

The strip hadn't been used by the Japanese and the grass was almost a metre high. Cutting this and removing the obstacles the Japanese had placed took time, but by 4 November aircraft from Port Moresby were landing regularly. Now 7th Division could rely on a steady stream of food (see the 'Cooking at Kokoda' sidebar), reinforcements and ammunition coming in while the wounded and sick could be flown out.

In the next battle after the recapture of Kokoda (see the following section), veterans who had fought along the track noticed the difference that the airstrip made. They commented that before Kokoda their mortars had to fire their bombs sparingly because every bomb had to be carried up the track. Now, they said, plenty of mortar bombs were available and the comforting sound of the bombs exploding on the enemy never seemed to stop.

# Exploiting the Decisive Moment: The Battle of Oivi–Gorari

The Battle of Kokoda is the official title of the fighting in Papua from the Japanese landing (on 21 July 1942 ) to the end of the Battle of Oivi–Gorari (on 11 November 1942).

That makes sense, even though Oivi is 16 kilometres east of Kokoda and not on the track, because until the Japanese defeat at Oivi–Gorari

- ✔ The Japanese themselves had not given up the idea of reinforcing Buna and once again advancing along the track
- ✔ The Australians weren't confident that they had the Japanese on the run and no repeat of the track fighting could occur

At Oivi, the Japanese had assembled the largest concentration for battle seen so far in Papua. This included 2,800 fighting troops and, just as important, all 15 artillery pieces that the Japanese had brought to Papua were in position.

The Japanese deployed in two parts. Half of the force, 41st Infantry Regiment with eight guns, held the heights of Oivi across the track from Kokoda to Sanananda near Buna. The other half of the Japanese force, 144 Regiment, was held in reserve near Gorari.

The regiment in Oivi was supported by combat engineers who were sent into the fight for the first time, perhaps a sign of desperation. Combat engineers were trained to fight, but were usually considered too valuable in their primary engineering task to be used in battle.

The Australians, too, had assembled a large force. Vasey had seven infantry battalions, although these had been reduced (by weeks of fighting) to fewer than 3,000 men. Together with supporting troops, the Australians had 3,700 men in action. They still had no artillery, but did have a dozen three-inch mortars and a Vickers gun per battalion. In the more open terrain, air support, too, was expected to be of greater assistance.

# Failing against the Japanese guns

Parallel to and south of the Kokoda–Sanananda track was another approach to Buna. Vasey sent a battalion along the approach to investigate the possibility of cutting the main track behind the Japanese. Meanwhile, he sent three battalions against Oivi heights, the big hills the Japanese were defending just west of Oivi Village.

The strength of the Japanese 41st Regiment, on good ground and with plenty of artillery support, was too much for the Australians. Attempts to get around both flanks of the Japanese at Oivi failed because the 41st Regiment was deployed on a broader front than the Australians had suspected.

Over three days, from 5 to 7 November, all attacks failed, at a cost of 33 dead and 81 wounded. American Boston medium bombers and Australian Beaufighters from 30 Squadron were called upon, but their bombing and strafing weren't powerful enough to materially alter the situation.

Vasey called off further ground attacks at Oivi because they weren't going to succeed and because of promising developments on the other track. From 8 to 11 November, the Australians at Oivi contented themselves with bombarding the Japanese, whose artillery retaliated. When the Australians probed the Japanese position at Oivi on the morning of 11 November, they found it abandoned. Because of Australian success on the other track, the Japanese had retreated towards the Kumusi River.

# Outmanoeuvring for victory

On the southern track, which ran parallel to the main northern track, Colonel Paul Cullen's 2/1st Battalion were looking for a track junction that turned north and led into the Japanese rear. They missed the junction and were almost at the Kumusi River before the error was realised.

Having lost a day, the battalion found the junction, which they called Leaney's Corner. Cullen's report to his brigade commander was passed to Vasey who decided that, especially as he was having no success at Oivi, he would send Eather with the 25th Brigade to join Cullen and take the 2/1st under command. Then the whole force, four battalions, would strike north towards Gorari.

The attack stepped off on 8 November and encountered the main body of 144 Regiment at Bariibe. Orokaiva scouts had warned Horii of Australians on the southern track. When Horii was certain that the Australians were on the southern track in large numbers, he committed 144 Regiment, until now held in reserve. Eather surrounded 144 Regiment with two battalions and pushed on up the track to Gorari. There, 2/33rd drove a Japanese battalion from Gorari while 2/1st Battalion encountered Horii's headquarters further east and attacked.

At this point, on 10 November, Japanese resistance collapsed. Horii's communications with his subordinates faltered and his own headquarters was scattered towards the Kumusi. Tsukamoto, now commanding 144 Regiment, decided, because he had heard nothing from Horii, to cut his way out east towards the coast. Yazawa's 41st Regiment, still at Oivi, waited until a runner from Horii got through, then he too withdrew.

## Chasing the Japanese across the Kumusi River

The battle became a pursuit after the Japanese dispersed at Oivi (refer to the preceding section). None of the Japanese guns could be moved across the river, though it was just low enough for 144 Regiment to wade across without much loss. The 41st Regiment couldn't at first find a ford and marched north for several days, pursued by the 3rd Battalion, before crossing the Kumusi River and turning towards Buna. Some 440 Japanese were killed in battle or during the pursuit. Another 380 wounded got away.

Half of the Japanese who arrived in Buna several days later had lost their rifles and all the Japanese supply dumps in the Kumusi area fell into Australian hands.

The Australians, who lost 121 killed and 225 wounded at Oivi–Gorari, erected a wire suspension bridge at the old Kumusi River crossing known as Wairopi (wire rope) and headed for Buna. Intelligence said that not many Japanese were at Buna. It seemed to Vasey that if the Australians got there quickly, and the Japanese had no time to send reinforcements from Rabaul, the rabble that he was now pursuing wouldn't by themselves be able to hold Buna.

The decisive battle of the Kokoda phase of the fighting in Papua wasn't actually fought on the track, but at Oivi and Gorari, 16 kilometres east of Kokoda on the track leading to the Japanese base at Buna.

# The death of General Horii

General Horii Tomitaro, 52 years old, a graduate of the Imperial Japanese Army Academy and commander of the Nankai Shitai, wasn't one of the survivors of the Battle of Oivi–Gorari.

When the Australian 2/1st Battalion found and attacked his headquarters on 9 November, Horii briefly took personal command of the defences. However, the headquarters staff and an infantry company were soon overwhelmed and scattered.

In the chaos, Horii and one aide fled north along the Kumusi River looking for a place to cross. They found a canoe and paddled to the sea. Several days later they reached the Kumusi River mouth on the Solomon Sea, 40 kilometres north of Buna. They then attempted to paddle the canoe south along the coast. A storm came up and the canoe was blown away from the shore. The canoe overturned and Horii drowned. His aide swam ashore, walked to Buna and reported the loss of the commander of the Nankai Shitai.

Horii's aide related that Horii had swum part of the way to shore when he said 'I have no strength left to swim any further. Tell the troops that Horii died here'. Horii shouted 'Banzai!', the shortened version of 'Tenno Heika banzai', meaning 'Long live the Emperor', and sank beneath the waves.

# Chapter 12

# Besieging the Japanese

## In This Chapter

▶ Closing in on Buna

▶ Struggling through the swamp

▶ Busting bunkers

▶ Driving the Japanese to the coast

▶ Ending the Japanese occupation of Papua and moving on to other battles

After Oivi–Gorari, the Japanese were on the run. They retreated to their Buna base (to the south-east of the central Japanese defence in Sananada; Gona was to the north-west) and, with their backs to the sea, resolved to hold on there. They hadn't yet given up on Papua and brought in reinforcements. The Japanese still hoped to win at Guadalcanal and were determined to keep their options open.

The war in Papua now entered its last act. The Battle of Buna–Gona was the last, largest and longest set piece battle of the Japanese occupation of Papua.

From the Allied perspective, haste was called for. If the Japanese didn't reinforce Buna, General MacArthur, the American commander of Allied land, sea and air forces in the south-west Pacific, might be able to take Buna quickly. If the Japanese did reinforce, it must be with troops who would otherwise have gone to Guadalcanal, which would benefit the American effort there. Either way, it was strategically important that the Allies made a strong and immediate attack on Buna.

In this chapter, I follow the Australian advance from the Australian crossing of the Kumusi River until the final battle at Buna, where the six-month Japanese sojourn in Papua came to an end.

# Advancing to the Sea

Under the command of Australian Lieutenant General Edmund Herring, the Allies advanced from two directions: General George Vasey's 7th Australian Division, which had just recaptured Kokoda, was pursuing the Japanese after their defeat at Oivi–Gorari (refer to Chapter 11), and from the southeast, advancing along the coast from Milne Bay, came the US 32nd Division under Major General Edwin Harding.

The lead element of Harding's prong of the advance, the Australian 2/6th Independent Company, was at Pongani 30 kilometres south of Buna. The 2/6th had arrived at Wanigela, 100 kilometres south of Buna, on 14 October and had been cautiously feeling their way north for a month.

Behind the experienced 2/6th (which had fought on the Kokoda Trail) was the 128th Regiment of the US 32nd Division, newly arrived in Papua. Commanded by Harding, the Americans moved along the coast towards Buna; their objective was by land, sea and air. Luggers, captured Japanese barges, indeed anything that would float, were pressed into service. The majority of troops and heavy equipment came from Milne Bay via Porlock Harbour, Oro Bay and Hariko. Airfields at Wanigela, Pongani and Sepia were built from scratch or from long-disused strips by American engineers.

As the Allies advanced on Buna, the Japanese made the decision to hold it. On 16 October, their command arrangements had changed. General Imamura Hitoshi opened the headquarters of 8th Area Army in Rabaul. He oversaw 17th Army under Hyakutake and 18th Army under Adachi. In both New Guinea and Guadalcanal, 17th Army had been running the war. Now Hyakutake was sent to Guadalcanal with responsibility for Guadalcanal only, while the new commander, Adachi, was in charge in New Guinea. Adachi set up his HQ in Lae and gave command of all forces in the Buna–Gona area to Major General Yamagata Tsuyuo. On 26 November, Imamura assured Yamagata that no retreat would occur from Buna and that additional troops would be sent there.

Incredibly, the Japanese knew nothing of the Allied advance from Milne Bay until 15 November. The next day they responded. Coastal barges used to move heavy equipment forwards from Wanigela were attacked by 14 Zeros off Cape Sudest. Four craft were sunk and two field guns were lost.

Another less successful part of the southern advance was the movement of 126th Regiment. They had marched over the Kapa Kapa track, parallel to the Kokoda Trail, and arrived, exhausted and hungry, at Pongani on 14 November. Nevertheless, by 16 November the Americans were ready to attack Buna from the south.

Figure 12-1 shows a map of part of this area of Papua New Guinea.

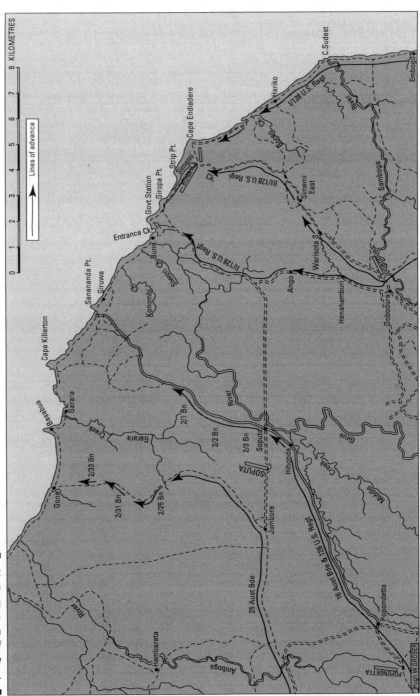

**Figure 12-1:** Map showing the north-eastern area of Papua New Guinea.

# Bunkering: The Battle of the Beachhead

The term 'nightmare terrain' might be overused describing the precipitous mountains on the Kokoda Trail or the mud at Milne Bay, but the Battle of Buna–Gona was, literally, fought in a swamp. The 20-kilometre wide tidal swamp had a number of causeways across it. The causeways were sometimes just a few metres wide, from just a few centimetres to two metres above the swamp, which was often deeper than a man could walk through. *Digging in* (digging a hole in which to hide and to fight from) was sometimes impossible because water was struck a short way below the surface, even on the causeways.

Though the Allies could often move through the swamp, they couldn't stay in it for long. Those who tried to stay had to sleep in trees to keep dry. Nor could the Allies easily be supplied in the swamp. One American colonel described his supply line to his forward troops as 'neck deep in mud and water'.

The curious lay of the land at Buna–Gona determined the deployment of the Japanese defences and channelled the Allied advance. The Battle of Buna–Gona was fought on four fronts on the four practical approaches to the central Japanese position at a place called Sanananda (the Japanese had men in one central bastion there, plus three outer fortifications covering its approaches). The four approaches and the main Allied units targeting each were:

- ✔ Toward Gona in the north — 16th Australian Brigade

- ✔ Straight at Sanananda in the centre — 25th Australian Brigade and 126th US Regiment

- ✔ The inland approach to Buna in the south — Urbana Force, part of US 126th Regiment

- ✔ The coastal route to Buna, via Cape Endiadere — Warren Force, part of 128th US Regiment and Australian 2/6th Independent Company

All four positions were independent of each other and each was, with the exception of the causeways, almost surrounded by swamp or sea.

Each bastion contained hundreds of bunkers, each holding 10 or 20 men. They were impervious to mortar fire and difficult for the guns of tanks and artillery to knock out. The typical bunker was a deep trench covered with several layers of coconut tree trunks. Connected to the bunkers were fire trenches. When the Allies bombarded, the Japanese hid in the bunker. When the Allied infantry attacked, half held the bunker and operated its one or two light machine guns, while the other half rushed out to man the trenches. To penetrate the line of bunkers, one had to be knocked out, then the others could be approached from the flank or rear — just the move the Japanese in trenches outside the bunker were there to prevent. If the attackers could get close enough, they could throw grenades into the firing slits in the bunker. Sometimes they crawled on top of the bunker with petrol and set it alight.

## Gathering the combatants

As the battle began, Vasey had 4,300 men north of the Giruwa River (on the Gona and Sanananda fronts) and Harding had 6,600 south of it on the Buna front. Both had elements of the other's force under their command. Vasey had two battalions of 126th Regiment while the Americans had the Australian 2/6th Independent Company and Australian artillery from 2/5th Field Regiment. All the Australian infantry battalions were worn down by several months campaigning against the Japanese. The Americans were fresh troops, but with little training and no fighting experience.

Air support was a combined Australian–American effort, as was air and sea supply. Allied air supply, intermittent in November, increased rapidly as new airfields were built at Dobodura, Popondetta and Soputa. By the end of the battle, 50 aircraft were arriving or departing each day from all the airfields.

On the Japanese side, reinforcements had arrived. The Allies had no idea that the Japanese had already been reinforced and that now almost as many Japanese were inside the position as Allied troops attacking it. However, the Japanese had a range of fresh and tired troops as well as many sick among their 11,000 army and navy personnel. About 2,000 were survivors of the fighting on the track or at Oivi–Gorari. One thousand more trained troops had never left Buna. Another 4,000 were base troops and civilian labourers who were armed and placed in the defences. They fought with courage but little skill. More than 2,000 fresh troops had recently arrived from Rabaul and the remainder, just less than 2,000, were too ill to fight, most of whom were in the main Japanese hospital at Giruwa near Sanananda.

## First attempts fail

The first Allied attacks on the Japanese beachhead fortress, over two weeks in the second half of November 1942, failed all along the line and cost 300 Australian and American lives. A difficulty for the Allies on all fronts was that they were unsure of the exact Japanese positions, and the first attacks failed in part for this reason.

At Gona, Brigadier Ken Eather's 25th Brigade attacked for a week beginning on 19 November, but the brigade was weak and its battalions less than half strength. Four field guns, flown in to a new strip at Popondetta, didn't provide enough support for the tired brigade to make headway. The 900 Japanese defenders — mostly non-combat service troops who had been armed, stiffened by a detachment of infantry from the 41st Regiment — were entrenched in a compact box of bunkers 300 metres square, with Gona Creek protecting their north and their rear on the Solomon Sea. Bunkers faced out on the other two sides. The defenders were mostly non-combat service troops who had been armed, stiffened by a detachment of infantry from 41st Regiment. The Australians attacked for a week but were unable to make progress.

The end of November saw the arrival of the third brigade of the Australian 7th Division. This brigade, the 21st, had fought on the Kokoda Trail, but hadn't been brought up to full strength since. However, the 21st attacked successfully around the Australian right to cut Gona off from the other Japanese positions, clearing the way for the Australians to attack Gona from two sides.

On the Sanananda front, Brigadier Lloyd's 16th Brigade attacked 1,000 Japanese from 144 and 41 Regiment, deployed to block the causeway along which ran the Sanananda Road, on 18 November. Cullen's 2/1st Battalion was able to work around the Japanese flanks and block the track in their rear. The Japanese retired that night into their main position on a narrower stretch of the causeway. The US 126th Regiment was brought up and worked their way through the swamp and again blocked the Sanananda Road behind the Japanese, at what became known as Huggins Roadblock. This time the Japanese refused to retreat and defied all Allied attacks here for two months.

The American Warren Force, with the Australian 2/6th Independent Company, advanced along the coastal approach to Buna on the Cape Endiadere track and the Simemi track with 3,900 men. Urbana Force, another 2,500 men, took an inland route to Buna through Dobodura and Ango. Opposing them, the Japanese Buna defences held 2,700 men, half of whom had recently arrived by barge at night. From 16 November to the end of the month the Allies made repeated attacks along both Buna approaches. The Americans lost 500 battle casualties, but didn't breach the Japanese defences.

IN THEIR OWN WORDS

# Mates at Gona

Dudley Warhurst told me about his experiences at Gona:

We were flown over to Popondetta with the new troops. Nothing like keen young fellahs to get the attack going in. Experience makes you cautious. A lot of people got premonitions that they won't come out of it and they don't. I was only young, a bushwacker, no experience communicating with people. I was a young fellah and the army looked after me.

At Gona we went smack into the middle of a Jap position of about 25 men. The higher ups said go in, I was one of the last to go in there. The Japs were up coconut trees and knew we were coming and said, 'Well OK, wait till they get through the swamp and then we would get him'. That is where Harry Saunders was killed — he was Aboriginal, the brother of Reg Saunders. Harry called his mate a white bastard and he called Harry a black bastard, and they were best of mates. No-one gave Harry a hard time. There was no hard times given to anyone, that was the secret of keeping the militia together, we were all volunteers and had to be mates. Couldn't work otherwise. Like a footy team, have to work together, rely on all of them. Need to rely on each other, that's what makes you a force. Mateship becomes thicker in battle than any other time.

You would see Japs come out to get their mates when they were wounded. I heard one call out to his mate and he came out of a bunker to get him. They were still in that bunker till about midnight, but we took that position after an artillery barrage, so I guess neither of them made it. You don't think about what you do before you do it. We took the top off the bunker and there were 16 Japs, half dead and half wounded, but they were quickly killed without afterthought. It was over before I knew it and no-one said anything. Wasn't my cup of tea, we never talked about it to the bloke that did it.

Officers found some Japs lying doggo [pretending to be dead] and we were ordered to clear up the area and one of them was alive. So we put him on a stretcher and the native carriers kept dropping him and walking over him. He died after a few days. We had the job of burying 22 of our chaps and 23 Japs that had fallen at that battle. Bloke found a cart and bought an injured guy down but he didn't make it. This become tough mentally. We became harsh. I was told to go with the padre to see if I could identify any of our fellahs had been killed. The body disintegrates in those conditions after a week but I knew a bloke with a gold tooth, so I was able to identify one of them. When you go back to parents, sisters and brothers this is one time that you tell lies. You say they were killed in battle and buried with full ceremony. I said to myself, No more. I just couldn't do it. I was only 21.

## *Casting about blame*

By the end of November, General MacArthur was a worried man. Not only had the Buna–Gona position not fallen, but neither had any progress been made in that direction. On the American front, some troops had refused to fight. An officer who flew in to see firsthand described the men as tired and listless and not hardened for jungle operations. MacArthur took his frustration out on his commanders. On 22 November, he ordered Harding to press on the next day 'regardless of cost'. Harding didn't obey the order.

A few days after issuing Harding the order to press on, MacArthur had had enough. He called forward the commander of 1st American Corps (32nd Division and 41st Division), General Robert Eichelberger, and told him to go to Buna and replace his own divisional commander, Harding. MacArthur said, 'Bob, I'm putting you in command at Buna. Relieve Harding, remove all officers who won't fight. I want you to take Buna or don't come back alive'.

MacArthur was under pressure from Blamey too (refer to Chapter 11 to find out more about Blamey). When the issue of sending the US 41st Division to Buna arose, Blamey told MacArthur that he would rather send Australians, because he knew they would fight. A witness to the conversation reported that MacArthur accepted the criticism of his troops and that it was a bitter pill for him to swallow after his own denigration of Australian fighting ability during the earlier Kokoda battles.

# *Progressing Towards Victory, December 1942*

December 1942 at Buna–Gona saw changes in the battle that indicated the Allies were probably going to win. How long it would take was another question. The Australians took Gona early in the month and Japanese reinforcements were no longer able to get through by sea from Rabaul after mid month. Increasing Allied air power, the arrival of additional troops and guns and Australian tanks in action for the first time in the war all indicated the tide was on the turn.

The Allies had begun the battle with about the same strength as the defenders, but by mid December they had been reinforced to a greater extent and lost slightly fewer men to sickness than the Japanese, who were running out of food and medicine. Japanese casualties too had been greater. By mid December, the Allies outnumbered the Japanese by two to one. Allied fighting ability was further increased by the arrival of more artillery and aircraft, and some tanks.

## Bringing up tanks and artillery

So far in Papua the Australians had rarely had artillery support. At Buna, the first two guns went into action a week after the Australians began their attack and, by the end of November, 12 guns were along the front against 25 Japanese guns of all types within their defences. Among the Allied guns was the 1st Australian Mountain Battery, with 3.7-inch howitzers. The Australians had been impressed by the Japanese mountain guns on the track and had created a battery of their own.

By the end at Buna–Gona, the number of Allied weapons had increased to 28, which did much to explain the Allies' success. Even so, this was still too few to provide proper support for the infantry. Normally a two division-size force should have had more than 100.

Support also included

- **Bren carriers (light armoured tracked reconnaissance vehicles):** While waiting for tanks to arrive, the infantry commanders were desperate for any help they could get. Five Australian Bren carriers were used in an assault on 5 December, but within 20 minutes all were knocked out.

- **Tanks:** Seven Australian tanks first went into action at Cape Endiadere, where the causeway of good ground was widest, on 18 December. They were M3 Stuart light tanks from the Australian 2/6th Armoured Regiment. Another squadron arrived soon after and the 20 tanks made a major contribution to the success of Allied attacks on the Buna front thereafter. Later a few tanks were moved, with great difficulty, to the Sanananda front where it could operate only along the road. As at Buna, Japanese anti-tank guns had some success knocking out the Stuarts.

## *Winning the air battle*

The air war on the track had been relatively low key because the Allied airpower was small and the Japanese devoted their main air effort to Guadalcanal (refer to Chapter 5).

However, by the start of December 1942, Allied airpower was growing and the Japanese, having determined to hold Buna, raised the tempo of air operations at Buna. But by the end of December, Allied air superiority over Buna was assured. The constant shuttle of supplies and reinforcements from Port Moresby to Dobodura and Popondetta airfields was hardly interrupted, and Australian Wirraways (light bomber/ground attack planes) of No. 4 Squadron were able to overfly Japanese positions without a fighter escort and adjust the fire of Allied artillery onto Japanese positions.

Conditions were not quite so safe for aircrew over Buna early in December 1942 when Pilot Officer John Archer and his radio operator/rear gunner Sergeant James Coulston encountered a far superior Zero fighter. Incredibly they shot it down. This is believed to be the only occasion when a Wirraway, not designed for air to air combat, shot down a Japanese aircraft.

Other changes from the middle of December were

- ✔ Allied airpower, projected in strength far out into the Solomon Sea, was able to prevent any more Japanese reinforcements coming to Buna from Rabaul.

- ✔ Medium bombers began making daily raids on Buna. Each Allied ground assault could now rely on the support of 10 to 20 tonnes of bombs.

## Gona's gone

Another Australian attack on Gona failed on 1 December, but Vasey felt obliged to attack again as soon as possible because a new problem had arisen. The Japanese were no longer able to land reinforcements directly into the Buna–Gona area, so were now building up a force of 2,500 men north of Gona between the Kumusi and Amboga rivers.

The new Japanese force, which had arrived by sea, included Major General Yamagata Tsuyuo. Yamagata was in command of the Buna–Gona area, but hadn't been able to get to his command. He hoped to march inland behind Gona with the new force and attack the Allied airfields and supply dumps at Soputa and Popondetta. His force was too small to change the outcome of the battle, but had he succeeded Allied supply would've been so disrupted that the defenders would've gained a breathing space of a few weeks.

To keep Yamagata's force away from Gona, Chaforce, a detached force drawn from 21st Brigade, held the area from north of Gona to the Amboga River.

On 8 December, the next attack on Gona commenced, with the last moderately fresh battalion on the front. This was 39th Battalion, another battalion that had fought on the Kokoda Trail, been rested at Port Moresby and was now flown back into battle. This time the attack was successful. The next day, Lieutenant Colonel Ralph Honner, commander of 39th Battalion, was able to advise his brigadier that 'Gona's gone'. Very few of the garrison escaped.

# Poet at Buna

The Australian poet David Campbell flew transport aircraft from Port Moresby, over the Owen Stanley Range to Dobodura during the battle. He later wrote a poem about it.

### Men in Green

Oh, there were fifteen men in green,
Each with a tommy-gun,
Who leapt into my plane at dawn;
We rose to meet the sun

We set our course towards the east
And climbed into the day
Till the ribbed jungle underneath
Like a giant fossil lay.

We climbed towards the distant range,
Where two white paws of cloud
Clutched at the shoulders of the pass;
The green men laughed aloud.

They did not fear the ape-like cloud
That climbed the mountain crest
And hung from ropes invisible
With lightning in its breast.

They did not fear the summer's sun
In whose hot centre lie
A hundred hissing cannon shells
For the unwatchful eye.

And when on Dobadura's field
We landed, each man raised

His thumb towards the open sky;
But to their right I gazed.

For fifteen men in jungle green
Rose from the kunai grass
And came towards the plane. My men
In silence watched them pass;
It seemed they looked upon themselves
In Time's prophetic glass.

Oh, there were some leaned on a stick
And some on stretchers lay,
But few walked on their own two feet
In the early green of day.

(They did not heed the ape-like cloud
That climbed the mountain crest;
They did not fear the summer sun
With bullets for their breast.)

Their eyes were bright, their looks were dull;
Their skin had turned to clay.
Nature had meet them in the night
And stalked them in the day.

And I think still of men in green
On the Soputa track,
With fifteen spitting tommy-guns
To keep the jungle back.

Now the Australians were able to turn their attention to Yamagata and his troops in the north. His advanced guard had driven Chaforce back, but by mid December the Australians had again advanced to the Amboga River. Here the front quietened down. Yamagata, unable to land most of the force for their planned offensive, abandoned it and instead decided to transfer the majority of his force on the Amboga River into the Sanananda defences by barge along the coast at night. The Royal Australian Navy and US PT boats (torpedo boats) unsuccessfully attempted to interrupt the Japanese coastal traffic by patrolling Holnicote Bay.

## *On the central front*

In the longest continual fighting at Buna–Gona, on the Sanananda Road, Japanese efforts to eliminate Huggins Roadblock failed as a small force of Americans held on.

Both sides faced the same problem. Huggins Roadblock cut off the main Japanese position, which in turn cut off Huggins Roadblock. The Allies and the Japanese were only intermittently able to get supplies through the swamp to their respective isolated forces. The US 126th Regiment and the Australian 30th Brigade failed in their attempts to link up with Huggins by overcoming the main Japanese position astride the road.

The Japanese had another blocking position beyond Huggins and later the Allies, once again by moving through the swamp on the flanks, established another of their own on the causeway beyond the Japanese causeway. The situation was peculiar, with Allied then Japanese then Allied then Japanese roadblocks like a string of beads along the causeway leading to Sanananda. Both sides struggled to supply their respective cut-off blocking positions while ambushing the supply parties of the enemy as they moved through the swamp.

IN THEIR OWN WORDS

# At Huggins Roadblock

Ben Love (an Australian soldier) explains more about the Huggins Roadblock:

At Sanananda we'd have a perimeter and there'd be a Jap just 50 yards in front and there could be another post of ours beyond that. Having established a perimeter, patrols would cut ways through to go around and see how far ahead the Japs had got. I remember vividly one instant. We were going up the track to relieve an American regiment that had been at Huggins a month. With casualties and sickness, they were 40 or 50 left out of three or four hundred and what was left of the Americans was coming back as we went in. At one spot there was a log across the track. As we came near to Huggins perimeter, we were told to stop before the log and get down and crawl,

because there were Jap snipers off in the bush or up in the trees. There was already a body, someone hadn't got down low enough. That was my first experience of war, crawling past a dead body.

Then we got to Huggins, a perimeter, two men to each dugout spaced more than a metre apart and 50 metres across so you got 300 men in twos all around it in a circle. During the night in each hole, there was one man on and one man off. Even through the day. The Japs were a bit crazy, they'd come at you. You hear a lot of stories about the atrocities of the Japs. The life of the enemy to them was of no consequence and their own life was of no consequence. We would come to a dug out where we knew they were. You'd pull your pin on your grenade. Our idea was not to take prisoners, it was just part of the game. I saw a couple of our fellows. The Jap was wounded and needed help to get up, so one of our chaps just shot him. They didn't want to be taken prisoner anyhow.

It was pretty dicey at night an hour on and an hour off in pits no deeper than a foot and a half. Because it rained every blessed day and your dugout was full of water. You'd only need to hear some kind of rustle in front of you and everyone was alert. It was a very trying and eerie position to be in. You are tense all the time. We didn't venture out but the Japs, they had a more suicidal, a different attitude to life and death. Even in the daytime later on I found. But at night evidently their leaders would send out two or three and in the dark they are creeping out. In the night in the jungle, nothing is moving so you can hear them. You'd wake your mate up if you thought there was somebody out there. You opened fire. Most of the time it was imagination I suppose, but you're not going to wait till they are right on you. Every now and then we'd go out in the morning and you'd find dead Japs. In the daytime, certain sections would be sent out on patrol, we were on the main track from Soputa to Sanananda, that's what we were guarding. And pushing them into the sea. We were about three kilometres from the ocean. During the day, it would be suicide to walk out on the main track.

At one stage, some of our chaps did get round and establish another perimeter on the main track on the other side of the Japs. I went out on one patrol on a small track just cut through the jungle. We came to a bend and as we came round the bend we came face to face, about 20 metres, with a patrol of Japs. It became a matter of who fired first. After we fired we thought, well, best part of valour was to get back. Only seemed to be two or three of them but we didn't know. We were lucky, one of my mates got hit in the face, chipped his nose.

We ourselves didn't get to the coast, It was a stalemate. We were there five weeks and the Japanese were going to fight to the last man. Soon you realised 7th Division cav [cavalry] wasn't going to do the job we were supposed to do. Later on a whole brigade was used. The 18th Brigade finished the job off. Our last job was going through and burying our own people. Our regiment went in about 350 and practically the whole regiment had malaria or dysentery. When we went back there were only about 47 or 48 of us. There was no way they helped us fight against malaria at that stage. Later on they came up with atebrin [anti-malarial medication] which made you yellow. Practically everybody suffered from malaria.

# Buna busted

The only small success on the American front in the first half of December was on the inland approach to Buna, where Urbana Force cut off Buna Village from the main Buna defences. The Japanese evacuated the pocket on 14 December.

To break the deadlock on the coastal Buna approach 18th Australian Brigade was brought up from Milne Bay in Royal Australian Navy corvettes. By now, the attacking infantry had the support of 20 artillery pieces, whose accuracy was improved by the aerial spotting of 4 Squadron, Royal Australian Air Force. Light tanks of 2/6th Armoured Regiment had also arrived. In six days, 18th Brigade cut their way through defences that had held up the Americans for six weeks. By the end of December, two-thirds of the Buna defences were in Allied hands and another American Regiment, the 127th, had arrived.

# Winning the Battle of Buna–Gona, January 1943

In December 1942, both sides still believed they could win the Battle of Buna–Gona, but by January 1943 neither the Japanese nor the Australians and Americans had any doubt that the battle would result in an Allied victory. The Allies began to bring from Australia to Papua the construction units that would turn Buna into a major Allied base as soon as the Japanese still in residence were disposed of. At the same time, the Japanese began to issue orders to evacuate Buna.

## 'Like an old time charge'

One last problem existed at Buna. A last-ditch defensive line the Japanese held along the edge of an old airstrip constructed before the war. On New Year's Day 1943, the 2/12th Battalion, Tasmanians and Queenslanders, charged across the old strip with tank, artillery, mortar and machine gun support, and took the position (both the coastal and inland approaches had met close to Buna). The following day, the Australians mopped up, the Americans of Urbana Force took a mission near Buna which another group of Japanese was attempting to turn into a strongpoint, and resistance was effectively ended in the area.

The charge of the 2/12th was a rare sight in the war in New Guinea: A full battalion assault over open flat ground. An American major who saw it described it as 'like an old time charge'. Those who ran across old strip say that it didn't look that grand. They crossed the open runway bent over against the Japanese fire and would've crawled instead, if allowed to.

The immense (by the standard of Buna–Gona) support received by the attacking infantry was also unusual. Half a dozen tanks, 12 medium machine guns, 14 mortars and 18 artillery pieces tore into the defences before and during the assault. Each man carried a one-kilogram demolition charge for use against bunkers. The tanks crossed the strip first, blasting holes in the bunkers, then the infantry threw their explosive charge though the hole. The attack was costly: 191 of the 590 men who charged across the strip were killed or wounded and the fighting on the Buna front was over.

Too late, the Japanese attempted a counterattack from Giruwa, south along the coast, to rescue their position at Buna. A battalion of infantry was brought down by sea from the Amboga River front for the purpose, but Colonel Yazawa, in charge of the operation, gave up the attempt when he saw that Buna was already lost.

Some 2,700 Japanese had defended Buna with 11 pieces of artillery. Four hundred Japanese escaped to Sanananda (see following section) but the remaining 2,300 died. The cost to the Allies on the Buna front was 2,870 battle casualties (dead and wounded), 913 of them Australian.

## Sanananda snaps

With the other three Buna–Gona positions taken, Allied attention now turned to the Sanananda Road. The Japanese force there had seen off attacks by three Australian brigades and one American regiment. Now the 18th Brigade and a few tanks were transferred to the Sanananda Road after their success at Buna, and the first regiment of the 41st US Division, the 163rd from Montana, arrived by air.

Together with 2/7th Cavalry Regiment and 36th Battalion, these units attacked the main Japanese position on 12 January 1943. This attack achieved little, but a subordinate move, to place a new roadblock even further into the Japanese rear, was a success. Allied troops from Gona and Sanananda were advancing on Cape Killerton when in mid January they found the Japanese positions all along the Sanananda Road were abandoned.

Closing in from all sides on the Sanananda bastion, the Allies overran the administrative centre of the Japanese position at Buna, finding hundreds of dead and dying Japanese. The ease with which the last defences were overcome came as a surprise. It finally dawned on the Allies that the Japanese had staged a massed breakout and that many of them had succeeded in getting away.

IN THEIR OWN WORDS

# A Japanese soldier at Buna

Nishimura Kokichi told me of his experiences at Buna, against the Americans:

I fought against the Americans at Buna. Before Buna, we were always able to find something to eat in the field but there we did not have any food. And at Buna I was the only survivor of my platoon and had no superior officer to help me. The soldiers of the other platoons would not give me any and it was impossible to leave the front-line to go in search of food.

It was at Buna that soldiers started eating human flesh. At first, we shot American soldiers close to our position to take the food they carried. At that time, we did not need to eat human flesh. But after some time, the American soldiers did not carry any food at all. In the end there was no way for us to survive without eating human flesh.

When the order came to break out I did it by walking in the sea out from the beach at night. I was alone because I did not want to join a group who would order me to do something and I thought a group would be more easily found by the enemy. I did not carry anything except two empty cans in case I found food to put in them. [Having escaped by moving along the coast well off the beach] I went slowly as I slept in the coconut trees in daytime and moved at night. I met other groups, one group went through the swamp, another inland to dry ground. I have no idea what happened to them. Eventually a small boat stopped for me and took me to Lae where I was given rice and treated for malaria.

There were some soldiers who committed suicide in Buna. They were not able to move because of their injuries. There was no order from the top about it. Some others were shot by the soldiers in the same group because the commander of that group believed they would be killed by the Allies later. And being killed by a comrade was much more honourable. Others were just left in the position. When we left wounded soldiers, we told a lie. We said that we would leave now to look for food, and promised to come back to rescue them.

# *Escaping towards Salamaua*

Early in January, Yamagata was informed by Imamura that Buna–Gona was to be abandoned. The Japanese held strong positions north along the coast and the remaining Buna–Gona force, about 5,000 men, was to break out to join them.

The first point the troops were to make for was the Amboga River, where a Japanese force held the line of the river against the Australians. Coastal barges would then transfer the weaker troops further north to Salamaua and Lae. The others were to walk.

The breakout was to begin on 20 January but Colonel Tsukamoto, in command on the Sanananda Road, decided not to wait. A week early he and his men abandoned their positions and, moving through the swamps, escaped to Amboga River. The Australians, believing Tsukamoto was retreating towards the coast, advanced on Cape Killerton and Sanananda. This had the effect of tightening the noose around the sole remaining Japanese position at Sanananda. When the breakout took place there on 20 January, it was much less successful than Tsukamoto's move.

Though the Battle of Buna–Gona officially terminated on 22 January, fighting between small Japanese groups escaping along the coast through the area held by the Australian 14th Brigade north of Gona continued for two weeks.

None of the Allied commanders was aware a Japanese breakout was contemplated, or even that it was occurring until too late. In general, the breakout was a success. About two-thirds of the Japanese who attempted to break out got away into the Territory of New Guinea.

Of 13,000 Japanese who fought in the Battle of Buna–Gona, or were present in a non-combat capacity, 3,200 completed the long retreat to Lae. The rest were dead. The Australian and American victors had committed 25,000 men, more than half of them Australians, to the Battle of Buna–Gona. Allied losses were 6,419 killed or wounded. Casualties to illness far exceeded this number.

## Finishing off the war in Papua

The Allies breathed a sigh of relief at the end of January 1943. At Buna–Gona, the Australians and Americans were fading fast due to casualties and illness. While the Japanese held on at Buna–Gona, a chance still existed that they might send reinforcements. But once Buna–Gona fell, for the Japanese to re-enter Papua would require a much greater effort than to reinforce what they already held and this was unlikely. In the month following the fall of Buna, the Japanese evacuated Guadalcanal.

It was clear to all that the Japanese had been forced onto the defensive. Imperial headquarters announced that Salamaua (in New Guinea) and New Georgia Island (in the Solomons, north-west of Guadalcanal) were the new front-line to be held at all costs. The way was now open for Allied offensives north towards Rabaul.

Japanese Army Chief of Staff Sugiyama Hajime foresaw the dangers. He wrote that 'We must hold the fronts in eastern New Guinea and Rabaul to the end. If they fall, not only will the Pacific Ocean be in peril, but it will allow the advance of MacArthur's counterattack through New Guinea and herald the fall of our dominion in the southern area'. He was right.

After Buna–Gona, a clear line of approach to Rabaul was available to MacArthur. He directed Blamey to plan a series of offensives along the coast of New Guinea from Buna to Lae, and to the Huon Peninsula with the aim of taking the western end of New Britain Island, on which Rabaul was situated. Meanwhile, Admiral Chester Nimitz directed the south Pacific theatre commander, Admiral William 'Bull' Halsey on Guadalcanal, to advance from there on Rabaul from the south-east, along the Solomon island chain. The post-Kokoda story of what happened in 1943 was an impressive succession of victories, when the Australians and Americans achieved all the goals they had set themselves after the fall of Buna.

# Understanding What the Australians Did Next

The advance of the Australians from Imita Ridge at the end of September 1942 was the beginning of a series of offensives that continued until the end of the war. Although in January and February of 1943 the Japanese drove back a small Australian group, Kanga Force, that was based 50 kilometres inland at Wau and operating against the Japanese garrisons at Lae and Salamaua, that was the last time the Australians were ever driven back by the Japanese, And when the AIF 17th Brigade arrived by air, the Australian troops pushed the Japanese back away from Wau's airstrip.

In early 1943, the Allies established a huge base at Buna from which they advanced north from Buna to the Huon Gulf, capturing Salamaua and Lae. Airfields were built on the Solomon Sea islands of Goodenough, Kirwina and Woodlark, and the now strong Allied air forces destroyed the last significant Japanese attempt to reinforce New Guinea by sea at the Battle of the Bismarck Sea in March.

With increasing command of the air and sea, MacArthur was informed by his superiors in Washington that he no longer needed to take Rabaul. His offensive should rather isolate and bypass it.

What happened next was this:

- **1943:** Towards the end of the year, the Australians captured Finschhafen and drove up the Markham Valley. The Americans landed on the western end of New Britain.

- **1944:** The Australians captured Madang, landed on New Britain and Bougainville, and advanced on Wewak. MacArthur landed in the Phillipines.

✔ **1945:** By this time, as fighting continued in rear areas, two AIF divisions landed in Borneo and seized the oil fields and refineries, the very things for which Japan had gone to war in the first place. Other important events included:

- The British took Burma

- Another American offensive across the central Pacific took Iwo Jima and Okinawa

- On 6 and 9 August 1945, atomic bombs were dropped on the Japanese cities of Hiroshima (home of most of the 41st Regiment men who had fought on the track) and Nagasaki

On 15 August 1945, Japan surrendered. The Pacific war was over.

# Chapter 13

# Defeating the Japanese Army: Why the Allies Won

*In This Chapter*

▶ Ending the war in Papua

▶ Working out why the Allies were the victors

▶ Improving skills and adapting to jungle warfare

▶ Assessing the cost

**M**any bigger battles were fought in the Pacific War than those that took place between the Allies and the Japanese in Papua. The importance of the Allied victory was more in its timing than its magnitude. The elimination of the last organised Japanese force in Papua in January 1943 was the first time since the war began 14 months before that the Allies had defeated a major Japanese invasion, and it was the Australians who made the main contribution to this defeat.

The Allied victory also taught vital lessons. The Allies had made many mistakes in 1942 but they learned from them, and the continual series of Allied advances from 1943 was a demonstration of the hard-earned knowledge gained from near disaster in 1942.

In this chapter, I explain why the Allies won, assess the results and point out what was learned.

## Working Out What the Allied Victory in Papua Achieved

The Battles of Kokoda, Milne Bay and Buna–Gona together make up the Papuan campaign, which was a strategic victory for the Australians and Americans. Port Moresby was secure so Japan couldn't invade Australia's east coast — because the Japanese needed a port and airfield complex near to Australia as a base from which to launch an invasion. The only large port and airfield close to north Queensland, which is where the Japanese would've landed, was Port Moresby.

But more than preventing the possible invasion of Australia had been achieved. Japanese plans had been thrown into disarray and a wide avenue of advance to the north had opened up with the fall of Buna. As the fighting in Papua commenced in July 1942, the Japanese were expecting an Allied counteroffensive and had decided on a line of defensive positions they wanted to hold, including Port Moresby and Milne Bay, with Buna as the base supporting both. On that line, they expected to defeat the counteroffensive. The Japanese failed to take either Port Moresby or Milne Bay and by January 1943 they had lost Buna too. Now Buna became the base for the Allied advance north towards Rabaul.

The end of the Papuan campaign came about because

- ✔ On the Kokoda Trail the Japanese advance on Port Moresby stalled.
- ✔ At Milne Bay the Japanese amphibious landing was defeated.
- ✔ At Buna–Gona the Japanese lost their last base in Papua.

# Understanding Why the Australians Won in Papua

The Allies won all the battles in Papua, but why did they win them? The most important reasons for the Australian victory in the Battle of Kokoda and the Australian and American triumphs in the other two battles in Papua (Milne Bay and Buna–Gona) can be summed up in three points (each of which are discussed in the sections below):

- ✔ Numerical superiority
- ✔ The Battle at Guadalcanal
- ✔ Better morale

## The big battalions

Napoleon I said victory goes to the big battalions, meaning that the side with the greater number of troops usually wins. That was certainly the outcome in Papua, where from July 1942 to January 1943 the Japanese committed 22,000 troops to almost double that number of Allied fighting troops (three-quarters of them Australians).

Neither side ever gathered together all their available men in Papua on one battlefield; the largest battle was Buna–Gona where 10,000 Japanese fought 20,000 Australians and Americans.

The Allies weren't always greatly superior in the numbers engaged in any given battle; rather, they could withdraw tired, exhausted and sick formations, and replace them with fresh ones much more often than could the Japanese for three reasons:

- ✔ Australia was closer to Papua than Japan and held a large reserve of Allied troops

- ✔ The Japanese had to commit huge numbers of soldiers elsewhere, such as China and the Dutch East Indies, to hold down their conquests

- ✔ The south-west Pacific front was a high priority for the Allies but, to begin with, a lower priority for the Japanese. However, when the Japanese got into trouble there, the south-west Pacific rose in their order of priority

Instances where the Australians and Americans were able to bring in additional numbers, or replace exhausted formations with some fresh troops, include

- ✔ On the Kokoda Trail from July to September, during the Japanese advance, the Australians generally fought the Japanese at about one to one. It wasn't until fresh Australian troops began the advance back along the track that Australian numbers began to make themselves felt. Meanwhile, the Australians who had fought in the July to September phase rested in Port Moresby and returned to the fight at Buna–Gona in November.

- ✔ Milne Bay in late August and early September, which involved the greatest Japanese intelligence failure of the campaign. They landed a 2,000-strong force expecting to find only a few hundred Australians defending. Instead, they found 10,000 Australians and Americans (though only half were combat troops). The majority of these Allied troops were brought forward to Buna–Gona in December.

- ✔ At Buna–Gona, where the Allies failed at first because their 10,000 men were no match for a similar number of heavily entrenched defenders. With the arrival of Allied reinforcements, particularly the US 32nd Division, and dozens of field guns and tanks that the Japanese couldn't match, the battle turned in the Allies' favour.

If the Australians hadn't been able to call on more fresh troops than the Japanese on the Kokoda Trail, they wouldn't have been able to drive back the Japanese. The Japanese landing at Milne Bay may have succeeded if the Australians hadn't been in far greater strength, much to the surprise of the Japanese. And at Buna–Gona, the Allies were supported by tanks, artillery and air power, together probably as important as their superior numerical strength.

# The Battle at Guadalcanal

Papua was one front of a two-front war in the south and south-west Pacific in 1942. The Allies had each front under a separate commander, US General Douglas MacArthur in New Guinea and Admiral William 'Bull' Halsey in Guadalcanal.

The Japanese had both fronts under one commander and considered the fronts interconnected. They had intended to put all their resources into the capture of Port Moresby, but when the United States Marines landed at Guadalcanal in August 1942 the Japanese had to decide which front was the most important. (Chapter 5 looks at the Guadalcanal campaign in more detail.)

Hyakutake, the commander in Rabaul, consulted with Imperial headquarters in Tokyo. They agreed that Guadalcanal was the more important and decided to send most of their troops and the striking force of the navy there. The Japanese failed repeatedly to retake Guadalcanal, but kept on trying. By January 1943, the fight had drawn in 40,000 troops on land, against the 22,000 Japanese sent to Papua. Had Imperial Headquarters decided the other way, at least another 20,000 troops, probably more, would've been available for Papua.

The Japanese also committed the bulk of their air force and their navy to Guadalcanal. Had these forces been available for operations in Papua, imagining the outcome of the campaign would've been as fortuitous for the Allies is difficult.

The period of greatest danger for the Allies was September 1942. The Kawaguchi Detachment, 7,500 men, was to reinforce General Horii, commander of the Nankai Shitai (South Seas Force), in that month for the attack on Port Moresby, but he was sent to Guadalcanal instead. With Kawaguchi and appropriate air and sea support, the Japanese may have taken Port Moresby.

# Bushido versus Bluey: Keeping up morale

The average Australian soldier (Bluey) didn't understand the Japanese soldier and despised him. The feeling among the Japanese was the same. Neither army understood the thinking of the other and, as a consequence, thought the other some kind of lesser being. In the midst of the clash of arms on the track was a clash of western and eastern thinking, a clash of cultures. The Japanese soldier was inculcated in the warrior's code, Bushido. The differences between Japanese troops and Australian troops included

- **Both sides had different views on surrendering.** The Australians thought surrendering to the enemy was acceptable, in certain circumstances. They quickly learned, though, that the Japanese wouldn't accept their surrender. The Japanese saw a willingness to surrender as unworthy behaviour for a soldier, an expression of an individual's concern for himself rather than for his country. It was, to the Japanese, typical of hedonistic and selfish westerners.

- **Bushido exalted winning by cunning.** To deceive the enemy was virtuous. Japanese tactics included:

  - Shouting at the Australians in English to confuse them.

  - Pretending to be dead when wounded ('lying doggo') until an Australian soldier came near. He then tried to kill him.

  The Australians saw this type of behaviour as underhanded, even insane.

- **Japanese troops fought to the death.** When a soldier left Japan he signed his life away to the Emperor and didn't expect to return home. Bushido is sometimes described as a soldier's search for a place to die. The Australians, on the other hand, fought to live. They wanted to go home after the war if at all possible. To the Australian, it made sense to run if the battle was lost; they saw no point in dying. A Japanese soldier inculcated with Bushido didn't want to survive if the battle was lost.

While the hatred between the two sides made for a particularly vicious kind of fighting, it also had implications for morale. At first on the Kokoda Trail, the Australians were shocked by their implacable enemy and morale suffered. Japanese morale was high; they were advancing and saw that the Australians would sometimes run before them.

When the Australians began their offensive along the Kokoda Trail and were able to bring in fresh soldiers (refer to the section 'The big battalions'), morale among the troops was boosted. At the same time, Bushido began to falter under hunger, sickness and defeat. Australian morale rose further when they saw that the Japanese could be beaten. In October 1942, for the first time in Papua, at the Battle of Second Eora–Templeton's, the Australians watched the Japanese run from the battlefield. At the beginning in Papua, high Japanese morale contributed to their success in battle. By October, Japanese morale was falling as that of the Allies rose.

Morale, built from training, experience, confidence in leaders and indoctrination, fades away with defeat, hunger, deprivation, sickness and an extended period in a hostile climate such as Papua.

# Learning From the Battle of Kokoda

The Australian army was later renown for its expertise in jungle fighting in the Malayan Emergency (1948 to 60) and in Vietnam (1962 to 72), but this expertise was not acquired in 1942. Rather, 1942 was the year that revealed a number of Australian shortcomings, though it ended in victory. In light of the experience of 1942, improvements were made and the Australian army underwent a number of fundamental changes to adapt to a new form of warfare in the jungle. Their unbroken series of victories from 1943 to 1945 show the Australians had learned a great deal from the near disaster of 1942.

In particular, the Australian forces learned to move and fight in the jungle, as well as to keep their men well fed and healthy there.

## Moving and fighting

The Australians arrived in Papua as a road-bound army that had to learn to move without roads. This required a restructuring of formations. The desert type of infantry battalion was slimmed down for jungle operations and the hundreds of vehicles a division usually had were deleted from the order of battle. The average Japanese division, normally with 4,000 horses and few vehicles, was much better suited to the terrain. Japanese officers rode horses where possible (see Chapter 17 for more about General Horii's white stallion) and the horses could be ridden over surprisingly rough terrain. However, most of the Japanese horses were small ponies used as beasts of burden.

A number of lessons were learned by both sides throughout the Battle of Kokoda:

✔ **Basic military tactics had to be adapted for jungle warfare.** The Australians became the experts at patrolling, ambushing the enemy and blocking a jungle track behind the enemy. The Japanese had been their superiors at these arts in 1942. By mid-1943, the Australians were the better tacticians and their casualties dropped accordingly.

> ✔ **Navigation in the jungle was a problem that had to be solved.** Both sides frequently found they became lost when attempting to move off the track to turn an enemy flank.

The Australians also learned that movement by air was a vital component of jungle war. In August 1942, the Australians had to assemble all kinds of transport aircraft from all over Australia to have a mere dozen for operations in Papua. The following year, at Nadzab, transport aircraft airdropped an American parachute regiment and an Australian artillery battery at an abandoned airfield west of Lae. Over the following two days, an entire brigade of infantry, more than 2,000 men, was landed at the strip. This was a far cry from Kokoda in July 1942, when the maximum number of troops that could be moved by air in one day was 150.

## Eating and shooting

The Australians discovered in Papua that the arrangements for supplying their troops in the front-line they had used in the Middle East didn't work in the mountainous jungle of the south Pacific.

The Australians developed from scratch a system of airdropping food and ammunition to the front-line troops, but this by itself didn't solve the problem of getting supplies to the front-line. The Australians also had to simplify and reduce what had to be sent forward. Packaging was lightened and inessentials dispensed with.

In the campaigns that followed Papua (such as the Huon Peninsula campaign of 1943), a new streamlined system of supply was introduced. At Lae and Finschhafen, the average infantry battalion fought and won with half the tonnage of deliveries that would've been considered essential when the same battalion fought in north Africa two years earlier.

## Keeping fit

The Australian army learned (from necessity) to fight malaria. Australian battle casualties in 1942 were over 6,000, but casualties to all illness (mostly malaria) were 29,000.

The deputy director of medical services wrote in a post-battle report in December 1942 that 'there was no deep consciousness in the force that malaria could destroy it as a fighting body and bring disaster to its operations. Malaria discipline was bad.'

General Blamey, the Allied land forces commander, acted immediately on the post-battle report, by

- Giving priority transport to supplies of quinine and other anti-malarial drugs to the front-line
- Instructing officers to take responsibility for malaria discipline among their men, and supplying troops with mosquito nets and training in anti-malarial precautions before they left Australia
- Sending malariologists such as Professor Frank Fenner to New Guinea
- Setting up a medical school in Queensland, to study and solve the problem of malaria

The anti-malaria program was very successful. By the end of 1943, the rate of sickness was one-third what it was a year earlier. By 1944 and 1945, the incidence of malaria was at tolerable levels.

Milne Bay, which had produced 6,000 malaria casualties by December 1942, was one of the worst areas. One thousand engineers were sent to Milne Bay to limit mosquito numbers by draining swamps, which were breeding grounds.

## The Americans in Papua and Guadalcanal

The United States 32nd Division fought in Papua for two months at the Battle of Buna–Gona. In this short period, the inexperienced force suffered even worse losses to illness than the Australians. Some 9,800 men of the division fought at Buna–Gona, of which 580 were killed in action and 1,900 were wounded. Medical casualties totalled 7,200, of which 3,000 were evacuated. This adds up to more than the division's entire strength, but the division wasn't really wiped out because the 4,200 men sick not evacuated were put back into the line as soon as they were well enough.

The Americans on Guadalcanal (refer to Chapter 5) didn't suffer quite so badly, except for the 1st Marine Division (which fought for five months, longer than any Australian or American unit in Papua), who lost 650 dead, 1,278 wounded and had 8,600 medical evacuations, which added together was almost the entire strength of the Division.

Overall numbers reveal that the rate of sickness for Americans in Papua was 67 per cent against 55 per cent on Guadalcanal. Battle casualties were also lower proportionally, given that a much larger force fought at Guadalcanal. An American study calculated that a greater proportion of any 100 US servicemen in Papua died from all causes than any 100 men on Guadalcanal. Three in each 100 at Guadalcanal died against 10 in every 100 in Papua.

# Counting Casualties at Kokoda

Brutal as it seems, armed forces use casualty statistics as one measure of success. After a victory, the number of men lost in battle and to sickness can be weighed against enemy casualties and the value of the objective, and a conclusion drawn about the relative value of the victory.

In battle, the attacker often loses more men than the defender, so the objective attained must be worth the victory. For example, at the Battle of Efogi on the Kokoda Trail on 8 September 1942 (refer to Chapter 8), the Japanese took a valuable Australian position and dispersed hundreds of Australians into the jungle — where the Australians were no longer in a position to contribute to the fighting. The victory was enhanced by the fact that Japanese casualties were slightly less than the Australians, losing 156 killed and wounded against 164 Australians.

## Calculating Kokoda battle casualties

On the track, both sides lost about 900 men killed and wounded during the Japanese advance from Buna to Ioribaiwa from July to September 1942.

The greatest losses were at Isurava where

- The Japanese lost well over one-third of their total of 900.
- The Australians lost 210 of their 900 casualties for the period.

(Refer to Chapter 8 for more on Isurava.)

When the Australian advance began in October, the first Australian victory, the second Battle of Eora–Templeton's (also discussed in Chapter 8), was a very expensive one, costing the attackers 412, to 244 Japanese. The Kokoda phase of the war in Papua ended with the decisive Australian victory at Oivi–Gorari, which once again turned the casualty count to Australian favour.

In all the fighting along the Kokoda Trail, the Australians suffered 1,760 battle casualties to 2,050 Japanese.

## Evaluating the cost of victory

In all of the fighting in Papua, Allied battle casualties on land were less than those of the Japanese, about 3,000 dead and 7,000 wounded against the Japanese loss of 13,000 dead and 4,000 wounded. But the Allies also lost more than 20,000 casualties to illness against a lesser number of Japanese. Most of the sick, like the wounded, would eventually recover and return to their units, but the loss was still important. Hence the loss to the Allies, from all causes, was about the same as those of the defeated Japanese. However, ridding Papua of Japanese was of vital strategic importance to the Allies. As armies assess things, the price was worth paying, but the victory was extremely expensive.

# Casualties by nationality and battle

Table 13-1 gives the full list of battle casualties and medical evacuations during the war in Papua from July 1942 to January 1943.

If you're not sure what some of the casualty terms mean, refer to the sidebar in Chapter 1.

| Table 13-1 | Number of casualties by nationality and battle |
| --- | --- |
| *Nationality and location of casualties* | *Number of casualties* |
| **Australian Army casualties** | |
| *Battle of Kokoda* | |
| Killed in action and missing presumed killed | 557 |
| Died of wounds | 66 |
| Wounded in action | 1,023 |
| **Total** | **1,646** |
| *Battle of Milne Bay* | |
| Killed in action and missing presumed killed | 172 |
| Died of wounds | 5 |
| Wounded in action | 206 |
| **Total** | **383** |
| *Battle of Buna–Gona* | |
| Killed in action and missing presumed killed | 1,033 |
| Died of wounds | 228 |
| Wounded in action | 2,210 |
| **Total** | **3,471** |

| Nationality and location of casualties | Number of casualties |
|---|---|
| *Goodenough Island engagement* | |
| Killed in action | 14 |
| Wounded in action | 18 |
| **Total** | **32** |
| *Other Australian battle casualties (including air raids at Port Moresby)* | |
| Killed in action | 13 |
| Wounded in action | 15 |
| **Total battle casualties Australian Army in Papua** | **5,560** |
| **Total evacuated sick Australian Army in Papua** | **29,100** |
| **Royal Australian Navy casualties** | |
| Killed in action | 5 |
| Wounded in action | 11 |
| **Royal Australian Air Force casualties** | |
| Killed in action | 310 |
| **Australian New Guinea Administration Unit** | |
| Killed or died on active service | 9 |
| **United States Army casualties for Papua, July 1942 to January 1943** | |
| Killed in action | 734 |
| Missing presumed killed | 176 |
| Wounded in action | 2,037 |
| **Total battle casualties United States Army in Papua** | **2,947** |
| **Total evacuated sick United States Army in Papua** | **8,259** |
| **United States Army Air Force casualties for Papua, air operations over land and sea, July 1942–January 1943** | |
| Killed and missing presumed killed | 525 |

*(continued)*

**Table 13-1** *(continued)*

| Nationality and location of casualties | Number of casualties |
|---|---|
| **New Guineans** | |
| *Papuan Infantry Battalion and Royal Papuan Constabulary* | |
| Killed in action | 14 |
| Died on active service | 4 |
| Wounded in action | 38 |
| *Other Papuans and New Guineans* | |
| Died while serving with Allies | 140 |
| Died while serving with Japanese | 1,200 |
| **Imperial Japanese Army** | |
| Killed in action | 8,400 |
| Evacuated wounded | 2,000 |
| Died of illness | 3,100 |
| Evacuated sick | 2,000 |
| **Total IJA casualties** | **15,500** |
| **Imperial Japanese Navy*** | |
| Killed in action | 1,800 |
| Evacuated wounded | 650 |
| Died of illness | 300 |
| Evacuated sick | 1,000 |
| **Total IJN casualties** | *3,750* |
| ***Total battle casualties Japanese Army and Navy in Papua*** | *13,600* |
| ***Total evacuated sick Japanese Army and Navy in Papua*** | *5,650* |
| **Total losses IJN and IJA in Papua** | 19,250 |

* Almost all aircraft flown by the Japanese in Papua were Imperial Japanese Navy aircraft. Their losses are included here.

# Part V
# Walking the Kokoda Trail

*Glenn Lumsden*

*'Can we go the way with the best mobile reception?'*

# In this part ...

**W**alking over the Owen Stanley Range requires considerable preparation, which should begin several months before you go. Walking a lot is good, but walking up and down steep slopes (even stairs) is better because that's the kind of walking you're going to be doing. If you're already fit, get fitter. You also need to sort out your paperwork, select a tour company, book flights, see a doctor and buy everything from insect repellant to socks.

In this part, I take you through a step-by-step guide, from thinking about trekking Kokoda to arriving in Papua New Guinea equipped and prepared. I also tell you what to do, and what not to do, once you're there.

# Chapter 14

# Preparing For the Big Walk

**W**alking the Kokoda Trail is certainly not for everyone. However, you're not just 'anybody'. Having made the decision to step up and take the challenge, don't take it lightly. Adventure is now your middle name, but unless you've recently trekked the Himalayas or scaled the heights of Kilimanjaro, this walk is like no other that you've ever attempted. You need to take special preparatory steps if you're to make your trip successful and memorable.

In this chapter, you examine your motivation for and commitment to walking the track. I also help you make the right decision in choosing a trekking company that caters to your needs, addressing the subjects of hiring a personal porter and deciding which direction to walk on the track.

## Checking Your Commitment

The hardest thing about trekking Kokoda isn't simply walking up a steep hill. Waking up the next morning, knowing full well that you need to do it all over again, day after day, is the hardest part. This point is where your commitment to tackle the track needs a reality check.

For some people, exercise is an occasional experience. If you need only the smallest of excuses to break your New Year's resolution to exercise, the track may not be for you.

However, if you're one of those people who can set her mind on the task and keep her eyes on the finish line, you're already halfway along the path to success. Kokoda is just as much a mental experience as a physical ordeal. Some say that your mind plays the greater role.

You don't need to be as fit as a marathon runner to walk the 96-kilometre track, but you need to start thinking like one. Mental discipline gets you to your next camp site before dark, so if you can wake up each morning and hit the pavement for one hour per day, rain, hail and shine, for ten consecutive days, you can proudly say, 'I'm starting my training for the Kokoda Trail!'

# Evaluating Why You're Trekking: History or Heart Rate

The first question you really need to ask yourself when considering which company to trek with is, 'What type of Kokoda experience am I looking for?' Some tour operators are adventure based, while others may be history-based operators that specialise in telling the story of the Kokoda fighting. Guides with some companies that emphasise undertaking the track as a purely physical challenge still tend to be swept up in the history and emotion as they stand at the Isurava Memorial and contemplate their surroundings. Whichever company you choose, the words on the memorial — Courage, Endurance, Mateship and Sacrifice — may mean a lot more to you once you've walked the track.

## Searching for history

The history of the Kokoda Trail is the motivation for some people to undertake such a gruelling ordeal. Why else would you risk life and limb, especially when other walks equally as challenging in other countries have modern infrastructure and are better equipped to get you out of trouble if an emergency arises?

History can put things into perspective as your leg muscles scream for a rest and that blister on your heel steps up a gear from 'painful' to 'totally unbearable'. Hopefully, around this time your trek leader pulls you aside and tells you the story of Corporal Lindsay Bear and Russ Fairburn of the 2/14th Battalion, AIF (see the sidebar '"I won't leave you mate" — the story of Russ Fairburn and Lindsay Bear' to read more about this). You then realise that you're walking the track for all the right reasons.

Some trek leaders only facilitate a little bit of history as you trudge along the track, while others are historians who conduct treks. Who would you prefer to walk with?

When selecting a tour company based on military history, do your homework and request to speak with the person leading your group across the track. Most tour companies have trek leaders who conduct tours as representatives of that particular company. Ensure from your first point of contact that you will have an opportunity to speak with the historian leading your group. Naturally, this person should know more about the history of the Kokoda campaign than you!

Examine the credentials of your tour guide and the company he represents (there are currently no female guides on the Kokoda Trail). Your guide doesn't need to hold a doctorate in military history from Australian National University, but he should have a good working knowledge of the campaign. To ensure a quality historical experience, ask these questions:

- ✔ Is he actively involved in the military history industry?

- ✔ Is he open to scrutiny on military history forums, or has he simply memorised a few facts from a book?

    Any historian worth your money, amateur or otherwise, should make herself available for interview or scrutiny.

- ✔ Which books does he recommend and, most importantly, can he offer you references? Question your guide about his information sources. You're paying for historical fact, not someone's version of the truth. You don't want to find out your so-called historian is a novice *after* you're on the track!

Some tour companies offer information sessions where you have the opportunity to view a presentation and ask questions about what the company can offer you. Other companies offer a free training session so your fitness can be assessed. The bottom line is the companies want your business. If a company can't or won't supply you with the knowledge you desire, choose another tour company.

So, your grandfather or your great-uncle Jim was a digger on the track, or you simply have an interest in one particular unit that served during the Kokoda campaign. You're going to be very disappointed if you pay a lot of money, train your heart out, and then learn very little about that particular group of soldiers. Your trek leader must be able to do more than ramble off some military facts or popular stories, parrot fashion. Your leader should possess the depth of knowledge that comes with years of research, not just cursory knowledge from having read one or two books on the Kokoda Trail. Do your research!

## 'I won't leave you mate' — the story of Russ Fairburn and Lindsay Bear

In early September 1942, the Australians were engaged in a vicious fighting withdrawal. The battle for Isurava had been fought and lost, and Brigadier Arnold Potts, the commander of the 21st Brigade, had no option other than to retreat. Among the wounded making their way back were two casualties whose injuries were so great that they deserved to be carried on a stretcher, but they were walking.

Corporal Lindsay A ('Teddy') Bear was wounded on 29 August 1942 by Japanese fire during the fighting at Isurava. Suffering from two gunshots to the right leg, one shot in the left heel and a bullet wound to the left hand, Bear was in a bad way but, like many wounded diggers on this day, he considered others were worse off than him and more deserving to be carried on a stretcher. Bear couldn't walk forward in the normal manner but, despite intense discomfort, he could move by shuffling sideways in a crab-like manner. This form of movement was slow and painful, but Bear knew the Japanese were behind them and they were coming. Bear knew that anybody captured by the Japanese would be given no quarter.

Bear's travelling companion, Corporal Russ Fairburn, had been shot in the stomach and the bullet had penetrated his abdomen, lodging near his spine. Walking was difficult enough for Russ, let alone looking after Bear, but together they made their way from Isurava back to Efogi North in the middle of the Owen Stanley Range. Knowing that Fairburn could make better progress on his own, Bear urged his mate to leave him. Fairburn ignored Bear's pleas and stuck with him, pushing Bear up the hills and preventing him from slipping down the muddy slopes at every treacherous descent. Forever loyal, whenever they reached a rest spot along the track, Fairburn would set his friend down and hunt around to source food and water for both men.

Through time bought by the self-sacrifice of their fighting comrades who were slowing the Japanese advance, both men made it back to safety. Bear would later recall, 'I shall never forget that night going up into Efogi. The rain was pelting down, darkness was closing in and things were rather miserable. Still Russ stuck to me, pushing me up that slope. But for him, I am sure I would have fallen back into the creek below'.

The history of the track is full of stories like this. Ample motivation for the trekker when times seem to get tough.

## Pumping up your heart rate

Some companies advertise themselves as adventure companies with an emphasis on team building and recreation; other companies focus on the historical events that took place in Kokoda.

Walking the track may be one of the most physically challenging feats you ever undertake. Many adventure companies aim at the corporate market, offering audacious and intrepid holiday experiences, usually by the most direct route on what some operators call the 'tourist trail'. In other words, the aim of this trek is to walk from start to finish with no deviations and in a timely manner.

The historic wartime track has many side trips you can make; however, many companies don't deviate from the main track to show you points of interest, such as the drop zones of Myola 1 and Myola 2. Many historical points along the track had a decisive influence on the outcome of the campaign.

# Working Out Which Direction to Walk

The direction you walk the track often comes down to personal preference. Some trekking companies don't offer a choice. A few people even decide to come back for a second time and walk in the opposite direction. Walking in either direction is historically correct, depending on which part of the campaign captures your interest.

You may desire to walk in a specific direction respective to a particular phase of the battle. For example, walking from Kokoda back to Owers' Corner gives you a better understanding of the Australian fighting withdrawal. This is largely the story of the militiamen of the 39th and 53rd infantry battalions, AMF, as well as that of the 21st Infantry Brigade (2/14th, 2/16th and 2/27th battalions, AIF) and, to a lesser extent, the 3rd Infantry Battalion and part of the 25th Brigade.

By trekking from Owers' Corner to Kokoda, you gain an appreciation for the Australian advance after the Japanese pulled back to the beachheads. This can be interpreted as the story of the 25th Brigade (2/25th, 2/31st and 2/33rd battalions) and the 16th Brigade (2/1st, 2/2nd and 2/3rd battalions, AIF) supported by the 3rd Infantry Battalion (AMF). Of course, many other support units also served on the track too.

The preference by some companies to start at Kokoda and walk in a southerly direction may be based on the trekker satisfaction of finishing under the archway at Owers' Corner. A visit to Bomana War Cemetery immediately after your walk brings home the emotional side of the experience. Seeing the thousands of graves, especially the graves of some of the men whose exploits were spoken about on the track, brings everything into perspective.

Kila Amuli, a Papuan trek master from Abuari Village, had more than 60 crossings to his name when he indicated his preference to walk from north to south (Kokoda back to Owers' Corner). In a contradictory manner that Papuan porters are famous for, Kila Amuli said, 'It's a little bit easier, but not really'.

# Going Along the Track with Others

Some say that walking the track is a once-in-a-lifetime opportunity. Not only is walking the track one of the most physically challenging feats you're likely to ever undertake in your life, but also the expedition can be a significant financial investment, so spend your money wisely.

In the next sections, I discuss how to find and research the available trekking options, whether you should hire someone to carry your pack (or do it yourself), and offer some tips for helping you get along with your fellow trekkers while you're on the track.

## Choosing a trekking company

Many Kokoda trekking companies are vying for your business. Luckily, making an educated decision on which trekking company to choose is only a click of the computer mouse away.

Like most trekking destinations around the world, a governing body manages and regulates the tourist traffic that passes along the track. The Kokoda Track Authority (KTA) is a Papua New Guinea–based organisation. The KTA manages the track as well as improving the life of the indigenous people who live between Owers' Corner and the village of Kokoda. Most Australians visualise the track as only a faraway battle site or a place to commemorate the sacrifices of a generation — and totally forget that the track is actually home for some Papuans.

In 2011, 78 licensed tour operators were listed on the website of the KTA. Almost all of these operators can provide you with a memorable experience. Some are operated by Australian or other foreign nationals, others by Papua New Guinean operators who may not have a flashy website, but who are equally adept at ensuring your health and safety across the track.

The Kokoda Track Authority's website is www.kokodatrackauthority.org. The information provided on the website of the KTA provides you with a firm foundation. You can learn enough to be able to ask the right questions to find a tour company that best suits your needs.

If you try to find the KTA by searching the Web using 'Kokoda Track Authority', be aware that some trekking companies are computer savvy and have worked their way up the web rankings. You may think you're navigating the KTA website when in fact you've been drawn into a commercial operator's web page.

A tour company should be licensed with the KTA, reliable and have all of the safety requirements in place. However, no company that offers escorted walks along the track can guarantee that all will go to plan and promise 100 per cent safety. As a trekker, you must remember that you're voluntarily attempting to negotiate some of the harshest terrain in the world in a tropical and unsanitary environment. Sadly, some trekkers have lost their lives in pursuit of achieving their goals. The trekking companies that led these unfortunate trekkers were all sound and reputable companies, and suggests no evidence of negligence on their part. The best that any tour company can do is minimise the risks and have sound contingency plans in place, so that personal hazards are kept to a minimum.

Your trekking company should carry certain items or adhere to conditions while on the track. Ask companies the following questions:

- ✔ Do you carry a comprehensive first aid kit? (This is in addition to the first aid kit that you pack for yourself. See Chapter 15 for tips on packing.)

- ✔ Do you have a Commercial Operations Licence under the Kokoda Track Authority?

- ✔ Do you provide duty of care to staff (porters), ensuring maximum pack weight of 25 kilograms?

- ✔ Is a written contingency plan in place to enable my evacuation in the event of an emergency?

- ✔ What's your maximum number of trekkers? (Or, what's the ratio of trekkers to tour guides?)

- ✔ Will a satellite telephone and tuned VHF track radio be carried at all times while on the track?

Ask your tour operator to respond in writing or email your questions and retain this information until you've returned safely from your trek, in case something goes wrong or you weren't satisfied with the tour. Hopefully, you won't need to refer to this information on your return.

## Walking in the dark

Sometimes a tour party falls behind schedule due to unforeseen circumstances. Some companies may simply wish to get you from 'A' to 'B' in the shortest possible time and may require you to walk in the dark to achieve this.

Walking at night can be dangerous and shouldn't be necessary. Consider finding a trekking company with a relaxed timetable. Ten days is a relaxed trip, five days is physically demanding and very difficult. Choose a company best suited to your fitness level.

# Carrying your own pack or hiring a porter

Deciding whether to carry your own pack is a big decision for trekkers when contemplating the track. Making this decision is a matter of self-assessment and personal preference. Unless you're a seasoned trekker with optimum fitness and have undertaken treks of a similar nature and duration before, use the services of a *porter* (someone who carries your pack for you). In fact, some companies require people over the age of 55 to hire a porter. You don't want to slow your group because you're struggling with your backpack.

The advantages of having a porter carry your pack include

- **Interacting with locals:** Your personal porter is likely to go out of his way to help you across the track and make your experience enjoyable. In some instances, he becomes your 'shadow' and you have the opportunity to learn more about his culture.

- **Providing employment for locals.** You're giving employment to a person who otherwise has limited opportunities to earn a living.

- **Safer trekking.** Not carrying your pack decreases the chances of injuring yourself due to overbalancing or back injuries.

- **Your own personal enjoyment.** You have more time to stop and 'smell the roses' (if you can get past the body odour!). The jungle of New Guinea is a beautiful place and you notice it more if you're not fatigued.

If you engage a personal carrier to carry your main pack for the duration of the trek, you need only carry a small day pack with your water, food for one day, snacks, poncho and your personal first aid kit.

In 2011, the cost of a porter varied from AU$600 to $700. This sum could cover the wages for the porter, the cost of the porter's return flight, food and accommodation. Don't base your decision about hiring a porter on cost alone. Changing your mind on the track when the going gets too much is difficult and expensive. First, you need to find a villager along the way who's prepared to be your carrier. Second, your tour company may require an added surcharge for administration purposes.

When the Western Australians of the 2/16th Battalion, AIF began their march to the start of the trail on 17 August 1942, each man carried between 45 to 60 pounds (20 to 27 kilograms) of equipment. Some diehard trekkers and history buffs insist on carrying their own pack in an attempt to experience some of the same hardship. Some live to regret it!

Group porters carry communal items, such as tents and cooking equipment. They may also carry trekker food items, communications equipment, ropes, shovels, machetes and emergency gear. Group carriers assist in the daily erection and dismantling of your tent.

## Getting along with others

Unless you're travelling with a group of lifelong friends, you're likely to find yourself going on a trek with strangers, which is one dynamic that always proves interesting. You may find yourself mixed with a group of complete strangers for more than a week, a situation that could provide you with lifelong friends who share a common bond, or prove a disaster.

To a small extent, trekking with strangers on the track may be compared to the experience of servicemen and women who enlisted during World War II. You're grouped with people who you normally may not choose to associate with. You're placed under conditions of hardship and duress, and you can do very little about the situation when on the track. Everybody in your group has one aim: To finish the track in one piece. You can do a lot to help yourself and your group, simply by doing your best to trek with a smile on your face and a bit of consideration for others. Keep in mind that the third word on the Isurava memorial is 'Mateship'.

I've given you some tips to help the trip go as smoothly as possible. Obviously, you can't control the behaviour of your fellow trekkers, but if you all try to do your part, you're sure to have a better experience:

- **Be prepared for a change in plans.** You're in a developing country where a wristwatch is merely a fashion accessory and everything happens in 'Papua New Guinea time'.

- **Bring a positive attitude.** Remember, you've signed up to this trek of your own free will. Everybody is feeling the same pain and those hills aren't going to get any less steep if you're sullen, always grumpy or constantly complaining. As the saying goes, 'It costs nothing to be nice!'

  A sign of a good tour company isn't that nothing ever goes wrong, but how the staff handle the problems when things do go awry. Remember Murphy's law: 'If something can go wrong, it will'. You're in New Guinea, so everything's possible. Welcome to the jungle!

- **Keep yourself and your kit organised.** Most days start early, so get into a morning routine. Have your belongings packed away in an orderly fashion, or at least have a system that facilitates a quick pack up.

- **Prepare yourself physically.** You need to train hard before your trek. Training ensures you can keep up with the pack. See the following section for further advice about training.

- **Try to keep your good humour.** Be encouraging and supportive, and never forget that during 1942, others did this trek a lot harder than you. Most of all, be grateful that nobody is shooting at you!

## Taking on training

The Australian Army has an expression: 'Train hard, fight easy'. If you're fit and well prepared, your Kokoda experience is much more enjoyable. Your group is limited in speed to the slowest person so your group also benefits if you're fit. People who are underprepared usually lag behind, which affects the group's morale. Trust me, I've seen it happen!

Potential trekkers should start their training well before they attempt the track. People who already regard themselves as fit and active should begin serious Kokoda training at least six months before departure.

If you're not fit, starting your training 12 months in advance is a very sound idea. Joining a gym is highly advisable because your gym instructor can tailor a physical fitness program specific to your task. You may even consider taking on the services of a personal trainer or undertaking group sessions, which can help keep you motivated.

## On hands and knees — two men of one mind

When we think about a victory won for the 'inner man', Paralympic champion Kurt Fearnley will always embody what it is to be a winner. Fearnley was born without the lower section of his spine and hasn't been able to use his legs since birth. However, his disability didn't prevent Fearnley from completing the track in November 2009. Fearnley completed the track in 11 days, propelling himself along on his hands and body. But he wasn't the first Australian to perform such a feat.

After the battle for Isurava Rest House, Captain Buckler of the 2/14th Infantry Battalion, AIF, found himself cut off from the main force. With two officers and 41 men, they set off through the jungle on an ordeal that lasted 42 days. Their party contained seven wounded soldiers and two men who had became very ill with fever. One of the wounded diggers was Corporal John Metson from Sale in Victoria. Suffering from a bullet wound to his ankle, Metson couldn't walk. He was also aware that it would require between six and eight of his comrades to carry him through the jungle on a stretcher. Metson flatly refused to encumber his mates and defiantly wrapped his hands and knees in bandages and strips of torn blanket. He then began to crawl along the jungle floor with the hapless party. Major William Russell of the 2/14th Battalion would later recall, 'for three weeks, chilled, rain soaked, mud caked, starved, exhausted — never complaining, always encouraging. With two stretcher cases, three walking wounded and one crawling, the party struck into the jungle in the darkness, reaching a point on the Eora Creek just before dawn.'

The pace was excruciatingly slow and the men grew weaker by the day. Eventually, Buckler had little option but to leave the sick and wounded in the care of a medical orderly, Private Tom Fletcher, at the village of Sengai. With the assurance that help would be sent back as soon as they reached the Australian lines, Buckler and his group paid the only tribute they could offer before departing. The men stood stiffly to attention and presented arms to their wounded comrades.

Buckler's party eventually made it back to safety, but sadly there would be no fortunate ending for John Metson and his wounded comrades. A Japanese patrol found Fletcher's party and executed the stretcher cases where they lay. For his selfless courage and display of sheer tenacity, Corporal John Metson was posthumously awarded the British Empire Medal. The four words on Isurava Memorial — Courage, Endurance, Mateship and Sacrifice — perfectly describe the spirit of such a man as John Metson; a story worth remembering when you feel a blister on your heel and your own resolve is put to the test.

Ask your trekking company whether they have any other clients living near you. Not only can you make a new friend, but you now share a common goal and can train together.

Here are a few activities that are Kokoda-specific and can complement your general fitness training program:

- **Hill training.** Naturally, this is the best form of training. The steeper, the better. However, start out gradually and don't push yourself too hard in the early stages of your training.

- **Pack training.** Regardless of whether you carry your main pack or not, start to train with something on your back so you get used to having a load on your back, even if you use just a small day pack with a light weight inside.

- **Soft sand/beach training.** When you think you're 'Kokoda ready', try a long walk on the beach, ensuring you walk on the soft sand (not the hard surface near the water line). This is great training and prepares you for that boot-sucking mud!

- **Walking stairs.** Some hills on the track are criss-crossed with exposed tree roots, so walking up and down stairs is excellent for Kokoda training. When you've mastered one step at a time, try alternating the number of treads taken. For example, take one step with your left leg, then climb up two steps with your right leg. This simulates the uneven steps naturally formed on the track by tree roots.

On the track, descending is always more stressful to the knee joints. If you suffer from bad knees, purchase a good-quality knee support to strap and support your joints. Train with the knee guard in place and walk with the same knee support when on the track.

# Chapter 15

# Packing Your Kit and Organising the Paperwork

*In This Chapter*

▶ Sorting out essential documents

▶ Packing the necessary equipment

▶ Working out what to wear

▶ Avoiding diseases

*B*efore going on any holiday, you need to decide 'What am I likely to need on this trip?' Most people have never been on a holiday like trekking on the Kokoda Trail. Once on the track, you simply can't dart down to the local shopping centre to purchase something you forgot to pack.

Most Kokoda trekkers pack too much gear. When you begin your trek, you can observe your porters to see what personal equipment they're carrying — not much. They cross the track regularly and don't take half the equipment many trekkers bring. Nobody's asking you to enter the wilderness with just a length of parachute cord and a hunting knife. However, you can and will survive without the creature comforts you use at home.

To survive (and enjoy) your Kokoda trek, you need to address some basic human needs: Health, energy levels, hunger and thirst, warmth, keeping dry and healthy feet. In this chapter, I address all of these elements with respect to walking the track.

With these factors covered, you have a good chance of surviving and completing the track. The Australian soldiers of 1942 enjoyed virtually no such indulgences and had to fight a war on top of that, so you're in a far better position than our forefathers.

# Arranging Your Paperwork

You need to organise a bit of paperwork before you leave Australia. This includes information regarding your next of kin, in the event of an (unlikely) emergency.

You also have forms to complete when you make a booking with the touring company that escorts you across the track (refer to Chapter 14 for tips on choosing a tour guide company). These forms provide information to the trekking company about any special needs you have. The forms are just as much for protection of the tour company as they are for you.

## Getting medical clearance

The trekking company needs to know you've had a medical examination by a licensed medical practitioner and you've been cleared to undertake strenuous activity.

Consult your family doctor before commencing any physical fitness program, especially if you don't exercise regularly. The track will always be there, so heed your doctor's advice.

If you suffer any ailments or have any physical limitations, discuss them with your tour company before making any bookings. In fact, from 2012, the Kokoda Track Authority requires each person on a trek to complete a detailed (standard) medical form and hand this into your trekking company. No form, no trek.

Your Kokoda experience is much richer if you're physically fit and mentally prepared. Put the time into your training, and no reason exists why you shouldn't finish what you've set out to achieve. See Chapter 14 for more on training before your trek.

If you think you may be pregnant, you shouldn't walk the track. Malaria is a very real risk and could be life threatening to both you and your unborn child. Some infections, such as listeriosis, are extremely hazardous to a foetus and certain medications are dangerous to the normal development of the unborn child. Ensure you undertake a pregnancy test before you depart.

# Checking your passport

Ordinary passports for adult Australian travellers are valid for ten years. Passports issued to children or senior citizens are valid for five years and cost less than adult passports.

If you don't already have a passport, allow ample time to acquire one (at least one month). The Australian Passport Office strives to have your passport ready within ten working days of receiving your application, as long as all of the relevant information is present and correct.

For entry into Papua New Guinea, ensure that your passport has at least six months' validity from your planned date of return to Australia.

Carry copies of a recent passport photo with you in case you need a replacement passport while overseas. Also take photocopies of the information page in your passport. Keep all these documents separate from your passport during travel.

# Applying for a visa

If you choose to ask your travel agent in Australia to organise a visa for entry to Papua New Guinea prior to your departure, bear in mind this means supplying your passport and trusting the mail system to return it safely. Tourists with pre-purchased visas simply pass through the immigration checkpoint, avoiding unnecessary stress and speeding up your arrival.

You can also purchase a visa when you arrive in Papua New Guinea. Visas cost 100 kina (approximately AU$50, at time of writing) and are valid for a period of 60 days from the date of arrival. Have your passport, immigration card and payment ready and stand in the queue requiring a visa (see Chapter 16 for more details about arriving in Immigration).

# Writing your will

Being organised is a good idea, so have a will prepared and keep your will in a safe place. You should also nominate an executor to your will.

The most dangerous part about any flight is the drive to the airport. However, tragedy can strike anywhere and, sadly, some Kokoda trekkers have lost their lives while chasing their dream. Having a will makes things easier for your family.

# Buying travel insurance

Travel insurance is essential and can be purchased easily online.

Ensure your travel insurance covers you for medical expenses in Papua New Guinea, including evacuation by helicopter if you're unable to walk out. Before departure, determine whether your insurance plan will make payments directly to the provider of the service, or reimburse you when you've returned to your own country. Some trekking companies recommend having your credit card details on you while you trek, in case your insurance company doesn't pay for evacuations upfront (or you can't get hold of them while you're on the track).

Not only the large corporate insurers cover evacuation. One Kokoda trekker who needed to be evacuated by chopper during 2009 was insured with a smaller, budget insurance company, and experienced no problems at all organising medical care.

Medical facilities in Papua New Guinea aren't as efficient as care provided in most western countries. The main hospital in PNG is the Port Moresby General Hospital, which is adequate but doesn't provide treatment as good as the treatment in Australia. Kokoda has a small hospital that can provide limited treatment. A common ailment for trekkers is dehydration. Kokoda hospital has intravenous saline capability and can help with minor cases of dehydration. (See the section 'Staying hydrated' later in the chapter for tips to avoid dehydration.)

# Sorting out malaria medication and other immunisations

Before visiting Papua New Guinea, you should take precautions against catching malaria while you're there. Other immunisations should also be seriously considered.

Take this book with you when consulting your doctor as he will need to consider prescribing some of the following medications for you.

### Anti-malarial medication

You may contract malaria and other mosquito-borne diseases in Papua New Guinea. An anti-malarial medication is essential when visiting all areas at altitudes less than 1,800 metres (5,906 feet), which is where mosquitoes are generally found. This includes Port Moresby and several parts of the track, especially the beachheads of Buna, Gona and Sanananda.

Malaria has flu-like symptoms that include

- ✔ chills
- ✔ diarrhoea
- ✔ fever
- ✔ general weakness
- ✔ muscular aches
- ✔ stomach pain
- ✔ sweating
- ✔ vomiting

Symptoms generally don't appear until 7 to 14 days after you're bitten and may not even occur until two to three months after exposure.

Many anti-malarial medications need to be started two days before your departure and continued throughout the trip until seven days after you arrive home.

If you're forgetful and are prescribed a malaria tablet to be administered daily, team up with another trekker who can remind you to take the medication every day.

Anti-malarial medication is not foolproof and the medication isn't guaranteed to prevent you from contracting malaria. Your best defence against malaria is to not get bitten by a mosquito.

Side-effects of anti-malarial medication may include

- ✔ dizziness
- ✔ insomnia and nightmares
- ✔ itching and a rash
- ✔ nausea and vomiting

In rare cases, severe reactions, such as depression, anxiety, psychosis, hallucinations and seizures, may occur.

### Immunisations

The following vaccinations are recommended for Papua New Guinea:

- ✔ **Hepatitis A:** This vaccine is recommended for all travellers to Kokoda. It should be given at least two weeks (preferably four weeks or more) before departure. A booster should be given 6 to 12 months later to confer long-term immunity.

- ✔ **Hepatitis B:** People vaccinated against Hepatitis A are sometimes also vaccinated against Hepatitis B. Discuss this vaccine with your doctor.

- ✔ **Japanese encephalitis:** This vaccine is recommended if you're lengthening your stay in Papua New Guinea, such as by walking other tracks or engaging in humanitarian work. While not commonly suffered by trekkers who fly in and out of Papua New Guinea on a two-week stay, cases of Japanese encephalitis have been reported sporadically from the Central and Western Provinces.

- ✔ **Tetanus-diphtheria:** Vaccination for tetanus-diphtheria is an absolute must for all trekkers who haven't received a tetanus-diphtheria immunisation within the last ten years. Even the smallest of open wounds can evolve into a tropical ulcer, if not treated correctly.

- ✔ **Typhoid:** This vaccine is recommended for all travellers who intend to travel to other parts of Papua New Guinea that are well away from the Kokoda Trail, but where Australians also served during World War II, such as Milne Bay or Lae. The vaccine can be administered orally or as an injection.

## Setting up a contingency plan

You're about to trek through one of the harshest environments on Earth. Something may go wrong and you should be prepared to accept some element of risk.

Injury may result from your trek (although the most common risk by far to a trekker on the track is gastro problems). Even the most cautious and hygienic person may be unlucky enough to be struck down by illness during the trek.

Should you suffer injury or illness that requires you to be evacuated from the track, you should have some type of contingency plan in place that guarantees the assistance of a support person.

Every trekking company has a duty of care that the company should abide by to ensure your safe passage across the track. However, the trekking company's duty of care generally ceases when you get on the plane to Australia.

If you require a medical evacuation, ensure you've nominated a person who can be contacted at any time while you're away. This person may be contacted by your tour company and informed that you need assistance the moment your aircraft returns to Australia.

In extreme cases, this person may need to board the first flight to Port Moresby to assist you while you're on the plane. Depending on the nature of your illness, you may need to be admitted to a hospital in Port Moresby and not permitted to fly until medical clearance is granted.

# Listing the Equipment You Need

When you're headed to Papua New Guinea for the trek, care must be taken in what you pack; not only general stuff, but also medication, insect protection, food, hydration products and sleeping gear.

## Packing general supplies

You may feel a bit overwhelmed at packing for such a remote environment. To help you out, I've compiled a list of what you need (and you only need what's on this list!):

- Biodegradable antiseptic soap (a must before meals). See the section 'Being careful with food and water'.
- Camera.
- Hand sanitiser (a must before meals). See the section 'Being careful with food and water'.
- Insect repellent (recommended if going to beachheads). See the section 'Choosing insect protection'.
- Large dry bag to keep your night clothes and sleeping bag dry.
- Lightweight cord (for instant clothes line) and six to eight pegs.
- Lightweight spoon/cup/bowl/utensils. The army 'dixie' cups are handy because they have a foldout handle. The dixie cup also fits outside the standard army water bottle, so is easily stored.
- Lightweight trekking poles to assist walking and stability (optional).

For that authentic Kokoda experience, ask your porter to cut you a stick from the bush. Strip the bark and ensure no borers are present. You may even pay your porter a small gratuity to engrave it for you (see Chapter 16). A wooden walking stick makes a great souvenir.

✔ Lycra tights, bike pants or 'skins' to prevent chafing (see the section 'Sidestepping chafing').

✔ Multipurpose pocket knife (optional, but ensure you pack the knife in your unaccompanied baggage during flights, because if you have it in your carry-on luggage as you board a plane the knife will be confiscated).

✔ One 60- to 70-litre lightweight backpack. Ensure all straps and the back support system are adjustable. An air flow system to cool the back is preferable. Train with this pack before your trek.

✔ One day pack (if not carrying your own backpack). Train with this pack before your trek. (See the sidebar 'What to carry if you're hiring a porter' for what to carry in your day pack.)

✔ One quick-dry sports towel. They're light and dry quickly.

✔ Personal medical kit (see the following section).

✔ Small dry bag to protect your camera and other items.

✔ Snacks and comfort food to maintain your morale and provide energy as you walk. Share your treats with your porter and you'll have a friend for life. See the section 'Keeping energy levels high'.

✔ Steel wool or dish pads to clean eating utensils.

✔ Sunglasses (essential if going to beachheads).

✔ Sunscreen (essential if going to beachheads).

✔ Toilet paper in a waterproof bag, or wet wipes.

✔ Toothbrush and toothpaste.

✔ Water purification tablets (very highly recommended).

## Bringing some basic medical goods

You're responsible for your own health, so bring an adequate supply of medication.

Certain substances may be legally held in your country, but not in Papua New Guinea. Retain all medications in their original packaging and ensure that the contents are clearly labelled.

If the medication was prescribed by your doctor, carry a signed and dated letter from your doctor.

# What to carry if you're hiring a porter

When hiring a porter (refer to Chapter 14), carry everything you need to be comfortable for one day. If you're travelling well and don't need special care by your porter, he may be used for other tasks, such as preparing a rope bridge at a creek crossing or forging ahead to set up camp. So you may be separated from your main pack.

Your day pack should include

✔ Camera

✔ Minimum of 2 litres of water

✔ One day's rations and eating utensils

✔ Personal medical kit

✔ Poncho or rain coat

✔ Small dry bag to keep your camera dry

✔ Toilet paper

✔ Torch (in case you're delayed and late getting into camp)

By separating your possessions in this way, you won't get caught out at any time without the items that you need to complete each leg of the trek. Your day pack may still weigh up to 6 kilograms, but is more comfortable than carrying a large pack.

People who treat themselves for conditions such as diabetes have successfully walked the track in the past. If you're carrying needles or syringes to self-administer insulin, ensure you have a letter from your doctor. Sharp items can't always be carried in your hand luggage and should be safely packed in your main luggage (but check with your airline for their specific requirements).

The following is a guide only (consult your doctor for more advice) but you may consider packing the following:

✔ Antibacterial disinfectant gel or alcohol-based hand sanitiser that kills germs without soap or water. Remember that 80 per cent of infections are transmitted by touching.

✔ Antibiotic ointment for cuts and blister wounds.

✔ Anti-diarrheal antibiotics (as prescribed by your doctor). Also consider a product called Travelan, which can be taken to reduce the risk of diarrhoea. Consult your doctor on this issue before usage.

✔ Ankle support guard (optional).

✔ Anti-chafing cream or gel.

✔ Antihistamine (optional) — useful as a decongestant for colds, allergies and insect bites and stings.

✔ Anti-inflammatory tablets (as prescribed by your doctor).

✔ Anti-malarial tablets (as prescribed by your doctor).

- Aspirin or paracetamol.

  Headache is one sign of dehydration. Ensure you take in plenty of fluids. (But be careful not to overdo it. You can drink too much water, resulting in death — see the sidebar 'How much water is too much?' for more details.)

- Blister packs, especially any commercial blister pack that acts as a second skin.

- One triangular bandage.

- Oral rehydration formula, sports drink or electrolyte powder.

  Purchase the flavoured variety of oral rehydration formula because natural flavour is very distasteful. At the end of every hard day, drink some, whether you feel you need to or not.

- Plastic bottle of antiseptic.

- Roll of adhesive strapping tape.

- Rubber surgeon's gloves.

- Safety pins.

- Scissors and tweezers (must be carried during flights in unaccompanied baggage).

- Sharp needle or splinter probe (to remove splinters or blister treatment).

- Sunscreen SPF 30 or stronger.

- Tropical strength mosquito repellent.

- Two elasticised bandages.

- Two knee support guards (essential for any person with knee problems).

- Waterproof plastic strips, such as Band Aids.

This may seem like a lot of items, but the trick is to keep your medical kit as small and light as possible:

- All bottled items should be small.

- Break the medical kit down into smaller packages in a logical manner; for example, one bag for open wounds, one bag for non-visible injury such as headache.

- Unless a substance is prescribed by a medical practitioner, remove all bulky commercial packaging.

- You'll use the dehydration prevention daily, so have it handy.

## Don't wear contact lenses!

In 2010, an Australian trek leader wearing contact lenses got an eye infection. The infection penetrated beneath his contact lenses either while the trek leader was bathing in a stream along the track, or as a result of using a sweat rag that had been dipped into a river, then used to wipe his forehead.

The effects of the infection were almost immediate and the trek leader lost vision in both eyes, necessitating evacuation by helicopter. After substantial treatment, he regained limited vision.

## *Choosing insect protection*

Unlike the soldiers of 1942, you're not likely to be placed in a weapons pit for sentry duty during the middle of the night. However, you'll face a common enemy: mosquitoes. Here are some tips for avoiding insect bites:

✔ **Buy a decent mosquito net.** When purchasing a mosquito net:

- Purchase the rectangular 'box' mosquito net, which is hung by four strings from each corner of the net. This type of mosquito net has been issued to members of the Australian Defence Force since the 1960s and is still used today.

- Avoid the type of mosquito net that's suspended from the ceiling by a single cord or string because they can become untucked as you turn in your sleep, exposing your lower legs.

- Ensure that the mesh size is less than 1.5 millimetres.

Army surplus mosquito nets can usually be purchased from any reputable disposal store or online auction house. You'll sometimes be sleeping in a Papuan guest house along the track, so plenty of hanging points are always available from which to hang your mosquito net.

Some tents have the ability to serve as a standalone insect protection net (without the outer fly fitted). They do, however, take up more room in your pack than a suspended mosquito net.

Most Anopheles mosquitoes are nocturnal and are very active around dawn and dusk, making the purchase of an adequate mosquito net a very sound investment.

✔ **Cover as much of your skin as possible.** Most trekkers prefer to wear short-sleeve shirts and shorts because of the heat and humidity on the track. However, to avoid being bitten by mosquitoes, cover as much as possible when trekking along the track. Light-coloured, loose-fitting clothing (including collared shirts) and covered footwear protects you from mosquitoes and the harsh effects of the sun.

✔ **Go to bed early.** You may be so tired that you won't see much of the night out and will be tucked up in your sleeping bag by 7 pm. Not only does an early bedtime give you rest, you minimise your chances of being bitten by a malaria-carrying mosquito.

✔ **Use an effective insect repellent.** Cover all portions of exposed skin with insect repellent. However, be aware that this protection diminishes when you sweat. Like sunscreen, insect repellent should be re-applied every few hours. Your insect repellent should contain 25 to 50 per cent DEET (N,N-diethyl-3-methylbenzamide) or 20 per cent picaridin. Check the manufacturer's labelling for further information.

## Keeping energy levels high

Your tour company should provide you with a suitable trekking menu and many include your meals as part of a package. A trek menu should include treats or comfort food to maintain your morale when the going gets tough. However, you may wish to supplement any purchased trek menu with your own selection of luxury food.

Here are some tips for food to bring (and how to keep down the weight of your backpack):

✔ **Breakfast oats:** The benefits of porridge to the trekker are great — porridge is a good energy source for the rest of the day. Add boiling water to the sachet contents and allow to stand for a few minutes.

✔ **Cashews:** If you enjoy nuts, consider buying a large packet of salted cashews. This luxury food item is craved by trekkers and satisfies the salt craving that's evident after profuse sweating.

✔ **Chocolate:** Chocolate is a good energy food, but is very susceptible to melting. Select a version that doesn't become a gooey mess, such as coated chocolate.

✔ **Dehydrated food:** Taking dehydrated food reduces weight (Papua New Guinea is not short of water to rehydrate your snacks!). Camping and outdoor stores stock many brands of dehydrated meals.

✔ **Instant noodles:** Quick and handy option (and very light!).

✔ **Instant powdered soup:** A good start to a trek meal.

✔ **Instant tea and coffee:** If you need your caffeine fix, you'll need plenty of teabags. A tube of condensed milk is the most palatable addition and adds a sweet touch; however, powdered milk and sugar sachets are the next best option.

✔ **Muesli bars:** A lightweight option for breakfast or a snack.

✔ **Sweets and lollies:** A must for any trek. Choose individually wrapped sweets, so that each article is protected from contamination from dirty fingers. (General food hygiene is described in the section 'Being careful with food and water'.) Hard boiled sweets that you suck on are good because they also occupy your mind to a small extent. Soft jelly lollies are also good because the chewing action is good for your morale (most people feel happy when they're eating, especially if they're eating something pleasant). They may be small comforts, but they all help.

## Staying hydrated

You're walking through a tropical country; the weather is hot and humid (although quite possibly very cold in the evenings). Avoiding dehydration is critical.

Contrary to what you might think, drinking too much water is also a danger; see the sidebar 'How much water is too much?' for more information.

Generally, carrying 3 litres of drinking water at any given time is sufficient (with at least 2 litres in your day pack). The water should be carried in three separate bottles of 1 litre each so you have enough water to drink while the sterilisation tablets sterilise the water in the other bottles. Here are some tips on how to carry all of this water in your pack:

✔ **Bottle with a screw-top lid:** The best type to use. The benefit of this design is that the portion of the bottle that touches your lips is protected from the outside elements beneath the cap, minimising the risk of gastro illness.

✔ **Camel pack (3-litre capacity):** Some people find it tiresome to constantly be removing a water bottle from their belt and unscrewing the lid. Subsequently, you may prefer to use a *camel pack*, a bladder that sits inside your backpack and feeds water to you by a tube to your mouth. This simplifies the method of administering water. However, the portion you suck on is easily contaminated by outside elements, so be cautious. (See the section 'Being careful with food and water' for tips on food and water hygiene.)

Many camel packs have ruptured on the track. If using a camel pack bladder, carry a backup water bottle.

✔ **Sport bottles:** These bottles aren't ideal, because the portion that touches your mouth is exposed to the elements. The lid is opened by pulling on the rubber outer, either with your fingers or your teeth. The lid may become contaminated if touched by dirty hands or by brushing against other equipment.

## *Getting a good night's sleep*

When you're using so much energy in the day, getting some down time and good rest in the evenings is vital. You may like to use this time to chat with other people on the trek, to debrief about what you've seen and done that day. If you're staying out, remember to cover up from mosquito attack because mosquitoes are most active at night.

## Weight — the vital factor on the Kokoda Trail

Think your pack is heavy? The troops on the track had to carry up to 27 kilograms each.

Prior to setting out along the track from Itiki on 15 August 1942, the men of the 2/14th & 2/16th infantry battalions AIF were instructed to prepare their kit and discard any excess weight. Emphasis was placed on the carriage of weapons and ammunition. Try as they may, the troops found it almost impossible to keep the load below 45 pounds (20 kilograms) and some soldiers carried up to 60 pounds (27 kilograms).

The load carrying equipment for Commonwealth troops of the World War II was 'Pattern 37' web equipment. These packs and shoulder straps had no padding or cushioning, so this would've proved uncomfortable.

During the Australian fight forward in the latter stages of the campaign, Sergeant Bede Tongs MM of the 3rd Infantry Battalion, AMF (Australian Military Force or militia), would find himself leading an eight-man patrol from Efogi

in a bid to locate the Japanese. They were the advanced element at this time and no other Australians were in front of them. Weight was such a crucial factor that they were required to cut the standard grey army blanket in half to reduce the load. Bede was forced to decide between carrying a spoon or a fork to eat his rations. He knew he couldn't carry both, so he chose the spoon.

However, some men chose to err on the side of caution. During the battle for Deniki at the start of the campaign, the soldiers of the 39th Infantry Battalion, AMF, were hurriedly instructed to move out. But the order also included a direction to bring as much food and ammunition with them as possible. Remembering the amount of rounds the 39th had been required to discharge over the last few days, one man of the 39th carried 1,100 rounds of .303 ammunition in cloth bandoliers with him, a phenomenal weight. He obviously planned on not being caught short.

For comfortable rest and sleep time, I recommend you pack

✔ An inflatable pillow.

✔ Lightweight clothes to wear during the evening. Long sleeves and trousers minimise your chance of being bitten by mosquitoes. The nights can get quite cold, so ensure your clothing can keep you warm.

✔ A mosquito net. Essential if you have the option to sleep in guest houses along the track (although your trekking company may supply a tent for every evening); see Figure 15-1 for a picture of the typical accommodation along the track. If you sleep in a tent, a mosquito net isn't essential, although I recommend that you bring a net. Refer to the section 'Choosing insect protection' for more information about buying a mosquito net.

✔ One lightweight sleeping bag.

✔ One sleeping mat (or self-inflating mattress).

✔ Sandals (preferably something robust, with straps). These shoes allow your feet to air out and dry when you enter camp at the end of the day.

✔ A small torch or head torch, and spare batteries.

**Figure 15-1:** Some village huts at Nauro.

Not a seasoned camper? Always have trouble finding anything in the dark? Here's a simple yet effective method of always having your torch within easy reach. When you get into your bed for the evening, hold your torch in your right hand, then lay flat on your back. With your arms stretched out adjacent to your body (just as if you're standing to attention, only lying down), place your torch next to your mattress without bending your arm. That way, when you wake up in the middle of the night, you need only to lay flat on your back with your arms by your side and your torch should be near your right hand. Works every time.

# How much water is too much?

Is it really possible to drink too much water? Yes! Drinking too much water can be fatal and, sadly, deaths have occurred on the track due to water intoxication (drinking too much water).

The danger arises when you drink too much water and electrolytes aren't properly replenished. Sodium levels in your body drop below 135 mmol/L (millimole per litre of blood), resulting in this hazardous condition.

Symptoms of water intoxication include:

- A change in behaviour or personality
- Drowsiness
- Headache
- Onset of confusion and/or irritability

These symptoms are sometimes followed by:

- Dulled senses
- Further thirst
- Muscle weakness, followed by twitching or cramping
- Nausea and vomiting
- Restricted breathing during times of exertion (such as trekking)

The treatment for water intoxication is to be evacuated immediately. No trekking group is trained or equipped to handle this situation on the track.

Mild cases may be alleviated by fluid restriction; however, this is still not a solution to the problem and, in the interests of the patient, evacuation and transportation to the nearest hospital is the best course of action.

As a precaution during your trek, supplement 1 litre of your drinking water per day with an additive that contains electrolytes. At the end of your day, when the sweating is over, drink one oral rehydration salt sachet.

# Finding Something to Wear

The best clothing for the track is clothing that makes you the most comfortable. Protection from the elements and insect attack are vital. Fortunately, a vast array of trekking gear is available to satisfy your clothing requirements.

Essentially, you need only two sets of clothes: One for day and the other for night. You can be kitted out without weighing you and your porter down if you follow these rules.

## Picking clothes for the walk

You're going to be wet during the day. Just accept this because you won't find a way around it! Rain and perspiration will soak you to the skin. That's why you need only one set of lightweight, quick-dry trek clothes to wear during the day.

You simply can't bring your whole wardrobe. You don't always have an opportunity to dry clothes, so you may experience one of the joys of trekking the Kokoda Trail: Waking up each morning and putting on a wet or smelly shirt! (Despite the heat, clothes rarely dry when hung out during the night.) Bringing more than one set of trek gear means you or your porter have to hump around a pack full of wet and heavy clothes.

Here's a guide to your clothing requirements:

- **A thin raincoat or poncho.** Ponchos are preferable because the poncho can be draped over your body and cover both yourself and your day pack during rain. An added bonus is you don't need to remove your day pack to apply the poncho. This item can also double as a ground sheet to sit on during short breaks, so carry it at all times in your day pack (if hiring a porter).

- **Broad brimmed hat (with a chinstrap).** The diggers wore a slouch hat for a reason. Baseball caps aren't effective at protecting your ears and the back of your neck from the harsh sunlight.

  When walking under jungle canopy, remove your hat while walking in shade to allow your head to cool.

- **One set of lightweight clothes for hiking during the day.** A long-sleeved shirt protects you from the sun and marauding mosquitoes. Shorts allow freedom of movement. You may like to purchase hike trousers that have zippered legs that can be removed or added. Ensure that the zippered ends don't chafe your skin.

## Caring for your feet

When preparing for your trek, don't forget socks and boots, or to address the problem of blisters.

### Buying new boots for the trek

Here are some tips for buying new boots for your Kokoda trek:

✔ Choose boots that are soft and comfortable, with a cushioned inner sole.

  Having plenty of toe room is paramount. The track has plenty of downhill walking, so your toes need ample space for your foot to slide slightly to the front of the boot.

✔ Don't rely on shoe sizes when purchasing your boots. Shoe sizes vary, so try on the boots to ensure a good fit.

  Most people also have one foot slightly larger than the other, so try on both shoes before you leave the shop.

✔ Go boot shopping during the middle or later part of the day. Your feet tend to swell as the day wears on, so try on boots when your feet are swollen, because they'll swell when you're on the track.

✔ Wear two pairs of the socks you're wearing on the track when you try on your boots (see the following section).

### Bringing the right kind of socks

I recommend you wear two pairs of socks at all times (one thick and one thin), so you need to bring:

✔ **Two pairs of thin sport socks, to wear under your thick socks.** The thin socks should be very close fitting so they hug your feet. This acts like an outer layer of skin. Wearing thin socks underneath your thick hiking socks helps to prevent blisters and hot spots from occurring (see the following section).

✔ **Two to three pairs of thick trek socks.** Wear the thick sock over the thin sock. The sport sock is tight against your skin, so the sport sock rubs against the inside surface of the hiking sock, not your skin, reducing the risk of a blister from developing.

Wash your socks in rivers or streams and alternate your pairs of socks each day. Just like your trek clothes (refer to the section 'Picking clothes for the walk'), your socks are likely to be constantly wet, but at least they'll be clean. Hang your wet socks out to dry at every opportunity.

### Preventing blisters

The most common problem for trekkers is blisters.

A blister is a lump that forms on your skin when the outer layer is injured. Fluid forms beneath the injured skin to protect the sensitive new skin under the wound. Your heels are susceptible to harsh rubbing if your boots are stiff or not formed to your foot shape.

When you experience discomfort or signs of rubbing on your heels, notify your trek leader and treat the source of the problem *before* a blister develops.

You have an obligation to your fellow trekkers not to slow the group through preventable injuries. If you try to tough it out, a blister may form, which will ruin everybody's day.

To avoid blisters, 'wear in' your boots before trekking by wearing them during training. However, with modern materials and designs, your hiking boots should be as comfortable as a pair of running shoes. If your boots are uncomfortable and give you blisters on your first training walk, you may need to try a different brand of boot. During your ten-day trek, you're going to be walking between five and eight hours each day, so your boots must be comfortable.

### Dealing with blisters

Despite your best efforts, you may develop blisters while on the track. If the wound is not too painful, keep the blister intact.

The outer layer of skin that contains the fluid is a natural barrier to bacteria (which flourishes inside a smelly boot) and decreases the possibility of the wound becoming infected.

You can apply an adhesive bandage blister, but the best covering is a second skin blister pack, which you can find in a chemist. As a last resort, if the pain is too intense and prevents you from walking, you may have to drain the fluid. Follow these steps to minimise infection:

1. **Wash your hands and the blister thoroughly with soap and water, then apply antiseptic hand gel to your skin, so that your hands are free from bacteria.**

2. **Apply antiseptic or iodine to the blistered area.**

3. **Use antiseptic or medical alcohol-based disinfectant to sterilise a sharp needle.**

4. **Puncture the blister near the edge of the wound with a couple of small holes, but *don't* tear or remove the outer skin.**

5. **Apply an antibiotic ointment to the blister and cover with a bandage or gauze.**

6. **Regularly clean and dress the wound.**

## Sidestepping chafing

Chafing is very common on the track because you're doing a lot of walking over consecutive days. The pain can come on quickly as a stinging or burning sensation.

Chafing is caused by a surface, such as your undergarments or clothing, rubbing constantly against your skin. This condition is accentuated by moisture, either from sweat or rain. Powders aren't the best preventative measure. On the track, chafing usually occurs on the inner thighs and women sometimes suffer chafing under the arms or breasts.

As soon as you begin to chafe, apply some anti-chafing gel or cream to the affected area and try to keep the cause of the chafing from further aggravating your skin. When you get into camp, thoroughly wash the affected area, apply more anti-chafing cream and rest the area overnight by leaving it uncovered.

Prevention is better than cure. To prevent chafing, wear a pair of tights, skins or bike pants that prevent rubbing against your skin. These items are lightweight and take up virtually no space in your pack.

# Taking Basic Sanitary Precautions

Papua New Guinea is not as sanitary as Australia or other countries in the western world. Dysentery, which causes severe diarrhoea, is the most common travel-related ailment suffered by modern-day trekkers. Prevention is your best weapon in the war against diarrhoea, and extreme caution should be practised with regards to your food and water intake.

## Being careful with food and water

By following some basic hygiene rules, you minimise the chance of contracting dysentery and diarrhoea. Here are some tips to keep you as healthy as possible during your trek:

- ✔ **Avoid 'hand to mouth' during food consumption.** For example, when eating items such as sweets or dried fruit from a packet, do your best to place the food item directly into your mouth from the packaging so the food doesn't make contact with your skin or fingers.

- ✔ **Disinfect your cutlery.** Disinfect your cutlery with antiseptic gel before use. This may make the first mouthful of food taste a little odd, but is far better than contracting 'Bali belly'!

✔ **Don't consume drinks that contain ice in Port Moresby before your trip.** You can't let your guard down at this stage and contract a belly disorder, just before you're to set out on your trek.

✔ **Don't drink water from any creek or stream unless given the 'all clear' by your chief porter.** The Papuans who act as your porters generally know the best source for fresh drinking water. The water may look clear and bacteria-free to you, but underlying factors may be present that render the water a risk to your health. One example is the mining operation upstream from the water supply at Ofi Creek, which often made the creek water brown.

✔ **Don't eat fruit or vegetables unless they've been peeled or cooked.**

✔ **Ensure you eat only piping hot cooked dishes.** Regardless of how tantalising that hotel buffet looks, avoid cooked foods that are no longer steaming hot. Meat products and cooked foods that have been standing for too long at room temperature may pose a health hazard.

✔ **Unpack before you eat.** When sitting down for a designated meal (breakfast, lunch or dinner), remove your meal from your back pack before washing and disinfecting your hands. You may recontaminate your hands when you rummage through your backpack.

✔ **Use soap and water — *and* antiseptic hand gel.** Before touching food or food packaging, thoroughly wash your hands with soap and water, then apply an antiseptic hand gel to disinfect your hands.

Due to the transient nature of your trek, you rarely have access to water that's been boiled and allowed to cool prior to consumption. Your only other option for worry-free drinking water is to chemically treat the water. A number of products are available from camping stores that purify your drinking water.

If you do contract severe diarrhoea, with blood in the stools, or if you get a fever with shaking chills and abdominal pain, forget about completing the Kokoda Trail. Unfortunately, once severe diarrhoea takes hold and you can't retain fluids, dehydration usually follows. This ailment can't be adequately treated in the field and medical attention should be sought.

When you're walking the track, only two ways back to civilisation are available — on foot or via helicopter evacuation. If you have dysentery, your option to walk out has been removed. A ride in a helicopter sounds like a fun way to see the track, but isn't the way that you or any other trekker intended to complete your Kokoda experience. Contracting dysentery could also mean the end of a companion's Kokoda journey because somebody has to accompany you to the nearest hospital to help you while you're too ill to help yourself.

## Watching out for other insect-borne illnesses

Most trekkers accept that the risk of contracting malaria is a possibility (which is why they take anti-malarial medication; refer to the section 'Sorting out malaria medication and other immunisations'), but other insects can also carry diseases, striking the unwary traveller in various parts of Papua New Guinea:

- **Dengue fever can be contracted from the Aedes mosquito.** Unlike the malaria-carrying mosquito, this type of insect is primarily active during the day in densely populated areas, although the mosquito is also found in rural environments. Dengue fever has flu-like symptoms and no vaccine is available.

- **Ross River fever is also transmitted via mosquito bite.** Fortunately, Ross River fever is not common among trekkers. Like dengue fever, the symptoms are flu-like and include fever, chills, headache, and aches and pains in the muscles and joints.

- **Scrub typhus is transmitted by tiny mites with six legs called chiggers.** The bite results in a bacterial infection that causes an itchy sore on the skin. Intense scratching by the sufferer may cause an open wound that can result in a secondary infection. This condition heals itself without treatment; however, cream or ointment that relieves the itch is helpful. Scrub typhus isn't really a problem for the Kokoda trekker, although it was widely suffered by soldiers during the Kokoda campaign.

## Staying away from HIV

Human immunodeficiency virus (HIV) has been reported in Papua New Guinea. You're most at risk if you have unprotected sex with someone who is contaminated, or use a contaminated needle intravenously.

If you need a blood transfusion, use your travel insurance and return to Australia on the next available flight so that you can receive treatment in an Australian hospital.

# Chapter 16

# Respecting the Locals and Keeping Yourself Safe

Australia and Papua New Guinea are close neighbours, but culturally, economically and often botanically they're very different. Travelling to a developing country can be frightening, and in some respects life is harder in Papua New Guinea. Exercise common sense and you have a very good chance of surviving your adventure holiday and having the photographs to prove it. By making slight changes to your daily routine and your personal conduct, you're likely to find your stay quite enjoyable.

In this chapter, I navigate you to the comfort of your hotel in Port Moresby, jumping through the legal hoops along the way. I examine how to handle Papua New Guinean currency, stay safe, purchase souvenirs and interact with the local people. If you follow these guidelines, your biggest worry will be getting up that first big hill!

# Climate Change — But Not the Global Type!

The moment you step off the plane in Papua New Guinea, you feel the humidity hit you square in the face.

This part of the world is very hot and you should dress accordingly. Always wear a hat and don't rely on sunscreen alone to protect you. Wear a lightweight, long-sleeved shirt to protect your arms and remember to drink enough fluids.

Take the first day slowly to acclimatise to the heat and humidity. You may experience dizziness or become lightheaded if you stand up too quickly. Spend your first day by the pool and relax because you'll be spending the next seven to ten days on your feet.

# Taking Care of Practical Matters

After landing in Port Moresby, you need to get from your plane to your hotel. Negotiating Immigration and customs is your first step and needn't be daunting, as long as you follow the rules. You also need to purchase and familiarise yourself with *kina*, the currency of Papua New Guinea, before you set off on your trek.

## Getting from the airport to your hotel

If you've chosen to trek with a reputable company, somebody should meet you at the airport.

When you step off the plane at Jackson International Airport, Port Moresby, your choice in trekking company makes a difference. Your tour manager or trek leader should've contacted you prior to leaving Australia to let you know where he'll meet you. If your tour company hasn't briefed you prior to leaving Australia, the company isn't earning its pay from the start.

If your tour leader is meeting you outside the airport, simply follow the crowd to Immigration as they leave the aircraft. Before leaving your aircraft, ensure your passport and immigration card are handy, yet secure. You don't want to drop papers in a crowd!

## Changing money

The currency used in Papua New Guinea is the kina. Having at least 100 kina in your possession prior to leaving Australia is wise. If you need more kina when you arrive in Papua New Guinea, you can find the currency exchange office on the other side of the baggage carousel at the airport.

The amount of kina you need varies from person to person, depending on your spending habits. If you don't spend a lot on souvenirs, AU$300 to AU$500 should be enough for a two-week stay. Most of your expenses should be covered in your tour package and a great deal of time is spent on the Kokoda Trail, so your daily expenses should be minimal.

Australian residents are already one step ahead in understanding the currency because all PNG denominations follow the same colour code as Australian dollars. For example, the AU$5 and PNG 5 kina notes are both pink, and the AU$10 and 10 kina notes are both blue. Remember, however, that they're not the same value!

### Buying bananas

When exchanging currency, ask for the smallest denominations possible. You need plenty of 2 kina and 5 kina notes for spending money along the track, to purchase those 'life saving' cans of soft drinks or packets of chips. (Warm fizzy drinks may not sound appetising now, but you'll be surprised how appealing they can be after your first big day on the track! Climb from Deniki to Isurava and warm soft drink will never taste so good!)

Local fruit may be available at each guest house. The bananas in New Guinea may be smaller than those in Australia, but they're fresh and chemical free. And you haven't tasted a great pineapple until you've sunk your teeth into a Sanananda-grown fruit. Prices vary from village to village, but small denominations are the order of the day. (Don't expect the locals to carry change.)

A number of sites on privately owned land are likely to arouse your curiosity. Entry fees vary between 5 and 10 kina. If you're short of change and need to break a 50 kina note, have your fellow trekkers give you their small denominations and pay the land holder with your large note. That gets rid of your large currency and keeps your wallet topped up with small notes.

## Negotiating Immigration

After leaving the aircraft, you need to pass through Immigration. A notice at the airport indicates which line you should take:

- ✔ Non-residents *with* a pre-purchased visa.
- ✔ Non-residents *without* a pre-purchased visa.

Simply take your place in the appropriate line and have your documents ready. (Refer to Chapter 15 for more information about applying for visas before or on arrival.)

When you've passed through Immigration, your backpack should be ready to claim from the baggage carousel.

## Pleasing customs officials

Don't bring anything dangerous or illicit into Papua New Guinea. Tell the truth, the whole truth and nothing but the truth on your customs declaration card. If in doubt, tick the box in the affirmative and let the customs official decide.

Most trekkers have food or treats in their luggage. If you take food into Papua New Guinea, tick 'yes' to food on the customs declaration card. PNG customs are used to seeing hundreds of Kokoda trekkers pass through. Simply explain to them that you possess 'trek food' and nine times out of ten they'll simply wave you through.

If you carry a knife to use on the track, tick 'yes' to the question regarding weapons on the customs declaration card because the knife will be picked up on the airport security scanner. Ensure that all sharp implements (including manicure scissors) are stored in your unaccompanied luggage or they'll be confiscated.

## Leaving the airport

Once you pass through customs, you're ushered through a set of doors to the main foyer of Jacksons International Airport. The airport is very well controlled by security. You should now be met by your tour guide. Once located, stick with your tour guide, who can lead you from this point on. However, if your tour guide isn't there, remain inside the main foyer of the airport until you have a game plan.

If you can't find your tour guide:

✔ Inform airport staff which hotel you're staying at — they should be more than happy to telephone your accommodation, in order to arrange a courtesy bus to transport you.

✔ Leave the foyer to wait for your courtesy bus, but don't despair. The front of the airport is within view of a security officer, and is generally a safe and secure environment. All airport officials and security officers speak English.

✔ As a last resort, hail a taxi to take you to your accommodation. Plenty will be waiting on the street in front of the airport.

## Taking care of valuables

Your hotel can be regarded as your safe haven (the barbed wire on the walls and security guard at the gate aren't there to keep you in!), but that doesn't mean the security is foolproof.

When you check into your hotel, most tour companies instruct you to prepare a bag that you won't be taking on your trek. This bag should contain a clean set of clothing for your return flight and other home-related items.

Don't leave any valuables or cash in the bag you leave at the hotel. A trekker learned that lesson the hard way during 2002, when AU$200 was stolen from luggage left in the 'safe' store room of a Port Moresby hotel.

Most hotels have a metal safe and are happy to store your valuables while you're away on the track, including your passport, return plane tickets and mobile phone. Whether you store valuables at your hotel is entirely your decision. (See the sidebar 'Leaving valuables at your hotel' for some tips.)

Any paperwork that you take with you on the track tends to attract moisture, despite your best efforts.

Bring an A4-sized envelope from home (your tour company may also provide you with one). Clearly mark the envelope with

✔ Your name

✔ The name of your tour company

✔ The date of your return from the track

## Leaving valuables at your hotel

I've put together some tips for surrendering the envelope of your important valuables:

- When surrendering your envelope, request to speak to the shift supervisor. The shift supervisor normally has control of the keys to the safe. Clearly instruct her that you'd like this envelope stored in the hotel safe and that you'll return on the specified date to retrieve your belongings.

- Obtain the name of the person to whom you handed your valuables. By recording her name and the time at which you gave the hotel your valuables, you're creating

an audit trail. Making a record of the shift supervisor's name in her presence clearly indicates you're holding her responsible for the safe keeping of your valuables, ensuring diligence on her part.

- Try to refrain from handing over your envelope when the front desk is extremely busy because even the most conscientious worker may get distracted.

- Confirm that your envelope has gone into the safe and thank the shift supervisor for her assistance.

Place your valuables inside the envelope and seal it, preferably with sticky tape or metal staples. See the sidebar 'Leaving valuables at your hotel' for some extra tips.

I've always stored my passport, plane tickets and mobile phone in the envelope that's locked away in the hotel safe and have never experienced any problems. However, some tour companies recommend you take your passport on the trek. In the unlikely event you have to be evacuated to Australia, it'll be convenient to have your passport to hand.

## Celebrating before you start walking

Excessive use of alcohol or other drugs may impair your sensibilities. You're about to undertake one of the most physically challenging activities of your life, so don't dehydrate yourself by drinking too much alcohol before you even start your trek. You can frequent the airport bar during other holidays.

## Meeting the Locals

That you're 'not in Kansas anymore, Toto' is obvious from the time you step off the plane. Papua New Guinea may be a developing country, but remember that you're a guest in the country. Papuan way of life is different and you must behave in a manner that is both lawful and respectful. To act differently invites trouble.

By observing a few basic principles, you can keep yourself safe while in Port Moresby. The serious souvenir hunter can also take home mementoes of the trek. Follow these guidelines and you'll remember your holiday for all of the right reasons.

## No mobile phone, no meetings, no stress

You're entering the Kokoda Zone now: A country where mobile phones are used, but are a luxury for some. Where timetables are a 'guide only' and where the wrist watch is a fashion accessory.

The locals operate on 'PNG time'; in other words, it happens when it happens. You're likely to learn that on the first occasion you ask your porter 'How much longer until the next camp site?' So leave your modern-day life behind you and lighten up. Your hectic schedule and workplace will still be there when you get home, so just go with the flow.

You're on holidays (although this may not seem obvious as you slug up the steep slope to Brigade Hill and your lungs burst out of your chest), so relax and enjoy yourself.

## Smile and say hello

One of the first things you learn about the Papuans is that they're willing to accommodate you in almost every way. Often they go out of their way to make you happy.

### Showing respect

No act of respect is greater than acknowledging the invaluable contribution the local Papuan people made during World War II. Express your gratitude for the assistance offered to our soldiers by the local population. You're likely to find this to be a good icebreaker and instils in Papuans a sense of pride in their heritage. Chances are the person to whom you're speaking is the descendant of an indigenous veteran or Fuzzy Wuzzy Angel.

The poem 'The Fuzzy Wuzzy Angels' was written by Sapper Herbert Beros during the Kokoda campaign at a place called Dump 66. Kokoda expert Soc Kienzle (son of Captain Herbert 'Bert' Kienzle, the architect of Kokoda) indicates that the real location of Dump 66 is the campsite now known as Goodwater, on the southern end of the track, between Goldie River and Imita Ridge. Goodwater is the most appropriate spot to read 'The Fuzzy Wuzzy Angels'.

'The mother's reply' was written in response to Beros's poem and is equally as moving.

While most Papuans are very friendly, that isn't to say that you can trust everybody that you meet with your wallet! A small minority of Papuans will take advantage if they can.

Generally, the population is friendly and pleasant to deal with. If you show outward signs of friendliness with a smile and 'hello', more often than not your friendliness will be reciprocated.

The only way to enjoy the full cultural experience in Papua New Guinea is to meet and speak with the locals. Be on your guard, but also be aware that the only motivation for most Papuans to talk to you is to engage you in friendly conversation. Being nice costs you nothing and you may benefit from the social interaction.

# Being Sensible When You're Not On the Track

Common sense is the key here. If you wouldn't do something at home or in front of a police officer in Australia, don't do the same thing in Papua New Guinea.

## Watching out for hazards

Travelling with another person, regardless of your gender, is preferable, although if you're a female traveller, travelling with a companion is always wise.

So long as you're not alone and stay in the public eye, Port Moresby and Poppondetta are both quite safe during daylight hours.

The local pets, particularly the dogs, are a very sorry looking lot and generally roam free around the domestic areas. Reports of animal bites aren't common, but these unfortunate animals may carry diseases, so don't attempt to pat or interact with the local dogs.

---

## An innocent name for not so innocent people

'Rascals' is a term often used to describe a criminal element within Papua New Guinea. The name may suggest a bunch of naughty children, but don't be fooled. Like most criminals around the world, rascals often prey on what they consider to be an easy target.

## Going out alone and staying out late

You're reasonably safe during daylight hours, but going out alone at night is a completely different story.

Going alone to a bar or nightclub as part of your pre- or post-trek celebrations is taking an unnecessary risk, especially if you've had a few drinks.

Nothing is wrong with being a part of a large group and travelling by taxi to a restaurant for a 'last supper'. In fact, some trekking companies encourage this as a part of their closing ceremony.

For any venue, travelling to and from the hotel by taxi is prudent and also supports the local economy; however, make sure you travel as a pair (or more), use hotel-recommended taxi services and only use taxis in the daytime. Never be the 'last man standing'. If your group decides to leave and return to the hotel, join them.

If you've survived walking the track and want to celebrate, you're encouraged to conduct your festivities within the confines of your hotel. Most accommodation venues provide a decent restaurant and a well-stocked bar. If you restrict your late night to the hotel where you're staying, you've less chance of coming to harm or being noticed by the police.

## Shopping around

Despite the best attempts by some trekking companies to cater for your every whim, sometimes you need to visit a supermarket and grab that last-minute item to see you comfortably across the track. Every company has a duty of care they stringently enforce, which may restrict your ability to simply wander off by yourself. However, time schedules are usually the main thing prohibiting a casual visit to the central business district.

I've visited various shopping centres within Papua New Guinea, including centres in Port Moresby, and Popondetta to the north (which is your main source of supplies when visiting the beachhead battlefields of Buna, Gona and Sanananda). As long as you follow some basic rules of common sense and safety, visiting a shopping centre in Papua New Guinea doesn't have to be dangerous.

Wandering through the shops and around town during business hours is generally safe. However, travelling with others is generally safest.

## Handling cash in public

Wandering the back alleys of any city with your wallet open and money bulging out of your pockets is foolish. Common sense should prevail while shopping, regardless of which country you may be visiting.

Key points to remember while shopping or handling cash in New Guinea are

- Have only enough money in your wallet or purse to buy the item you need.
- Store the bulk of your money in a secure place on your person, such as a money belt worn underneath your outer clothing.
- If you need to access your money belt, notify your travelling companion and ask this person to be your 'eyes and ears' while your mind is occupied and your defences are down.
- Go to a quiet corner of the shop or complex to access the cash you've secreted away.
- Refrain from using your credit card if you possibly can to minimise the risk of credit card fraud.
- In parts of Port Moresby, modern and secure ATM banking services are available. If you need to use an ATM, try your hotel first. Most reputable hotels have a teller machine in the lobby.
- As a last resort, inform your tour manager or trek leader, who may be able to organise a representative of your trekking company to accompany you in a taxi while you visit a bank.

## Bringing home souvenirs

If you wish to take home a souvenir, make enquiries with your tour company in Australia prior to making a booking. Most Kokoda trekking itineraries are very tight and don't have time for souvenir hunting.

Peddlers of New Guinean art can sometimes be found vending on the side of the street near the hotels. Inform your tour manager or leader if you leave the hotel. Others in your group may wish to accompany you and the hotel security guard can keep a protective eye on you.

Purchase souvenirs after you return from the track. You don't want to carry the extra load over the track (and you can't expect your porter to carry unnecessary weight).

If you trek in a northerly direction and finish your journey at the beachheads, you can find ample opportunity to purchase arts and crafts on the coast. In particular, the local women in beautiful Sanananda Village are likely to gladly bring out their handmade crafts for you to peruse.

Be wary of any item made with sea shells because they may be difficult to get through Australian customs. Ensure the shells are thoroughly clean and devoid of sea life. Check all wood carvings and timber products for signs of borers and termites before you purchase them. You need to declare these items when you come back to Australia.

From an historical perspective, a great souvenir is a jungle cut walking stick. The famous movie footage and photographs taken by acclaimed war correspondent Damien Parer shows men of the 39th Battalion carrying their walking sticks. Without this walking aide, many soldiers would've found the going very tough indeed. Modern-day trekkers are no different. When your porter cuts a stick for you at the start of the trek, obtain a knife and peel the bark off as soon as possible. This allows time for the stick to dry out over the next week or so and allows easy examination for borers when you get to customs in Australia.

A walking stick can make a fine memento of your trip, especially when your porter is kind enough to engrave it for you. Some porters are expert wood carvers and can adorn your stick with the date of the trek and other inscriptions (it would be polite to offer your porter a small gratuity for any carvings — consult your trek leader with regards to an appropriate price).

Removing any relic from the track is illegal. Unexploded ordnance and bullets are unstable and pose a serious risk to life and limb, as well as to your aircraft and other passengers during your return flight. Leave relics in situ and allow other Kokoda trekkers to enjoy them. Large fines may apply for the attempted removal of any artefacts from Papua New Guinea.

# Travelling To and From the Track

When driving to or from Owers' Corner, travel before the afternoon rains. Most minibuses in Papua New Guinea aren't 4WD capable and the final stretch of road to Owers' Corner is unsealed dirt. This road can be very slippery when wet.

## Souvenir bullets

In the beachhead area, the local craftsmen have a penchant for creating necklaces with beads adorning a spent projectile head or bullet as a 'hanger' to the necklace. These bullets can be found in all calibres, both Allied (Australian .303 and American .30 calibre) and Japanese (6.5 and 7.7 calibre). The necklace makes a nice souvenir and I've always been fortunate to have mine passed by customs officials. Declare this item on your customs card when returning to Australia and don't risk a fine.

Safe travelling from your hotel to the start (or finish) of the track shouldn't be your problem. This is the responsibility of your trekking company and the reason you're paying them good money.

# Relating to the Papuans on the Track

Group porters accompany you across the track and you may also choose to hire a personal porter. Show respect for these porters and treat them as you'd expect to be treated.

## Meeting your porters

Your porters are men and women from the local villages who live on the track. From Buna in the north to small settlements near Owers' Corner, porters work within the tourism industry and your business is often their only source of employment.

At the start, your porters are complete strangers, but if you open yourself up to these remarkable people, by the end of your journey they may have become lifelong friends. Such a strong bond can develop between trekker and porter that a tear or two may be shed when you part company.

Forget the stories of rascals along the track (refer to the sidebar 'An innocent name for not so innocent people' to read about the rascals). You're safe when you're with your porters. Porters often immerse themselves in icy water on either side of a log crossing just to hold your hands to prevent you from getting your boots wet (see Figure 16-1 for an example of how porters can help you across rivers). They'll pull you up an incline and hold your hand on a treacherous descent. They'll even build you a stretcher or carry you on their back, should you injure yourself.

**Figure 16-1:**
Porters help
trekkers in
many ways,
including
assisting
them to
cross rivers.

The grandchildren of the Fuzzy Wuzzy Angels of 1942 are now guardian angels for the modern-day trekker. Sadly, you may never see these people again. But should you return to PNG, you're likely to be warmly remembered and greeted.

## Showing respect for your porters

We all like to be treated fairly and with respect. Life is also a lot more enjoyable when the people around us are happy and amiable. So if you 'do unto others', you're off to a good start. This is especially the case if you use the services of a porter.

Here are some tips on getting off to a good start with your porter:

✔ Remember that your porter is a person too. Like you, he has feelings. And despite the fact that he encounters tourists on a regular basis, your porter may still have a shy manner.

✔ Don't be offended by shyness. By nature, the local people are generally not boisterous or as outgoing in the same way as westerners, so you probably need to break the ice.

✔ Start with a smile. You get only one chance to make a first impression and a warm smile is a great way to start.

✔ Some porters understand English well, others don't, but they all have an overwhelming desire to make your life easier as you walk the track. Take every opportunity to talk to your porter. He'll certainly appreciate your friendliness.

✔ Remember that the porters get tired too. Your porter may have crossed the track a number of times and appear to be handling the hills with ease, but he too can get tired and run down. If you experience a tough day and feel completely worn out, chances are your porter is feeling much the same, he just won't show it.

✔ Share your treats. Sharing your sweets or other treats with your porter buys you a lot of respect. Other porters will also love you if you have enough to go around!

Often your porter does more than just carry your pack. He may offer his hand to support and pull you up a hill, or cut protruding foliage so it doesn't brush against your face, or forge ahead and prepare a rope at a creek crossing. The occasional soft drink or banana goes a long way to building a good relationship with your porter.

## Avoiding overloading your porters

The maximum carrying load for a porter is 20 kilograms. However, a porter's physical ability must be considered when carrying a load. The weight carried by a porter must be consistent with international standards set down for porters in the International Porter Protection Group.

If you hire the services of a personal porter, do your best to carry as much weight yourself as you possibly can. Refer to Chapter 15 for tips on what to pack.

## Displaying Appropriate Behaviour On the Track

As discussed in Chapter 14, your personal demeanour on the track is important for group morale. This also includes the manner in which you conduct yourself in times of hardship.

You also need to respect the cultural sensitivities of the people who live along the track. Here is a short guide on respectable behaviour on the track:

- ✔ Don't treat the locals simply as objects to be photographed. Always ask permission before snapping away with a camera.

- ✔ Refrain from using offensive language. The majority of villagers and porters practice Christian beliefs. Respect the culture of the local people and their values at all times.

- ✔ Remove rubbish responsibly. When deciding what food and snacks to bring with you for your trek, consider the packaging and how you intend to dispose of it. Rubbish disposal practices vary from one tour company to another, but remember to leave only footprints, take only photographs.

- ✔ Some trekkers may choose to carry a small hip flask or have a tot of rum. Use alcohol responsibly and discreetly.

- ✔ The track involves little 'public' land. The land is owned by someone or by a village. Use only campsites and fire places that have been agreed upon by the local landowner or authorised by the Kokoda Track Authority.

- ✔ Use designated toilet facilities where provided. If in the jungle, make all attempts to relieve yourself downhill from the track and away from any water courses. Cover any human waste with dirt or leaf litter.

- ✔ Use only biodegradable soap.

- ✔ Use only designated bathing areas; your intended site for a bath can be another man's supply of drinking water.

- ✔ Wear respectable and appropriate clothing.

Your tour company should supply a communal garbage bag for you to responsibly dispose of your rubbish each evening. During the day, store your refuse in your day pack until you get into camp.

# Part VI
# The Part of Tens

*Glenn Lumsden*

*'We were only outnumbered fifty to one,
so naturally the enemy didn't
stand a chance.'*

# In this part ...

This part is a chance for me to change your mind about some myths you may have heard about the fighting in Papua, and about walking the track today. Some of the myths on my list are more for amusement than vital to understand the fighting. But other myths may surprise you by challenging what you may have already heard about Kokoda. This part is also an opportunity to point out a few oddities (not all of them easily found) that you may see along the track, and to include some great stories I haven't been able to fit in elsewhere.

# Chapter 17

# Ten Legends about the Kokoda Trail

## In This Chapter

▶ Disposing of myths and legends

▶ Relaxing about creepy crawlies on the track

The two best known words in Australian military history are Gallipoli and Kokoda. They're both great stories, but elements of the stories have grown to legendary status. Often, when the evidence is checked, the legend is revealed. Here are ten of the legends of Kokoda.

## The Japanese Weren't Little

Australian veterans say they were told the Japanese were small, with buck teeth and poor eyesight, and that they had Coke bottle (thick) glasses.

The veteran's view, as expressed by one, was that when they met the Japanese in battle they found they had been misinformed: 'All we had heard about the Japs was they were little blokes with big glasses, which was completely wrong. They were big fellas, and we learned the hard way that we were up against an implacable enemy and if we wanted to exist we had to fight them'. No Australian who fought in Papua disputes that 'implacable' is a suitable description for the Japanese soldier.

No statistics exist about the relative dental condition of the armies, nor the proportion of men on either side with glasses — or monocles in the case of several fashionable captains in the Japanese 41st Regiment — but the Japanese were in fact, on average, smaller than the Australians.

The average Australian soldier in 1942 weighed 71 kilograms and at 170 centimetres was 10 centimetres taller than the average Japanese soldier, who weighed 58 kilograms.

As these numbers show, neither army was composed of heavy set men. Lean and muscly is a good description of both. It follows that the average Australian soldier should need more food than the average Japanese and this was so.

An Australian's daily ration pack, provided he was getting his full allowance (and many didn't), contained 15 per cent more kilojoules than those of the Japanese. (You can read about what the ration packs contained in Chapter 10.)

# The Australians Were Outnumbered

The Australian retreat from Kokoda to Ioribaiwa from July to September 1942 (described in Chapters 7 and 8) is usually described as a fight against overwhelming numbers of Japanese. The series of Australian defeats in this period is normally explained by the Australians fighting 'impossible odds'.

The Japanese supposedly outnumbered the Australians many times over, by from four to one to six to one. The Battle of Isurava, for instance, has been compared to Thermopylae, where a small force of Spartans and other Greeks was overwhelmed by a huge Persian army in 480BC.

The truth is the Australians were not significantly outnumbered in their retreat along the Kokoda Trail. The soldiers were convinced that they were, but in the jungle very few enemy were seen, even during battle, and believing the enemy were strong everywhere was a natural response. The Japanese suffered from the same misperception and also thought they were outnumbered.

The actual numbers of Japanese and Australians (with their Papuan allies) engaged in the fights along the Kokoda Trail during their retreat are described in Table 17-1.

| Table 17-1 | Number of troops on either side, listed by battle | |
|---|---|---|
| *Event* | *Number of Australian and Papuan troops* | *Number of Japanese troops* |
| Oivi | 150 | 230 |
| First Kokoda | 130 | 210 |
| Second Kokoda | 430 | 660 |
| Deniki | 470 | 450 |
| Isurava | About 2,300 | About 2,300 |
| First Eora | 700 | 1,300 |
| Efogi | 1,550 | 1,570 |
| Ioribaiwa | 2,900 | 1,700 |

# The Japanese Thought a Road Over the Mountains Existed

If you read a lot of the Japanese soldiers' diaries, you find some unusual ideas. For example, in early 1942 rumours went around the Japanese forces who were going to the south Pacific that

- ✔ Papua and New Guinea were states of Australia

- ✔ The Australians were considering making peace with Japan

- ✔ When they got to Queensland, the Japanese would find the best bananas in the world

They were only right about the last one — the first two weren't true.

But the biggest, and probably most disappointing, myth was about an apparent road to Port Moresby. When the Japanese Army arrived in Rabaul and heard they would be landing on the north coast of Papua and marching over a mountain range to Port Moresby, another rumour did the rounds: A road had been laid over the mountains and they could drive most of the way to their objective.

The problem with this myth is that those who believed it were privates and other low-ranking soldiers who had no access to the intelligence reports of their senior officers.

The Imperial Japanese Army and Navy had been sending spies to Papua for several years (refer to Chapter 5) and knew no road was available, only a rough track, over the Owen Stanley Range. The reports written by these spies, all of whom were officers of the army or the navy, and one of whom became the senior intelligence officer of the force that marched along the track, listed all roads in Papua that could be driven on.

The senior officers who planned the operation with these reports had no doubts that the roads about Buna, Milne Bay and Port Moresby were short and didn't connect any one of the three places with the others. But they didn't tell the lower ranks, who were surprised when they discovered that if they wanted to get to Port Moresby they would have to walk the whole way.

# The Australians Inflicted Huge Casualties on the Japanese

Many descriptions of the battles along the Kokoda Trail say something like this: 'The Japanese came forward in waves and as each was cut down by Australian fire another wave clambered over the bodies of their dead and pressed on'. If this description was accurate, the Australians must have killed enormous numbers of the enemy at Kokoda, Isurava, Eora, Efogi and Ioribaiwa.

In fact, they didn't. In 1942, the Japanese rarely made the mass attack called the 'banzai charge' (they grew fonder of it later in the war) and casualty claims from both sides made at the time are extremely dubious. The Australians claimed to have killed 500 Japanese at Isurava, but the actual number was one quarter of that. The Japanese claimed to have killed 930 Australians in the same battle, but the actual number was 100.

The problem was that at the time casualty claims could only be estimates. As the Australians retreated from Isurava, they had no way of knowing how many Japanese they'd killed. The Japanese held the field and a week later one of their officers was given the job of making an accurate count of Australian dead by finding the bodies. He reported he had found 105, not far from the correct number.

Extreme claims make better reading and, unfortunately, records often aren't checked after the war to establish correct figures. A good example of this overclaiming comes from the day after the Battle of Ioribaiwa, 17 September 1942. There, in a famous ambush on the main Ioribaiwa to Imita track, C Company of the Australian 2/33rd Battalion led a large

Japanese patrol into a trap. A few Australians showed themselves and the Japanese advanced on them until they were suddenly fired on from three sides. The Australians fired thousands of rounds, claimed to have killed 50 and presumably wounded many more, though another, even more dramatic version states that no Japanese survived. Then the Australians retreated to Imita Ridge so were unable to check how many enemy they'd killed. The story of this brilliantly successful ambush, in which the Australians took no losses and slaughtered the Japanese patrol, has become a minor classic of Kokoda and the site is still visited today.

Even on the face of it, the number 50 dead seems high, because in the prior three-day battle on Ioribaiwa Ridge, the Japanese had captured the ridge from the Australians at a cost of only 40 killed. In fact, Japanese records show that in the famous ambush their losses were only two wounded, one of whom later died. The ambush was the only fighting of the day and the records of the 3/144 Battalion, from which the Japanese came, show only these casualties. The commander of the ambushed patrol, Lieutenant Okabayashi Shintaro, survived the war and wrote an account of it.

On 17 September, Okabayashi reported his patrol was advancing down the main track when they saw a few enemy and chased them, but they were then fired on 'from all sides'. Okabayashi then withdrew with two men wounded, one of whom died soon after.

# The Australians' Fighting Retreat Saved Port Moresby

It appeared to the Australians fighting along the track that their dogged retreat slowed and eventually halted the Japanese advance to Port Moresby. In fact, the Japanese advance slowed and stopped because the Japanese commanders changed their minds.

The Japanese landed at Buna with the intent of taking Port Moresby, but the American attack on the Japanese-held Guadalcanal Island prompted the Japanese commanders to reconsider their position. They concluded, just before the Battle of Isurava was fought in late August 1942, that they didn't have the resources for a total effort on both fronts at the same time. They had to decide if they would capture Port Moresby first, and leave Guadalcanal until later, or the other way around.

Imperial Headquarters in Tokyo considered the dilemma for a few days before ordering Hyakutake, the general in Rabaul who commanded Japanese land forces in the south Pacific, to capture Guadalcanal first. He told his subordinate, General Horii, commander of the Nankai Shitai, that the new troops arriving in the region wouldn't join Horii in Papua, but would be used at Guadalcanal instead. The Port Moresby operation, Horii was informed, would be postponed. Meanwhile, Horii was permitted to send a smaller force along the track to advance to secure a forward position from which the attack on Port Moresby would be launched as soon as the Guadalcanal problem was solved.

As things turned out, the Japanese kept losing battles on Guadalcanal and in the surrounding sea, and never did solve 'the Guadalcanal problem'. Consequently, Horii wasn't given the reinforcements he needed, nor permission to go for Port Moresby. Of course, none of the Australians present knew this at the time. But with a bit of hindsight, we can see that the Australians didn't save Port Moresby; rather, the Japanese on the track had called off their plan to capture the town.

Refer to Chapter 5 for more about Guadalcanal.

# General Horii's White Horse

The legend goes that General Horii had a white horse and that he rode it up the track, at least as far as Efogi, where the horse died. (Its carcass was pointed out by locals to the Australians as they advanced in October 1942.) A similar story says that Horii's white stallion died on Ioribaiwa Ridge, the furthest point of the Japanese advance, and another version has General Horii's horse's bones found by the Kumusi River east of Kokoda. (Apparently, the horse drowned, along with General Horii, when the two tried to cross the Kumusi River after the Japanese defeat at Oivi–Gorari in November.)

The bones of Horii's horse must have possessed some mystical quality, like the bones of Christopher Columbus, which I saw in a glass case in a cathedral in the Dominican Republic in 1984. I was taken aback when a month later I visited a church in Seville in Spain and Columbus's bones were again featured, also in a glass case with a large sign.

One part of the legend about Horii's horse is entirely true. Horii definitely had a horse, a pure white stallion. No-one now knows what its name was. Unfortunately for the legend, in 1942 a white stallion was the most common type of horse in the Imperial Japanese Army, from the rank of major and above. Colonel Yokoyama, who served under Horii, had one, as did Colonel Tsukamoto. Even Major Horie, commander of the Stanley Detachment, had a white stallion; a Japanese infantryman noted in his diary that while resting at Kokoda he saw Horie galloping through in October on his way to Buna. About 20 white stallions were landed at Buna by the Japanese Army. When the Japanese advance took them beyond Kokoda to the foot of the Owen Stanleys, officers' horses were stabled there in the care of a veterinary unit. The 200 or so horses that went as far into the mountains as Ioribaiwa were small, sturdy ponies that carried supplies and weapons. The bones found at Efogi were probably one of these.

When the Japanese retreated, the officers' horses were sent to Buna where some perished and some were captured by the Australians and Americans when they captured the Japanese base in Buna in January 1943. Horii's stallion was probably there, but what happened to the horse isn't known for certain.

# United States Troops Were No Good at Buna

US troops at the Battle of Buna–Gona are often said not to have been very good fighters, certainly not as good as the Australians. After their first failed attacks in November 1942, the American soldiers were described as tired and listless, with low morale. MacArthur discussed with Blamey the necessity to send reinforcements and proposed sending more Americans, 41st Division, then in Australia. Blamey replied that he would prefer to send more Australians, because at least he knew that they would fight.

The course of the battle seemed to bear out Blamey's criticism. Of the two fortified areas on the northern and southern flanks of the Japanese position, Gona and Buna, the Australians took Gona first in early December. Buna, where the Americans were, fell only in early January 1943 after the Australian 18th Brigade was brought forward to assist the Americans. In a few days, the Australians took positions that the Japanese had held against the Americans for six weeks.

However, all this is a bit deceptive. The Australians on the Gona front were against 900 second-rate Japanese troops, mostly rear area non-combat troops, many of whom were ill from the effects of having been in Papua for five months. At Buna the Americans faced a much larger Japanese force, over half of which were fresh troops recently landed. The Japanese also valued their position at Buna more than Gona, so had placed the majority of their artillery there. Moreover, when the Australian 18th Brigade arrived it was accompanied by tanks, which the Americans didn't have, and tanks proved to be the decisive weapon in breaking open the Japanese defences. In any case, comparing the men of the American 32nd Division to the Australian 18th Brigade is unfair. The former were National Guard, had no experience of war and were, until recently, part-time soldiers comparable to the Australian militia. The Australian 18th Brigade, in contrast, was a battle-hardened, successful AIF formation.

As with many myths, a grain of truth can be found in this one. The Americans didn't do well at Buna, but when all the factors are considered their task was a harder one than that of the Australians at Gona, and an Australian militia division would probably have done no better had it attacked Buna. While the Australian and American senior officers both were disappointed by the performance of the 32nd Division, they never expected that the division could behave as well as an equivalent AIF formation.

# The Japanese at Buna Should've Been Left to Starve

Thousands of Australians and Americans were killed or wounded eliminating the Japanese stronghold of Buna. After the war, some historians argued this was a mistake and instead the Japanese at Buna should've been left to 'wither on the vine'. *Wither on the vine* refers to a strategy that would save lives. Attacking and destroying isolated Japanese forces wasn't necessary; rather, the Japanese force should be cordoned off in the area they held and left there. Denied supply from their own rear areas, the Japanese would slowly wither away, as does the fruit of the vine if denied water.

This view is argued from hindsight and fails to understand the importance of Buna to the Allies. Now that we know the outcome of the war, we can see that leaving the Japanese in Buna to starve might've been a possibility in late 1942 and would've saved Allied lives. But no-one in 1942 knew what the outcome of the war would be. The Allied commanders who decided the strategy weren't even confident they would win the war. What the Allied commanders did know in late 1942 was that leaving Buna alone was too risky and they needed Buna for their own future advance towards Lae and Rabaul. The following factors were behind this thinking:

✔ The Battle of Guadalcanal was still undecided. The Japanese might possibly win, in which case they would send thousands more troops to Buna and try to break out of their base there.

✔ The Japanese fleet was still strong and easily capable of protecting the transport ships taking reinforcements to Buna, or even staging a new invasion of Papua elsewhere. In December 1942, Blamey still insisted on keeping a strong garrison at Milne Bay because he believed the Japanese still had the capacity to make another attempt to capture it.

✔ The plains south-west of Buna were one of the few places on the north coast of Papua suitable for a large airfield complex, which the Allies needed to support their advance north in 1943 (refer to Chapter 5).

Now we know that the Japanese lost at Guadalcanal and their fleet never again won an important naval battle, so to leave the Japanese alone at Buna would've been a possible alternative strategy. But, without an Allied air base at Buna, the advance north in 1943 would've been weakened, in turn costing more lives, possibly more than would've been saved had the 'wither on the vine' strategy been adopted at Buna.

No easy solutions are usually available to the problems faced by generals in war. Looking back with hindsight and saying what they should've done, however, is easy, if unfair.

# The Papuans Willingly Fought with the Australians

The story of the Fuzzy Wuzzy Angels is well known. These young Papuan men carried wounded Australian soldiers on stretchers over the track to hospitals, saving many Australian lives.

This is quite true, but only a small number were volunteers. Most Papuans were conscripted. From mid 1942, the Australian administration was empowered to conscript local labour for up to three years at a time. More than 10,000 Papuans were conscripted under this law in 1942. Papuans who deserted or didn't work to the Australians' satisfaction were faced with beatings, fines or imprisonment.

Not all the Papuans and New Guineans fought on the Australian side. When the Japanese landed at Buna, they brought along more than 2,000 men from New Britain who, with some pressure applied, had signed on to carry supplies for the Japanese in Papua. The Orokaiva people of the Buna region also joined the Japanese, some as supply carriers and some as armed scouts. Perhaps 200 to 300 served in the latter capacity. Orokaiva scouts may have captured Captain Sam Templeton at Oivi in July of 1942 and handed him over to the Japanese. (Chapter 7 has more about the fate of Templeton.)

The Papuans had no special reason to favour either side beyond the normal considerations of inter-tribal politics. A warlike people, the Papuans had had frequent clashes with the Australian administrators of Papua. In the 1920s and 1930s, white miners were sometimes murdered and Australian officered police expeditions would extract revenge by killing dozens of people from the offending tribe. The tribal opponent of those who killed the miners would co-operate with the Australian authorities if they saw an advantage in doing so.

The arrival of the Japanese was, from the Papuan perspective, the intrusion of another powerful group into the ever-changing alliances between tribes. At first, the Japanese looked like being victorious so Papuans who found themselves in a Japanese-occupied area were naturally cooperative and threw in their lot with the Japanese.

By November 1942, the Australians were in the ascendancy and Papuans switched sides if it was possible. The carriers from New Britain deserted the Japanese if they could and at least 40 Orokaiva were killed by the Japanese, mostly for attempting to desert. When the Australians recovered the Orokaiva homeland, they also hanged a number of Orokaiva who, while working for the Japanese, had killed Australian civilians or shot down aircrew.

So the Papuans did fight with the Australians but, for the most part, their fighting was done unwillingly. The majority of Papuans sided with the Australians and the Americans, but that was because they believed the Allies would win the war.

# Leeches, Crocs, Snakes and Spiders

Many trekkers believe they're going to be inundated with a multitude of unpleasant creatures, great and small, along the track. But Gary Traynor, who is a guide for trekkers, reports that's not really so:

> Before walking the Kokoda Trail, my imagination ran wild. I had this misconception that I was going to be attacked from all angles by blood-sucking leeches, dodging snakes and surprised by all manner of spiders. Not to mention the occasional croc at every deep river crossing.
>
> The reality was the complete opposite. Not that I am complaining! While I have only completed ten crossings of the track, my dates of travel have varied from April to October and every month in between. Call me lucky, but I have probably only seen about three leeches during those treks. I have never had to pick a leech from myself; nor have any of my trekkers. They are hardly noticeable at all.

*As for the snakes, I could count the number I've seen on one hand. With a Papuan guide armed with a menacing 'bush knife' at the front of our group, any snake is usually sushi by the time our trekkers cross the hapless reptile's path. (However, we did see a python once and he was a monster! But he was coiled up and sleeping in a tree which was well off the track, so he was certainly not interested in us.)*

*In New Guinea, you do come across some huge spider webs, but we are never in a place long enough to be bothered by spiders, who might crawl into your tent if you left it open for several days.*

*The Papua New Guinea croc is generally found in freshwater marshes, mainly in the interior portion of the island and is generally only seen in the river system if it's normal habitat becomes too dry. The croc is a nocturnal feeder and I have never seen one in any of the rivers or creeks. Having spent a fair bit of time at Sanananda, the locals tell me that there are saltwater crocs about, but again I have never seen one. The villagers of Sanananda practically live in the ocean and they also tell me that no person has ever been taken by a shark or a croc while swimming. And that is just the way that we trek guides like it.*

# Chapter 18

# Ten Things to Look For On the Kokoda Trail

*H*ere are ten locations that should be listed on your Kokoda itinerary. Many are off the beaten track, but are well worth the effort and are fundamental parts of the Kokoda story. Don't take for granted that your tour company visits each and every location because visiting these places of interest adds extra time to your trek, so question your prospective tour company before you make a booking.

## Australian 25-Pounder Field Gun, Owers' Corner

One of the first things you notice when you arrive at Owers' Corner is the presence of an Australian 25-pounder field gun. This isn't one of the original artillery pieces used at Owers' Corner, but is a good example of the type. The only difference between this artillery piece and the three guns hauled to Owers' Corner in mid September 1942 is that the large protective metal shield had been removed from the 1942 guns. This made them slightly lighter and only marginally easier to manhandle to Owers' Corner.

Two guns of the 53rd Battery, 14th Field Regiment RAA (Royal Australian Artillery) fired their first shots in the Kokoda campaign at exactly 1500 hours on 21 September 1942. Spotters deployed on Imita Ridge signalled the artillerymen their target distance. The first few rounds fired were range-finding smoke markers. The shells took approximately 25 seconds to fly the 10 kilometres to their intended targets on Ioribaiwa Ridge; over the next few days, 700 high-explosive rounds would be fired on the Japanese positions.

One story to emerge from this incident drew upon the comments of a Western Australian soldier who served with the 2/16th Infantry Battalion. Corporal Alan Haddy would often taunt the Japanese with the call 'mix that with your rice, you bastards' as he launched a grenade in their general direction. This verbal tirade obviously became legend within 2/16th circles; when the Western Australians were dug in on Imita Ridge and they heard this artillery sail over their heads for the first time in the campaign, one wag recited the 'Alan Haddy taunt', which is said to have brought roars of laughter from all within earshot.

As these two guns engaged targets on Ioribaiwa, the third gun was laboriously manhandled across the Goldie River and to the vicinity of Uberi. However, the Japanese withdrew before this piece could be brought to bear upon the enemy and the gun didn't fire any rounds in this part of the campaign.

# The Golden Stairs

The Golden Stairs refers to a series of steps cut into the side of a steep incline, with bush timber as a tread and reinforced with stakes to hold each log in place. The steps were treacherous and often included small pools of water and mud.

Much conjecture and debate has revolved around the location of the Golden Stairs. Based on photographs held by the Australian War Memorial, personal diaries and unit records, it can be established that stairs had been constructed on at least three different points at the southern end of the Kokoda Trail. Subsequently, the name 'Golden Stairs' could've been applied to any or all of these features. Common sense suggests the first set of stairs to be built on the track was on the southern slope of Imita Ridge, because this was the first major incline to be encountered by the engineers as they advanced from Owers' Corner.

When the 39th Battalion first started off along the track on 7 July, no stairs existed at all. Wartime journalist Osmar White gives a good insight into this on page 187 of his book *Green Armour*, where he states that it took 17 hours for the battalion to travel just 600 yards up one clay slope. Doctor Geoffrey Vernon set out along the track on 20 July 1942 in order to catch up with the forward elements of the 39th Battalion. He wrote an account that related how, on the following day, his party negotiated a well-stepped path up the southern slope of Imita. This stepped path ceased at the gap beyond Uberi; however, he came across some diggers who were cutting steps into a particularly steep descent, to make it easier for the carriers. This descent appears to be the northern slope of Imita Ridge. Vernon's account makes it clear that more than one set of stairs was built on the Kokoda Trail.

Stepping out along the track himself around 20 August 1942, Osmar White wrote that after leaving Uberi, the track slanted up a razorback into which 1,000 steps had been cut by engineers. White also reported that 4,000 steps had been cut into the 2,500-foot (762-metre) ridge that led up to Ioribaiwa Village. The passage of time has erased any positive evidence of the stairs built by the engineers during 1942.

One short section of the modern track to Ioribaiwa does resemble a common photo of the Golden Stairs credited to Colonel A F Hobson of HQ 7th Division. By carrying a copy of this image, trekkers who still have the energy may wish to keep an eye out for this razorback as they slug it out during the steep climb. You can see the photo by visiting this page of the Australian War Memorial website: `http://cas.awm.gov.au/item/P02423.009`

# Japanese Trenches, Above Ofi Creek

A Japanese trench system lies slightly off the track, on the edge of a ridge to the northern side of Ofi Creek. As you walk towards Kokoda from the direction of Owers' Corner, the trench is on the right side of the track and is easily overlooked. This excavation consists of a main trench that acted as a communication trench connecting a series of small posts. This position was almost certainly developed between 11 and 16 September 1942 to control Japanese artillery positions, possibly as an observation and command post for directing fire towards the Australian positions, which at that time were dug in on Ioribaiwa.

The Japanese had two types of artillery deployed in or near the trench system on Ioribaiwa Ridge. The shell casings of expended artillery rounds can still be found in the area.

# Ammunition Dump, Myola 1

The ammunition dump situated adjacent to Myola 1 is the best preserved Australian ammunition dump on the track. As you approach Myola 1, the dump is on a side track to the left and is indicated by a sign. The land is privately owned and a small tariff is paid to the land owner.

Myola 1 was opened as a supply dump by Captain Herbert 'Bert' Kienzle, who located this feature on 3 August 1942 when a dropping zone and supply area was desperately needed. The area consists of a large, undulating, grassy plain with patches of swampy ground. Movie footage filmed by wartime cinematographer Damien Parer shows Douglas DC3 aircraft (colloquially known as the biscuit bombers) dropping food and equipment to the waiting troops. However, advancing Japanese forced Myola 1 to be abandoned on 4 September 1942. Orders were given to the troops to consume as much food as possible and destroy the rest to deprive the enemy of any spoils. Troops exchanged torn and muddied uniforms for fresh clothing, and carried whatever ammunition they could.

A large amount of *ordnance* (weaponry) was buried during the evacuation, resulting in this dump. The predominant military hardware consists of Australian 2-inch and 3-inch mortar rounds. A lot of No. 36M hand grenades were also buried, all of which are still live.

Don't handle any live ordnance because unexploded rounds may be unstable.

Other odds and ends of military hardware can be found littering the area, and a lot still lies hidden. One curiosity is the large amount of heel plates that can be found. The boots worn by Australian troops during World War II had a small, metal horseshoe-shaped plate on the heel to prevent excessive wear. From the amount of rusty heel plates, clearly a large stock of boots was once in this area.

# Crashed P-40 fighter, Myola 2

Perhaps the best aircraft crash site on the track, in terms of recognisable aircraft wreckage, is the US Army P-40 Warhawk fighter near Myola 2. Elements of the American 5th Army Air Force engaged Japanese forces in the Myola area from 6 September to 4 October 1942. Up to six P-40 fighters were lost in this general area.

The aircraft crash near Myola 2 may be the aircraft piloted by First Lieutenant (later Captain) Ralph L Wire of the 9th Fighter Squadron, 49th Fighter Group. This fighter squadron was operating from Port Moresby. Lieutenant Wire is credited with three confirmed victories to his tally; however, his aircraft didn't crash as a result of battle damage.

The aircraft is believed to have crashed on 22 November 1942 because of mechanical failure or fuel starvation. The pilot parachuted to safety and made his way back to friendly lines, arriving at Kokoda station, which by then had been in Australian hands for nearly three weeks.

The Curtiss P-40 Warhawk (called the Kittyhawk in Australian service) was a single seat, all metal fighter and was in front-line service in various models during the Pacific war. The Curtiss P-40 Warhawk was the third-most produced American fighter after the P-51 Mustang and the P-47 Thunderbolt.

Bits and pieces of wreckage have been gathered by the local people and deposited in one pile, but many parts of the aircraft are recognisable. The engine and both wings are present and the .50-calibre machine guns are clearly visible. The under surface of one wing bears the word 'Army', signifying that the P-40 was of US Army Air Force stock. Of particular interest is the heavy steel armour plating that was built in behind the cockpit and protected the pilot when being fired upon from the rear. This aircraft wreck is out of the way, but well worth the time and effort required to view it.

# Stakes In the Ground, Brigade Hill and Templeton's Crossing

At two locations on the track, you may see a curious arrangement of stakes in the ground. These symbolise the location of 1942 gravesites. One such location is on the knoll of Brigade Hill (on the bare grassed section adjacent to the memorial) and the other is at Templeton's Crossing on the Kagi side of Eora Creek (see Figure 18-1).

Cut timber in New Guinea rots and the stakes may not be there. However, the local landowners often replace these markers out of respect for the people once buried there. In the case of Templeton's Crossing, the more cynical may perceive this as a way of enticing the curious trekker to view the cemetery and collection of relics, so the landowner earns a gratuity.

**Figure 18-1:**
Stakes in
the ground,
Templeton's
Crossing.

No formal graves are on the track. A wartime cemetery was established at Bomana during the campaign and the Commonwealth War Graves Commission is now tasked with its maintenance (refer to Chapter 2 for information about this organisation).

However, human remains are buried along the track. All known wartime graves were exhumed and bones re-interred at Bomana, but whenever a body was exhumed, not all of the bones may have been removed and reburied at Bomana. Some believe that only the major bones, such as the skull and thigh bones, were removed. Finding documentation that details the percentage of remains of each individual re-interred is virtually impossible. The important thing is each and every person who made the supreme sacrifice is commemorated by either a headstone or their name recorded on the memorial to the missing.

# Bede Tongs's Plaque, Eora Creek

A number of commemorative plaques are placed along the track, but one that deserves particular mention is the bronze panel dedicated to the 3rd Infantry Battalion, Australian Military Force.

The 3rd Battalion, colloquially known as the 3rd Militia Battalion, was the longest continuously serving unit on the track, passing through Owers' Corner on 5 September 1942 and in action until relieved at Gona on 4 December, a period of nearly three months.

Situated on the western side of Eora Creek (at the location probably incorrectly called Eora Creek Village), the plaque is to the south-west of the Japanese mountain gun position. This panel also has the distinction of being the only plaque laid by a veteran of the Kokoda campaign, Bede Tongs, because he retraced his own footsteps across the track. Bede was one day short of his fifty-ninth birthday when he laid the plaque at Eora Creek on 26 June 1980. Bede was the subject of the documentary film produced for Peter Luck's *The Australians* as he walked across the track. At the time of this dedication in 1980, the 3rd Battalion Commemorative panel was the only plaque between Owers' Corner and Kokoda Plateau.

Bede trekked the track again in 1983 with his son and grandson, perhaps the only time that three generations of the same family have made the crossing. With the exception of Kokoda legend Bert Kienzle, who resided in New Guinea before and after World War II, Bede Tongs may hold the record for the number of postwar crossings by any Kokoda veteran. In 1983, Bede and his son carried cement across the track, to reinforce the plaque that had originally been glued to the rock.

# Japanese Mountain Gun Position, Eora Creek

The battle for Eora Creek began on 22 October 1942 (refer to Chapter 11) and was the largest battle on the Australian advance back to Kokoda station. A short climb from the current Eora Creek Crossing is an area known as the Japanese Mountain Gun position.

Located on the edge of a steep hill, why the Japanese chose this position to site the Model 92 and Model 94 guns is clear. One Japanese gun pit gives a commanding view of the small plateau on the opposite side of Eora Creek, where the Australians had a number of huts for a supply and rest area in August 1942 (the area that's often mistakenly referred to as Eora Creek Village). This Japanese position also provided the only water supply on the hill. The Japanese didn't occupy the higher ground near their artillery position, and so it was from there that the Australians launched a flanking attack that took the position in late October 1942.

Of interest in this area is a Japanese tunnel and a sizeable ordnance dump, containing a number of discharged Model 92 casings and a number of Model 94 rounds that are still live. Other items, such as rusty Japanese helmets, Australian grenades and a Japanese Type 89 mortar (incorrectly called a 'knee mortar') are also present.

This land is privately owned and a small tariff applies to view the site.

# Con's Rock, Isurava Rest House

Not all diggers who served on the track were Australian born and bred.

Greek-born Constantine Vafiopulous served as a medical orderly with the 2/14th Infantry Battalion during World War II. Later known as Con Vapp, he saw service in Syria and was seriously wounded during this fierce campaign. Captured by Sengalese troops fighting for the Vichy French, Con was exchanged in a prisoner swap and returned to Australia.

Shipped to New Guinea in 1942, Con Vapp took part in fighting along the track. On or around 30 August 1942, during the evacuation from the Isurava Rest House position, this medical orderly, with only basic training, performed an emergency amputation on an Australian soldier.

This operation is reported to have been performed on a flat-topped rock just south of the rest house (the rock was also known as 'Surgeon's Rock'). The shape of the rock is unmistakable and the flat surface can easily be compared to that of an operating table. The patient's name, the limb amputated and whether he survived the operation isn't known. Imagining what was going through Con's mind as he performed such an operation with the basic, inadequate tools at hand isn't difficult, however.

The surgical procedure was merely the start of the ordeal suffered by the injured soldier. About 70 kilometres of torturous track was ahead of him before he received treatment in a hospital.

Con returned to this location in 2002 and indicated that, to the best of his memory, this rock was the location where the emergency amputation was performed. However, Con has since passed away and little else is known about that moment in time. So spare a thought for Constantine Vafiopulous (and the soldier he operated on) as you pass this flat-topped rock.

# Crashed Japanese Plane, Isurava

Between modern-day Isurava Village and the 1942 battle site lies the wreckage of a Japanese aircraft.

The aircraft was originally believed to be an Aichi D3A dive bomber, but aircraft pieces indicate that the aircraft was manufactured by Mitsubishi. One panel bears the number '5194', which is a number pertaining to Mitsubishi — although this doesn't provide conclusive proof of the aircraft type. The wreckage may be that of a Mitsubishi Ki-30 light bomber or a Mitsubishi Ki-51, both of which have a fixed undercarriage. However, the wreckage bears many features of a G4M1 Betty, a much larger, twin engine bomber.

This wreck above Isurava is of a heavy structure and includes multiple bomb racks (the Betty had two lines of racks in the bomb bays). The aircraft appears to have protected internal fuel tanks and, judging by the size of the wing tip and Hinomaru (the round red symbol of the Japan, as found on the national flag), the wreckage may be that of a multi-engine plane. If this is true, the wreck isn't complete and the remainder of the aircraft is yet to be found. At least six G4M1 aircraft were lost over the Owen Stanley Range as the Japanese made attacks upon Port Moresby.

A Type 92 machine gun, on display at the Alola museum, is almost certainly from this crash site. The machine gun barrel is bent, consistent with having been involved in an aircraft crash. All three Mitsubishi aircraft mentioned carried Type 92 machine guns as part of their defensive armament.

Found near the top of a very steep incline on the high side of the track, the climb up to the crash site is very tiring. Allow 20 to 60 minutes to climb to this location, depending on your fitness and energy levels. The difficulty of the climb explains why very few Kokoda trekkers make the effort.

# Chapter 19

# Ten Veteran Stories

## In This Chapter

▶ Recording veteran interviews

▶ Ambushing the enemy

▶ Flying raids in the south-west Pacific

▶ Returning to Japan

In 1993, I recorded my first veteran interview, with Howard Pope from Adelaide. He was the last surviving World War I veteran of the South Australian 27th Infantry Battalion. The interview was so good I went back the next day to record more of what Howard had to say. But before I could transcribe the interview I lost the tape recording. I'm still irritated about that, but I learned a lesson and have taken much better care of the veteran interviews I've done since. Excerpts from a lot of these interviews are in earlier chapters, but I have other interviews that relate to the war in Papua that it seems a pity to leave out, so I've placed them in this chapter. The interviews have been edited for clarity.

Think of this chapter as one long In Their Own Words paragraph. Everything below is the words of these veterans and their families, except the explanatory text in italics at the start of the sections.

## Mal Bishop

*When the Japanese landed in Papua, Kanga Force was cut off in the Territory of New Guinea, almost 200 kilometres north of Kokoda. They had an important influence on the Papuan campaign because documents Kanga Force captured during a June 1942 raid on Salamaua indicated that the Japanese might be about to land at Buna. Mal Bishop, then a lieutenant, was on the raid.*

First we went to a forward base at Mubo, which was a few hours' walk out of Salamaua. Then we went in by dark down to Salamaua. We had three main positions to attack and we had the support of one mortar with 100 bombs, which were carried for us by the natives. There was the group I was with at Kela Point, there was another group at Kela and another group over the other side of the airstrip.

On the waterfront at my spot at Kela Point, there was a line of Chinese trade stores and these were built on concrete slabs with the entrances from the roadway through double doors. We had to decide whether to go in through the back or through the front. The other chap and I went to try to find this track to get in around the back of these Chinese stores and we found there were so many empty tins, bottles and rubbish in the sand that we would never have got there without making a hell of a lot of noise. So we decided to go over the road to the sea wall to face these trade stores from the front. Well, we did that, we were all ready, and in front of the building there were some seats. It was just cracking on dawn and you could see them, there were some Japanese soldiers there and they are having a rare old time with a couple of marys [indigenous women]. The marys were giggling and carrying on, the soldiers were carrying on.

So we were in position a few minutes, then suddenly around Kela things started, that was the signal. Either a certain time or the first shot. So we were off across the road and into these blokes. Well, looking back, it was quite funny to see all these Japanese soldiers trying to get through the front door of the building. The doors opened outwards and they were fighting each other to get in, about six of them. I had a sticky bomb with hessian around two slabs of one pound each of TNT explosive. Sticking out was the handle, so you pulled the wire on the thing and held it in your hand like an ordinary grenade and when you threw it, it went off in seven seconds.

I galloped across the track, about 20 yards to the hut, I must have been yelling like a banshee, firing a pistol and I had the bomb in my right hand. This is where sudden thoughts strike you. The Japanese are fighting one another to get through this door and I am shooting with this pistol. They got through the door and slammed it and I went to throw the bomb. And I thought, by God, have I pulled the pin? So I'm trying to find out and I've got this pistol in my hand. So I threw the pistol away so I could use two hands. And the pistol was on a lanyard round my neck and it flew round and hit me hard in the backside. I threw the bomb and turned to get back down to cover because these things have got a mighty explosion. As I started to turn away one of the Japs must have shot from inside and he got me in the back and down I went. I got up again as the bomb went off inside the building, the roof went up and the walls went outward and down it came. I staggered across the road and got down behind the seawall and a native who'd been with me all the time was holding my Tommy gun. He said 'Master quick, killim Japan, killim Japan' and shoved this Tommy gun at me. So I started to fire and then we charged across, and the Japs were yelling and screaming and running, so we got stuck in to them. By that time I'm bleeding fairly heavily. Then we got the order to withdraw.

I walked for a while then found I couldn't walk, so they carried me. They carried me back to Mubo that night. We had a doctor there and he operated on me in a native hut. Then they took me back to Wau and I spent six weeks there. So that was the raid.

# Ryozo Kawate

I was ordered to go back along a track and get some food from an enemy dump we had captured. One of the NCOs, a man from Fukuyama City, told me to bring a pistol, not my rifle because then I could carry more food back to my company. When we were walking to the food depot, we were suddenly shot at from high up a slope. I told my friend, 'Don't use a grenade. It might fall back down on us. I will go up and shoot him'. I first went down and around about 50 metres to one side and then started climbing up the hill behind him. On top of the hill, I could see the Australian soldier's head. I thought, 'OK, I can get him'. And I started approaching him very quietly. It took a while. When I came to within 15 metres of the enemy soldier, I rested my pistol on a branch and pulled the trigger. It is easy to tell the difference when the target gets shot or not. I was often hunting wild birds with air rifles back home in the country, and I could tell that the bullet hit the target.

My friend, who had approached the Australian from the other side, called my name and asked me, 'Did you get him?' I replied, 'Yeah, I think so'. I ran to the enemy and my friend came as well. The white man, who looked about 28 or 29, was still alive, blinking his eyes. I saw his helmet, and I saw that his submachine gun was still attached to him by a sling. So, I shot him once more to let him die. Then, we checked his bag and looked for food, but nothing was in there, probably because the Australians must have been under the same severe conditions as us. We found no food, but we found a photo of his family. Must have been his wife and kids. Both of us saw it together and we kept silent for a while. Then, we started saying to each other, 'We had nothing to do with this man. Why did we have to kill him?' We both had family photos with us, too, and we could understand how the Australian soldier was thinking about his family. Perhaps he was conscripted, too, like us, and was always thinking about his family.

# Matt Power

On the track, I was a sergeant in C Company 2/14th Battalion. We were brought hurriedly down to Brisbane and sailed to the north, not knowing where we were going. At Port Moresby, American transport vehicles took us straight up to Sogeri that afternoon. We started up the track two days later. It was extremely tough, carrying 45 pounds, rifle, and moving eight miles a day. You were knackered at the end of each day, but you recover extremely quickly as we were so fit.

The second day, I will always remember this, it was up the golden staircase. The last mile or so up the hill, a lot of people found it difficult to get up. Those who were fit, as soon as they dropped their kit at the top, they came back down the hill and picked up the others' kit. So we all got to the top. You sweat a heck of a lot in a campaign like that, the salt was starting to show through your shirt when it dries. When we got in each night, we gorged on these cups of really hot tea with plenty of sugar. It was well organised. At every night stop, we had a militia group and their job was to organise a meal for us.

We reached Isurava about 4 o'clock in the afternoon of 26 August. While our Lieutenant, Boddington, was briefed by the 39th Battalion officers, we sat chatting to the 39th about the tactics the Japanese were using. Boddington, he was a New Zealander. We were happy to go into action with him but the company commander was a bit suss. Then Boddington came back to allot us our positions. My section was way out on our own on the extreme left of C Company. You couldn't see anything, just a glimpse of a native garden. I had nine men so I placed three forward, three on the right, three on the left. Me in the middle. Then night fell. It was a fairly eerie experience because we had been trained for open warfare in the Middle East. The Japanese move around at night, they were calling out you see, so the first night was very uncomfortable. You didn't know where you were. You didn't have any maps. They would call out something in English, 'Hello', trying to draw your fire. That was the first night.

The following morning I had a better idea of what the situation was. I could see 7 Section about 100 yards away, but there was nothing in between us. We didn't have enough men to man a closely formed perimeter. In the morning, the lads tried to build up rough defences. Nothing happened that day and the night of the 27th it rained very heavily. Just across from my little gully, Bill Maxwell, a great friend of mine, was there with Harry Barnes, who wasn't very bright and terribly excitable. Bill and Harry must have dozed off, and Bill suddenly woke up to realise that there was a figure standing over him. Bill realised it must be an enemy, so he lashed out with his foot and that came up just at the time the Japanese thrust his bayonet which caught Bill in the hand. He lost that finger. And the Jap turned and ran back, and Harry in his excitement threw a grenade and forgot to pull the pin out.

On the 28th, the battle started in earnest. I went around the section to make sure everything was okay and that is where I got knocked over by a sniper. I imagine he was in the native garden. The bullet went in and lodged in the sciatic nerve, it is still there now. I went to the aid post to get a dressing and the doctor said it is a bit more serious than you might think, so I ought to go back [to Port Moresby]. I was a bit dumbfounded, really, so I thought I would go back to the section and see if everybody is okay and tell them what's happened. I got halfway back and everyone was there. They had pulled back because the Japanese had attacked. Boddington was dead and what was left of the platoon was in a semicircle holding on. Then I was told to get walking. I came back with a group like myself, of walking wounded. I walked all the way back. At Port Moresby we were shot on to the hospital ship and came back to Brisbane.

# Honda Minoru

At Oita, I trained to be a fighter pilot in 1941. I was very bad at shooting. I couldn't hit anything. One day, I was in the middle of shooting training and was chasing after another Type 95 fighter that had a target banner behind it. When I pulled the trigger, the bullets were supposed to hit the target banner behind the airplane but my bullets hit the plane. I panicked and almost crashed my aircraft. I knew I would be in big trouble and I was. Later in the air-to-air shooting course I did it again. I am surprised that they passed me and allowed me [to] do battle with Japan's enemies.

The strongest memories I have about places I went are New Guinea and Guadalcanal. For six months I fought there almost every day. My flight log shows one week at Rabaul where I was in the air for 47 hours. Each morning flying was like going to the office. One day I flew to Port Moresby, next to Guadalcanal, or Milne Bay or Buna. I was exhausted. I always slept under my plane, not in tents. Otherwise, I would not even have time to run to my plane when there was an air raid. Sometimes, I was too tired to get into the cockpit and I asked the ground crew to push me. Pilots died from exhaustion. Many men who survived combat died on the way back to our base. There were two major causes to kill them: Weather and exhaustion.

The weather dramatically and rapidly changed. Once I became confused in clouds and fell into vertigo on the way back to Rabaul. The level gauge on the instrument panel showed a funny angle but I felt sure that I was flying horizontally. If I hadn't recovered from the disorientation, I would have flown into the ocean or a mountain. Many men were lost in thick cloud and died.

The other cause was exhaustion. We were all very tired because we had to fly and fight every day for five or six hours. After combat ended, the survivors all returned to the base in Rabaul. However, on the way back, some of them fell asleep. It was easy to tell who was sleeping. Once they fell asleep, their airplane started slowly going down to the ocean and crashed straight in. I saw such cases all the time, but there was nothing I could do but pray for them to wake up. I believe five out of every ten pilots recorded as killed in action died either by bad weather or sleeping. I thought this was about to happen again on the way back from Guadalcanal one day. I found a Zero fighter flying low ahead of me near Munda Island. It was one of my friends, Sergeant Nakajima. His plane was hit somewhere and was declining in altitude. He made an emergency landing on the ocean and started swimming toward Munda. Then I saw hundreds of sharks were heading toward him. I was shocked. I dove and started shooting at the sharks. After I shot once, I flew past them and turned around to go again, but Nakajima had disappeared.

Decades after the war, he appeared in front of me on a street in Japan. He was alive! He told me that he reached the island and was rescued by the local people, then was later handed over to the Americans then to the Australians. He was sent to Sydney and then to a camp. He stayed there till the end of the war. He said that the sharks I had shot at were really dolphins.

# Neil Russell

*In the 1930s, Sydney and Melbourne each had a Capstan Clock advertising Capstan cigarettes. The advertisement said 'Look at the Capstan Clock every time you pass. Make a habit of checking your watch by it, and as you do so, remember it's "Time for a Capstan"'.*

Got engaged in 1942 but I was on 12 hours' notice to leave so we were arranged to get married on the next weekend, but then I got called to Milne Bay. It was a solemn area. You are sleeping in tents, there is water everywhere, very wet place, wasn't very comfortable there at all. The Japs landed just after we got there and the South Australians, the 2/10th, they were the first battalion of our brigade in. Didn't do much good, either. They got scared of these tanks, but they didn't realise how small the tanks were when they heard the noise of them. They didn't have their anti-tank rifles. So they thought the safest thing was to get out and fight another day.

Then us, the 2/12th, was given the job to counterattack. Right at the very start, Geoff Swan got hit and was evacuated, so my company commander was gone before we even started and then the second in command, Harry Ivy, he took over. He said, 'Righto, 16th Platoon, you lead off followed by me with 17th Platoon'. We had only been going five minutes and he got killed. So they said, 'Righto, Russell, you can take charge of your platoon and his platoon and carry on with the attack'. And off I went with the command of these two platoons. This was our counterattack, we lost a lot, sad, one of the disappointing things you have to do, I had to do.

As we went along the coastal strip, which is not very wide, the jungle comes down to the track and there were all these side tracks. I had to send a section up each track as we came up to them. It was curly, not a very pleasant thing to do for these fellahs, send them up the side tracks not knowing what was ahead of them, you know, to make sure there were no Japs there. We did this several times and eventually we got to KB mission. There was some fighting and there were Japs, sometimes lying doggo, who weren't really dead. You had to watch out for that. The mission was a hut on stilts and there is a green oval, not a big one. We knew the Japs would be over on the other side in a bit of wooded country, bit of cover for them. We had to get across this open space and I thought, God what are we going to do here? Right, bayonet charge. I said, 'What's the time? And the lads said, 'Time for a Capstan, sir!' You had to gee them up, you know. I said, 'We'll fix bayonets and charge'. Then I said, 'Charge, let's go!' I was in the middle of the charge. You take your badges of rank off and carry your rifle like everybody else so then they don't know who the platoon commander is. That is what you do.

We got there, and it had had its effect because the Japs had retreated. The bayonet charge was putting on a bit of a show to put the breeze up [the Japanese] so they would piss off. And it worked. So we got across, we lost a few blokes, a few fellahs got killed, some wonderful blokes. I didn't see any Japs, they had gone by the time I got there. So that turned out to be successful. Both platoons behaved perfectly.

# Hori Kameji

I was in Rabaul when the war ended. Until 14 August, a few enemy airplanes were coming and bombing us, but on 15 August they started dropping papers instead of bombs. The papers said, 'Peace treaty has been concluded'. At first I didn't realise we had lost the war. I thought we might have to return New Guinea to Australia, but the Philippines would stay a part of Japanese territory. I was in Rabaul until May 1946 and was cultivating farms, working for the Australian occupation forces until then.

I got on a ship to go back to Japan at last. I was so glad to leave Rabaul and tears came from my eyes. Someone on the ship started a song and we sang together: 'We are like the cloud in the sky. Our blood once boiled for war but it has now all gone for nothing and we don't know where we are going from here'. Twelve days later, we saw land and someone screamed, 'It's Japan!'

I cannot explain how I felt when I saw home after five years, since the beginning of the war. I promised myself that I would be a man who believes in faith and peace for the rest of my life.

When I arrived at my house, it was after 10 o'clock at night. My family had no idea I was coming back and they went crazy with joy. My mother said, 'We must tell your father that you have come back alive'. So she took me to the Buddhist shrine and we prayed to the spirit of my father. I also returned the protective charm my mother had given me. Next morning she told me, 'After you went to bed last night, I went into your room and touched your legs'. You see, in Japan we believe a ghost has no legs, so when Mother felt my legs she was finally convinced that I had returned alive. She said, 'Nothing else can make me happier than this'. She also told me that the charm really did not protect me. It had no power to do so. It was really my belief in the charm that helped me to survive. But now I did not need a charm, so she burnt it. From now on, she said, I should work hard so everyone is proud of me. It was a fresh start; though I was 20 when I went away and was now 25, Mother said that I am 20 again now and I can make a fresh start today.

Other strange things happened to me after my return from the war. One night, I was about to fall asleep. Then I saw an old lady who lived next door suddenly come into my room and disappear. I got up and told my mother, 'The lady next door might have died!' My mother said, 'Don't say such a thing!' But then, a few hours later, the family next door came to my house and told us that their grandmother had died. My mother said the strange things happened to me because my body was back at home but my spirit was still at war.

# Paul Cullen

The brigadier told me the battalion I commanded had to capture the bridges [over Eora Creek] by dawn tomorrow morning. I said, 'Goodo'. So I said to the adjutant, Jeffrey Cox, 'Come on, we will go with the intelligence officer, and Sergeant Mackenzie [to see the objective]'. So we went down, it was dark by then, the roaring of Eora Creek at full blast, no need to [be quiet]. The Japanese weren't very active, so we crawled down all through our dead men from the previous attack and got in position just near the end of the bridge. In the moonlight, you could see the Japanese bunker with the machine gun sticking out. By this time, it was getting on towards midnight, so I said, 'Come on Jeff [let's] crawl across this bridge'. So we said our goodbyes [to each other] and set off. The machine gun never fired at us. Jeff Cox got to the bunker and dropped a hand grenade in it so that solved that problem. I said, 'Jeff, this is a wonderful opportunity', so we crawled back across the bridge [to bring forward more troops]. We got back and I said to John Burrell, tell the [men] to come down as quickly as possible, we are going to go over this bridge while it is still dark. So he went away and that took several hours because everyone was in their little bivouacs all over the bloody jungle.

So we waited, I don't know what time it is, perhaps it's 4 o'clock, [The first company] came down, noise didn't matter, Eora Creek roars away. I led them across, Cox, Burrell, MacKenzie and I led them across the first bridge again, and then you go around and prepare to cross Eora Creek. So I said charge [across the second bridge] and the first man was killed, of course. We captured the flat [ground] on the other side. The commander of A Company, Captain Sanderson, he was killed. He had a German submachine gun. He was a great big strong man and he was surrounded by dozens of dead Japanese. But he got separated from his company somehow or other, by maybe 30 yards. He was in the front of it you see, he was caught out at the attack across the bridge. I always think it is a supreme example of good training and high morale that he was there just at the critical time and it was bad luck that he was killed. Poor old Sandy with his Schmeisser! That's war, pretty useless, stumbling around in the jungle in a situation of that nature. It couldn't have been a more critical, testing time, but there Sanderson was, on the spot.

Goodness knows how beneficial our attack was across the bridge, but we established ourselves on the other side. From my point of view, to get across that bridge was the supreme test of a good infantry battalion's morale and efficiency. I got a Military Cross for that. It was quite a hazardous thing to do. Was that my job to do that? [Lead his battalion's attack across Eora Creek] Please define leadership! I have a reputation and confidence, and a fear of shame. What drives anyone to do a battalion commander's job?

# Bernie Lewis

We picked up one prisoner lying beside the track who was sick and emaciated. Much later, we came across a few of them in little makeshift tents out in the open. They were obviously dying, and I saw four of them and all they had on was shirts, they had dysentery, it was pouring out of them, and they were dying and I very much regret to say that they were shot by our fellows, much to the distress of the padre. One fellow who I challenged about it said it was a merciful release. But that didn't always happen, didn't always happen at all. And I will give you an example. When we went on to the river Kumusi, we were held up, we weren't the first battalion to strike. We were held up a few days, we were running the signals line behind our battalion headquarters and we had to move around near the Kumusi to see where we would decide to set up. And in heavy brush right alongside of us, a tiny emaciated little wispy bearded Jap walked out. He was carrying in his hand a Japanese signal box. He walked up to Tommy, our sergeant. We weren't wearing any insignia but somehow he knew Tommy was in charge, and he came up and offered him this phone and bowed down to him. Tommy was so nonplussed that he bowed back and took it! He bowed again and Tommy took the phone and patted him on the back and said, 'You poor little bastard'. And, do you know, we gave him a couple of biscuits, and took him back, handed him over to the regimental police who were ordered to take good care of him, because obviously a Japanese prisoner, who voluntarily gave himself up, well, he would talk. And it is my opinion he waited until he saw us signallers, then he decided to come out of the bush. He saw the signal box, saw that we were sigs, saw us as soul mates so thought we might take him in.

## Mrs Tsukamoto Yukiko

I would like to tell the Australians who read your book that Japan and Australia should be very good friends and never go to war again. I would also like to tell you a story about my husband.

After the war, Mr Tsukamoto and I went to all the reunions of his regiment. As they got older, the veterans always said that the best day each year was the one when they could meet up with their old army comrades. One day at a reunion, a man I did not know very well told me, 'Your husband never complained about anything in the war. He always went through the toughest situations before anyone else. He was always the first to advance. I know your husband never shows off about what he did and that is another reason why I admire him so much. We all do. So please, take good care of him, because you are taking care of him for us, too.'

My husband is still frightened of the sound of thunder. It makes him remember the enemy and the artillery, the sound of bombs. The war was 60 years ago but he still wakes me up at night. Not so often these days, though. He is getting better.

## Allen Sullivan

After Oivi, the Japs moved down the river so we were chasing them as we had information from the natives. And there were Japs along the river who had hung themselves. They climbed out along a bough and jumped in the water, just individuals along the way. I wondered what sort of blokes they were to do that. Then we went back to the Wairopi crossing. The bridge!

Wires swinging, walking on a plank, a hundred yards long, the flaming river rushing below, it was terrifying. In the flaming middle of this thing your feet were underwater. I think we lost a couple of blokes off the bridge. I'll never forget it.

Then we got down to Gona. We were hanging around the edges at Gona, patrolling around the area. Getting toward the end at Gona all the 3rd Battalion, well there wasn't many of us left. We were heading up a track. I was the second scout, bloke in front of me and another behind me, crawling up this track. And, out of nowhere, mortars. The bombs landing right in the middle of us on the track, we were crawling along, all hell broke loose. Alex Mundy had a Bren gun but it was such a surprise we couldn't react. Only went for a few minutes but was a total bombardment, we were covered in dirt and grass. Behind me they disappeared, dead. Teddy had both legs blasted to bits, Jim lost a foot. It lasted only a minute or two. The Japs had picked out this spot on the track and we had walked into it.

So, suddenly, this bombardment stops. And there was silence and we had to get back. Blokes wounded trying to get back, bloke with side of his face gone, trying to run on broken legs, they had to rebuild his face. Bren gunner was just gone. He got killed there. What happened then, trying to get back, one of the officers trying to carry injured on his back, told me to go get ground sheets to drag out the wounded. So I had to go back down the flaming track, another session out in the open. Belting down the flaming track, Crack! Crack! Trying to get down under cover and get the flaming groundsheets the officer wanted. I got them and I thought, Well, this is lovely. Now I have to get back with the groundsheets, past the snipers, again. Head down, arse up, away I went. Got back and the Japs would have heard us all carrying on with our wounded. Had to get Teddy Young out, getting blokes on each corner of the groundsheet and drag him 50 yards to get under cover. Got him on a stretcher, flashes getting close to you, Crack! They had three or four shots. Crack! That's the sound it makes. We get Teddy down to the first aid post, then down to the battalion one. They couldn't do anything for him and we carried him further. He survived the war, lost his legs, would never talk about it.

The Japs had that part of the track marked and were waiting for us. Only lasted a minute, boom, boom, trying to bury yourself in the dirt, stand up and see if you could stand up, never seen Alec again, blown up, such a shambles. That was the finish of the 3rd Battalion at Gona.

# Appendix

● ● ● ● ● ● ● ● ● ● ● ● ● ● ● ● ● ● ● ● ● ● ● ● ● ● ● ● ● ● ● ● ●

This appendix is about organisations and definitions. If you want to know exactly what armies mean by words like campaign or battle, how armies were structured in 1942, or what a flank or a reinforcement is, read on.

## Sorting Out Wars, Campaigns and Battles

When armed forces fight other armed forces, they carefully divide the violence into categories depending on the size and scale of the violence. That's why we have terms (in descending order, by size) such as wars, campaigns, battles, actions, engagements, ambushes and skirmishes.

You don't need to know many of these terms to understand *Kokoda For Dummies*, but knowing a few can certainly help, as follows:

- **World War II:** This war lasted from 1939 to 1945, and was called a world war because fighting occurred on most continents and in most oceans.

- **The Pacific War:** A term used to distinguish the period of World War II when Japan entered the war (1941 to 45) and the fighting took place in the Pacific Ocean and in Asia.

- **The Papuan Campaign:** Wars are usually divided into campaigns. This is an extended period of fighting in some defined geographical area like Papua. The Papuan Campaign lasted from July 1942, when the Japanese arrived, to January 1943, when the Australians ejected them with a little American help.

- **The Battle of Kokoda:** The term 'Kokoda' is sometimes used as shorthand for all the fighting in Papua but, in fact, the Papuan Campaign is divided into three battles: The battles of Kokoda, Milne Bay and Buna–Gona. The Battle of Kokoda lasted from 23 July to 13 November 1942.

> ✔ **The Battles of Milne Bay and Buna–Gona:** Milne Bay was a short battle, from 25 August to 7 September 1942. Buna–Gona, the last and bloodiest of the three battles of the Papuan Campaign, was fought from 16 November 1942 to 22 January 1943.

# Working Out the Difference Between Actions and Engagements

*Battles* are divided into actions and engagements. More important or larger events in battles are known as *actions*. As Table A-1 shows, the Battle of Kokoda is divided into certain actions.

| Table A-1 | Key Actions in the Battle of Kokoda | |
|---|---|---|
| *Location of Action* | *Date of Action* | *Chapter in this Book Where this Action is Discussed* |
| Isurava | 15–30 August 1942 | 8 |
| Ioribaiwa | 10–28 September 1942 | 8 |
| Eora–Templeton's II | 8–30 October 1942 | 11 |
| Oivi–Gorari | 4–13 November 1942 | 11 |

The smaller and less important events in a war are known as *engagements*, and the key engagements are outlined in Table A-2.

| Table A-2 | Key Engagements in the Battle of Kokoda | |
|---|---|---|
| *Location of Action* | *Date of Action* | *Chapter in this Book Where this Action is Discussed* |
| Kokoda–Deniki | 25 July–14 August 1942 | 7 |
| Eora–Templeton's I | 31 August–5 September 1942 | 8 |
| Efogi | 6–9 September 1942 | 8 |

You don't need to remember all the information in this appendix, but seeing the way armies divide things is interesting. For example, in the rest of the book, I talk about seven distinct clashes that took place between the Papuan–Australian forces and the Japanese in the period 25 July to 14 August, but the Official Nomenclature Committee who decided these things has, in its wisdom, called the whole period the Kokoda–Deniki engagement.

The Official Nomenclature Committee was set up in London after the war to define all the campaigns, battles, actions and engagements of Commonwealth armies. The Official Nomenclature Committee did concede that the words 'battle', 'action' and 'engagement' aren't absolutely rigidly defined and that the considerations used in classifying an encounter are its magnitude, the size of the forces, intensity of fighting, strategic or tactical importance and public sentiment. The last consideration is important for us, because in 'public sentiment' all the clashes along the Kokoda Trail are called battles.

I stay with public sentiment on this one and describe a part of the fighting as a battle without bothering with the technical terms.

# Making Sense of Different Army Structures

Armies, navies and air forces were all involved in the fighting in Papua but, because the fighting was on land, I mostly discuss armies. Armies have special ways of organising themselves and some familiarity with this organisation helps you understand the course of events.

The Australian and American armies have slightly different military organisations to the Japanese Army, so I've included definitions for both the Allied (Australians and Americans) and the Japanese military organisations. Papuan units were organised along Australian lines.

## Australian and American Armies

The Australian and American armies define their military groupings as follows (listed by size, in descending order):

- **Army:** Two or more corps, commanded by a general. The Australian land force in Papua in 1942 wasn't big enough to require an army level command in Port Moresby.

- **Corps:** At least 30,000 men, with two or more divisions. As the Australians increased in strength during 1942, New Guinea Force, the HQ in Port Moresby, became a corps command under a lieutenant general.

- **Division:** 15,000 to 20,000 men in three brigades (plus supporting units not in the infantry bridades) commanded by a major general. The Australian 7th Division was the major formation fighting on the Kokoda Trail.

- **Brigade:** Up to 3,000 men in three battalions commanded by a brigadier. A US regiment was similar to an Australian brigade. The Australian 21st Brigade, a part of 7th Division, was the first large formation to fight in Papua.

- **Battalion:** 500 to 1,000 men with four rifle companies commanded by a colonel or a lieutenant colonel.

- **Company:** 100 to 150 men in three platoons under a captain or major. The company-size Australian and Papuan formation that first engaged the Japanese in Papua was called Maroubra Force. It later grew to divisional size, by which time the name Maroubra Force was no longer used.

- **Platoon:** 30 to 60 men in three sections under a lieutenant.

- **Section:** 10 to 15 men under a corporal or sergeant. In the US army, a section was called a *squad*.

## The Japanese Army

The Japanese Army, which was formed in 1871, was organised roughly along the lines of European armies, but the forces that fought in Papua and Guadalcanal were slightly different. The Japanese Army was organised as follows:

- **Area army:** The 8th Area Army was established in Rabaul in November 1942 to control the increasing numbers of troops pouring into the region. What the Australians and Americans called an army the Japanese called an area army. An area army controlled two or more armies.

- **Army:** A corps-size formation under a general. The 17th Army, under a major general, was responsible for the fighting in Papua.

- **Division:** The Nankai Shitai, the force that fought in Papua, was a light division with two instead of the normal three regiments.

- **Regiment:** Up to 3,000 men in three or four battalions under a colonel. Like the Americans, the Japanese referred to their brigades as regiments.

- **Battalion:** 500 to 1,000 men, with three or four rifle companies under a lieutenant colonel or major.

From company to section level, the order of Battle of the Japanese was almost the same as that of the Australians. Refer to the preceding section for those definitions.

# Learning Jargon

Here are explanations for 15 words used by armies and by historians who want to explain how battles work. You can understand the battles much better if you learn a few of these explanations:

- **Amphibious operations:** An amphibian is an animal comfortable on land and in water. An amphibious operation involves landing troops from the sea, where they're very uncomfortable, to the shore, which they feel to be their natural habitat.

- **Bombardment:** Occurs when artillery or mortars use their ability to fire at long ranges on the enemy, usually as preparation for an infantry assault.

- **Defensive:** Holding a position to prevent it falling to the enemy. When possible, the defender is in trenches or fighting pits.

- **Flank:** The left or right end of the front-line. Attacking the enemy flank is usually more effective than attacking frontally.

- **Front-line:** The side of the military formation facing the enemy.

- **Manoeuvre:** The movement of a group of troops is known as a manoeuvre.

- **Morale:** Refers to how well trained, confident and optimistic the soldiers feel. Soldiers with high morale stay and do their duty in battle. Those with low morale run away.

- **Offensive:** How armies describe any occasion when an armed force is the aggressor and is advancing, attacking or assaulting towards the enemy.

- **Pinning attack:** A frontal attack on the enemy to keep them busy, and hopefully draw in their reserve, while the attacker makes the main effort elsewhere, probably on a flank, is known as a pinning attack.

- ✔ **Rear:** Behind an army, a vulnerable array of non-fighting units, supplies and equipment is always present. Attacking an army's rear is even better than attacking its flank.

- ✔ **Reinforce:** Occurs when fresh troops are brought from another area, either from another part of the battlefield or elsewhere, to support those troops already present.

- ✔ **Reserve:** Behind the front-line should be a reserve that isn't involved at the start of a battle. The reserve is held out of the fight by the commander until he can see he has a problem, or spots a chance to win the battle, then he commits his reserve to the battle.

- ✔ **Strategy:** The broad perspective, outside the battlefield, concerned with the use of military resources to achieve a goal. For example, the Allied strategy in 1942 was to prevent the Japanese capturing Port Moresby.

- ✔ **Supply:** Armies require the delivery of a constant stream of food, ammunition and other supplies from their rear base so they can continue to fight.

- ✔ **Tactics:** Refers to the combination of fire and manoeuvre used on the battlefield to defeat the enemy.

# Index

## • R •

## • S •

## • T •

# Notes

# Notes

## Health, Fitness & Pregnancy

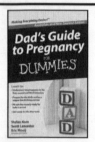

978-0-73037-735-1
$29.95

978-1-74216-972-9
$39.95

978-0-73037-739-9
$39.95

978-1-74216-946-0
$39.95

978-1-74246-844-0
$39.95

978-0-73140-760-6
$34.95

978-0-73037-500-5
$39.95

978-0-73037-664-4
$39.95

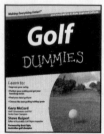

978-0-73037-536-4
$39.95

978-1-74216-984-2
$39.95

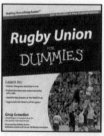

978-1-74031-073-4
$39.95

978-0-73037-660-6
$39.95

# FOR DUMMIES®

## Reference

978-1-74216-999-6
$39.95

978-1-74216-982-8
$39.95

978-1-74216-983-5
$45.00

978-0-73140-909-9
$39.95

978-1-74216-945-3
$39.95

978-0-73140-722-4
$29.95

978-0-73140-784-2
$34.95

978-0-73140-752-1
$34.95

## Technology

978-0-47049-743-2
$32.95

978-1-74246-896-9
$39.95

978-1-74216-998-9
$45.00

978-0-47048-998-7
$39.95

# FOR DUMMIES®

## Business & Investing

978-1-74216-971-2
$39.95

978-1-74216-853-1
$39.95

978-1-74216-853-1
$39.95

978-1-74216-962-0
$19.95

978-0-73037-668-2
$19.95

978-0-73037-556-2
$29.95

978-0-73037-715-3
$29.95

978-0-73037-807-5
$29.95

978-1-73037-695-8
$39.95

978-1-74216-942-2
$39.95

978-1-74246-889-1
$39.95

978-1-74246-848-8
$34.95